D1082801

THE
SPUTNIK
CHALLENGE

THE

SPUTNIK

CHALLENGE

Robert A. Divine

New York   Oxford
OXFORD UNIVERSITY PRESS
1993

Oxford University Press

Oxford   New York   Toronto
Delhi   Bombay   Calcutta   Madras   Karachi
Kuala Lumpur   Singapore   Hong Kong   Tokyo
Nairobi   Dar es Salaam   Cape Town
Melbourne   Auckland   Madrid

and associated companies in
Berlin   Ibadan

Published by Oxford University Press, Inc.,
200 Madison Avenue, New York, New York 10016

Oxford is a registered trademark of Oxford University Press

Library of Congress Cataloging-in-Publication Data
Divine, Robert A.
The Sputnik Challenge / Robert A. Divine.
p. cm.
Includes bibliographical references and index.
ISBN 0–19–505008–8
1. United States—Politics and government—1953–1961.
2. Eisenhower, Dwight D. (Dwight David), 1890–1969. 3. Artificial
satellites—Social aspects—United States. I. Title.
E8735.D535 1993
973.921—dc20   93-8835

2 4 6 8 9 7 5 3 1

Printed in the United States of America
on acid-free paper

72338

To Alex and Thomas

PREFACE

As the Cold War passes from the realm of current events into history, *Sputnik* remains one of its most enduring landmarks. The Soviet launch of the world's first artificial earth satellite created a crisis in confidence for the American people. How could a backward Communist nation beat the United States into space? Many citizens reacted by questioning the vitality of an entire way of life, expressing concern that *Sputnik* signaled the weakness of American science, the failure of American schools, and the complacency of American political leadership. Worst of all, they feared that the Soviet Union had gained a lead in developing long-range missiles, thereby threatening the very security of the United States in the nuclear age.

The panicky response to *Sputnik* had long-lasting effects on American life. It opened a debate over the state of education, science, space exploration, and national security that lasted well into the 1960s. The *Sputnik* furor contributed significantly to the election of John F. Kennedy in 1960, to the passage of massive federal aid-to-education measures under Lyndon B. Johnson, and to the decision to send American astronauts to the moon. In a sense, the anxiety raised by *Sputnik* did not end until Neil Armstrong and Buzz Aldrin took their historic steps in July 1969.

Dwight D. Eisenhower was one of the few Americans who was not impressed by the Soviet feat. Contemporaries saw his calm reaction as proof of his complacency, if not senility, and condemned him for a lack of leadership. The passage of time has confirmed the wisdom of the president's response. He believed that American science and American education were much sounder than critics charged, and, above all, he was confident that the United States held a commanding lead over the Soviet Union in strategic striking power. His refusal to support hasty or extreme measures in the wake of *Sputnik* proved fully justified.

Yet Eisenhower, for all his prudence and restraint, failed to meet one of the crucial tests of presidential leadership: convincing the American people that all was well in the world. His inability to understand the profound uneasiness and sense of impending doom that gripped the American public as a result of *Sputnik* was a political failure of the first order. He simply could not comprehend why the nation refused to accept his reassurances; he finally was forced to go against his deeply ingrained fiscal conservatism and approve defense expenditures he did not believe were really needed.

In this book, I have focused on Eisenhower's response to *Sputnik,* viewing the crisis from a White House perspective. This approach was made possible by the richness of the files at the Dwight D. Eisenhower Library, which stand as a tribute to a military man's insistence on keeping a detailed record of all the deliberations involved in the decision-making process.

In particular, I owe a deep debt of gratitude to three remarkable individuals. Andrew Goodpaster, the president's staff secretary, regularly sat in on all Oval Office meetings relating to national security. Within a few hours, or a day or two at most, he prepared lengthy memoranda of the White House meetings that laid out the ideas, suggestions, and conclusions of Eisenhower and his advisers. The result is a reliable record of the key decisions of the Eisenhower administration that appears to be free of Goodpaster's own feelings and views. L. Arthur Minnich was the assistant staff secretary who took minutes of both cabinet meetings and the president's regular sessions with congressional leaders. In addition to preparing the formal summary of these meetings, Minnich kept a handwritten notebook that contains many candid comments by both Eisenhower and those trying to influence him. Many of the most revealing statements cited in the pages that follow come from Minnich's invaluable notes. Finally, Ann C. Whitman, the president's devoted private secretary, kept a diary that gives an insight into the mood of the Eisenhower White House and the state of the president's emotions. Intensely loyal, Whitman not only recorded her own feelings about the impact of *Sputnik* on Eisenhower but also persuaded the president to dictate occasional diary notes for posterity.

I wish to acknowledge the help of a number of archivists and librarians who assisted me with the research of this book: John Wickman and Martin M. Teasley at the Dwight D. Eisenhower Library in Abilene, Kansas; Claudia Anderson at the Lyndon B. Johnson Library in Austin, Texas; Lynn Wolf Gentzler at the Western Historical Manuscript Collection at the University of Missouri Library, Columbia, Missouri; and Sheryl B. Vogt at the Richard B. Russell Memorial Library, University of Georgia, Athens, Georgia.

The award of a semester free from teaching by the Research Institute of the University of Texas at Austin enabled me to begin research for this study. I wish to thank Bill Brands for his advice and counsel and Peter Felten for preparing the index.

Once again, I am indebted to Gerard McCauley, a resourceful and gracious literary agent, and to Sheldon Meyer, a wise and patient editor. India Cooper proved to be alert, intelligent, and tactful in helping prepare the manuscript for publication. My wife, Barbara Renick Divine, prodded me gently to finish what began to seem like a never-ending project and provided companionship during the long days of research and writing. I am grateful for her support and her willingness to accompany me to distant archives. Finally, I am dedicating this book to my grandchildren; may the next generation enjoy a world free of the nuclear peril that has cast such a long shadow over all our lives.

Austin, Texas   R. A. D.
September 1992

CONTENTS

INTRODUCTION

On Friday evening, October 4, 1957, some fifty American scientists involved in the celebration of the International Geophysical Year (IGY) were attending a reception given by their Russian counterparts at the Soviet embassy in Washington. A few minutes before seven, word arrived that Moscow radio was broadcasting the astonishing news that the Soviet Union had launched the world's first artificial satellite, which it dubbed *Sputnik.*

The American scientists were caught completely by surprise. Dr. John Hagan, in charge of Vanguard, the American satellite program, knew that the first U.S. satellite would not be ready before early 1958. Yet the government, in a series of announcements, had led the American people to believe that the United States would be first in space. Indeed, an elaborate astronomical team of observers, dubbed Operation Moonwatch, had been formed to track *Vanguard.* Dr. Frederick Whipple, director of the Smithsonian Astrophysical Observatory outside Boston, was flying back from the Washington IGY meeting when *Sputnik* was announced. Upon learning the news, Whipple responded by focusing the Moonwatch network on a search for the elusive Soviet satellite in the sky. Moonwatch teams soon determined its track from its radio signals which were on a different frequency from the American satellite's, and thus difficult to monitor. Eventually Moonwatch telescopes observed the orbiting Soviet rocket that had launched *Sputnik,* but they never could identify the satellite itself, which was painted black.[1]

Sputnik was a sphere about twenty-two inches in diameter, weighing 184 pounds, compared with only 3.5 pounds for the six-inch American *Vanguard.* Composed of aluminum panels, it traveled at a speed of up to eighteen thousand miles per hour in an orbit some 550 miles above the earth. Its most distinctive feature was an "eerie beep . . . beep . . . beep from somewhere out in space" that was picked up and broadcast by commercial radio stations in the United States, even though only Soviet scientists could decode the signals. Indeed, it was a tape recording of that "beep-beep-beep" that enabled A. A. Blagonrov, a leading Soviet scientist, to confirm to the American IGY team at the Soviet embassy on October 4 that the satellite was the Soviet *Sputnik*. "That is the voice," he said. "I recognize it."[2]

The stunned American scientists were quick to congratulate their Russian colleagues. Physicist Lloyd Berkner proposed a toast in honor of *Sputnik;* Joseph Kaplan, chairman of the U.S. National Committee for the IGY, called it "a remarkable achievement on their part." Another American scientist added, "We are all elated that it is up there." Two days later, Detlev W. Bronk, president of the U.S. National Academy of Sciences, sent a letter congratulating the head of the Soviet Academy of Sciences for "placing an earth satellite in orbit." "This is a brilliant contribution," Bronk stated, "to the furtherance of science."[3]

I

The White House tried to minimize the significance of the *Sputnik* launch. President Dwight D. Eisenhower had left on Friday morning for a weekend of golf at Gettysburg. Press Secretary James C. Hagerty informed him of the Soviet achievement on Saturday morning, but Eisenhower let Hagerty and Secretary of State John Foster Dulles handle the initial administration response. Hagerty and Dulles quickly agreed to say that *Sputnik* came as "no surprise," and they decided not to mention an earlier U.S. proposal for the peaceful use of outer space in order not to "appear scared." Accordingly, Hagerty briefed the White House press corps, stressing that the administration was not caught by surprise and stating that the president was being kept informed of *Sputnik* as a matter "of great scientific interest." When reporters asked if the White House was upset that Russia had beaten the United States into space, Hagerty replied, "We never thought of our program as one which was in a race with the Soviets."[4]

Public reaction was very different. *Time* and *Newsweek* saw *Sputnik* as both a striking scientific feat and an ominous event in the Cold War. On the one hand, they hailed the orbiting satellite as a first step "toward the conquest of outer space," thus "opening a bright new chapter in mankind's conquest of the natural environment." But at the same time, they regretted that "man's greatest technological triumph since the atomic bomb" had been scored by "the controlled scientists of a despotic state." The editors of the *New Republic* compared *Sputnik* to "the discovery by Columbus of America" but feared that it was "proof of the fact that the Soviet Union has gained a commanding lead in certain vital sectors of the race for world scientific and technological

supremacy." Even more widespread was the belief that the true significance of *Sputnik* transcended the obvious fact that it marked the
beginning of the space age. The Russians, by using a rocket powerful
enough to put a 184-pound satellite into orbit, demonstrated that they
might well be close to perfecting the world's first intercontinental
ballistic missile—an ICBM capable of carrying a nuclear warhead the
thousands of miles that separated the two superpowers.[5]

Democrats quickly picked up this theme. Ardent Cold Warriors
such as Senators Henry M. Jackson of Washington and Stuart Symington of Missouri had been charging for years that the Eisenhower
administration had not been spending enough on national defense.
Jackson called *Sputnik* "a devastating blow to the prestige of the
United States as the leader in the scientific and technical world," and
Symington asked Eisenhower to call Congress into special session. In a
telegram to Senator Richard Russell, chairman of the Senate Armed
Services Committee, Symington said the Soviet satellite was "proof of
growing Communist superiority in the all-important missile field."
Russell apparently agreed, telling a Georgia audience on October 5,
"We now know beyond a doubt that the Russians have the ultimate
weapon—a long range missile capable of delivering atomic and hydrogen explosives across continents and oceans." Two weeks later, the
Democratic Advisory Council, which included former President
Harry Truman and defeated presidential candidate Adlai Stevenson,
accused the Eisenhower administration of "unilateral disarmament at
the expense of our national security." "The all-out effort of the Soviets
to establish themselves as master of space around us," the statement
concluded, "must be met by all-out efforts of our own."[6]

These partisan charges led to exaggerated efforts by Republicans to
play down the significance of *Sputnik*. Senator Alexander Wiley of
Wisconsin dismissed the Soviet feat as "a great propaganda stunt."
Outgoing Secretary of Defense Charles E. Wilson told reporters at his
last press conference that *Sputnik* was only "a nice scientific trick"
without any real significance. White House Chief of Staff Sherman
Adams was equally unimpressed, saying the United States had no
plans to engage in "an outer space basketball game" with the Russians.
Other administration spokesmen continued to play down *Sputnik* despite growing public concern. On October 18 presidential assistant
Maxwell Rabb said the satellite was "without military significance";
four days later, trade adviser Clarence Randall made the most memorable comment of all, labeling *Sputnik* "a silly bauble."[7]

Few Americans agreed. James R. Killian, president of MIT and
soon to become White House science adviser, wrote that *Sputnik*
caused "a crisis of confidence" among the American people. The conservative *U.S. News & World Report* likened *Sputnik* to "the first split-
ting of the atom." The most frequent comparison was with Pearl Harbor. Edward Teller, known as the "father of the H-bomb," told a

television audience that the United States had lost "a battle more important and greater than Pearl Harbor." The *Reporter* went even further, saying, "Sputnik as a name for a great national emergency is to Pearl Harbor what Pearl Harbor was to the sinking of the *Maine*."[8]

While many observers stressed the military danger implicit in *Sputnik,* others saw it primarily as a cultural challenge. The most often quoted comment was the one that Senator Styles Bridges made on October 5. "The time has clearly come," said this New England Republican, "to be less concerned with the depth of pile on the new broadloom rug or the height of the tail fin on the car and to be more prepared to shed blood, sweat and tears if this country and the Free World are to survive." Pundits such as Walter Lippmann and Norman Cousins joined in the chorus advising Americans to give up their love affair with material goods and strive instead to improve education, science, and the quality of national life.[9]

Whether they viewed *Sputnik* in a military or a cultural context, most observers agreed on one point—the nation faced a crucial challenge. The editors of *Life* compared the Soviet satellite to the shots fired at Lexington and Concord and urged Americans to respond as the Minutemen had done then. "Those 'beeps' are the ticking of a clock that Soviet technology has given the American people, who can certainly put the Russian timepiece to good use," wrote Max Ascoli in the *Reporter.* In the months ahead, he continued, "every citizen must take upon himself an extra load of worry and of responsibilities commensurate with his capacity to think and to act." *Sputnik* was a hard jolt, Ascoli concluded, "and that is very good indeed, for nobody can defeat us but ourselves."[10]

II

Not all commentators shared the sense of common danger. Many scientists were more alarmed by the public overreaction to *Sputnik* than by the Soviet feat itself. Harvard astronomer Harlow Shapley pointed out that the Soviets had simply applied well-known scientific principles to achieve an engineering triumph. The only surprises were the weight of the satellite, which was much larger than expected, and the "public frenzy" over the launch. The editors of *Science* felt that the only thing that *Sputnik* demonstrated was the falsity of the popular conception that Soviet science was way behind Western. Two European émigrés felt equally perplexed by the public outcry. Hungarian-born Theodore von Karman of Cal Tech warned that "fear and hysteria are not the right reactions," preferring instead to see Americans concentrate on achieving their own satellite. Walter R. Dornberger, who headed the German rocket program in World War II, agreed. "We should not be afraid," he claimed, "but we should look at it as a very necessary push for us to go ahead."[11]

Dornberger played down a suggestion that captured German scientists had been responsible for the Soviet satellite. He and others pointed out that the United States captured nearly all the important German rocket scientists in 1945; the Soviets did take over some of the V-2 factories and a number of technicians, but they relied far more heavily on a strong scientific tradition of their own in rocket research. Perhaps the most famous of the German rocket scientists, Wernher Von Braun, would later tell a Senate committee, "The sputniks are definitely the result of a Russian program with little if any German assisstance." Nevertheless, *U.S. News & World Report* claimed that Russian spies, in a move similar to the treachery of the Rosenbergs, stole vital rocket information from the United States after World War II, and in early 1958 *Look* magazine ran a two-part series on how careless Americans in postwar Germany "let the missile secrets get away."[12]

These charges confirmed the view of some observers that a major scientific advance had served only to heighten Cold War tensions. Norman Cousins found it regrettable that "the chill of the cold war had fixed itself upon the event." Sociologist C. Wright Mills warned against making a blind, irrational effort to catch up with and surpass the Russians in space. "Who wants to go to the moon anyway?" Mills asked, claiming that "the whole space gambol" is "a lot of malarky."[13]

Two journals at opposite ends of the political spectrum agreed that the American people were making too much of *Sputnik*. Voicing conservative views, David Lawrence, the editor of *U.S. News & World Report,* denied that the Soviet satellite damaged American prestige or showed that the Russians were ahead in the race for the ICBM. "No military advantage has been added or subtracted by the launching of the earth satellite," he contended. The editors of the *Nation* lamented the fact that the national reaction to *Sputnik* had "settled fairly rapidly into the old familiar cold-war fixation." Instead of giving the Russians the "congratulations for a major scientific achievement" to which they were entitled, the United States seemed determined to embark on "an orgy of defense spending."[14]

Some felt that the real lesson of *Sputnik* was to point up the bankruptcy of traditional defense efforts. Commenting that "our security policies have failed to bring any promise of security," Walter Millis urged that *Sputnik* become the occasion for "a fresh national appraisal of the real world" and an effort to free the nation from the limitations of the Cold War. Retired General Omar Bradley concurred. In a speech entitled "Greater than the Conquest of Space," he argued that there was no security in science or technology, only in diplomatic solutions. Historian Frederick L. Schuman urged a new effort at diplomacy with the Soviet Union on the same grounds. "Safety in our time," he wrote, "requires co-existence, disengagement and the negotiation of a modus vivendi."[15]

III

Despite these varied responses to *Sputnik,* the overwhelming public feeling was a deeply felt sense of national crisis. The figure everyone turned to for reassurance was Dwight D. Eisenhower. For five years he had presided over the country as a benign father figure. He had calmed the nation by ending the Korean War after only six months in office and contributing, however indirectly, to the demise of McCarthy and the ugly Red Scare. Recovering from a serious heart attack in 1955, he had easily won reelection the following year, despite a bout with ileitis. Placing himself above party, he had carefully nurtured his popularity with the people by avoiding partisan struggles with Congress, but he now faced a potentially damaging political assault by those who had suddenly found an issue that seemed to cry out for decisive presidential leadership.

Republicans as well as Democrats began to criticize Eisenhower for not responding swiftly and boldly enough to *Sputnik.* In the Senate, Ralph Flanders of Vermont and John Sherman Cooper of Kentucky condemned the administration for complacency. Former Congresswoman Clare Booth Luce spoke out against "a decade of American pretensions that the American way of life was a gilt-edged guarantee of our material prosperity." Arthur Krock noted that newspapers that had always backed Ike in the past were accusing the president of "not leading the country in a crisis." *Time* commented that the criticisms directed against the president were "the worst Dwight Eisenhower has ever suffered," and William Lawrence wrote that "one of the results of the sputnik's quick trips around the world has been to strip from the President his reputation for infallible judgment in military matters."[16]

The heart of the problem was the popular belief in American supremacy in science and technology. "It is this faith," wrote one British observer, "which has been affronted by the Russian satellite achievement and which is now crying out with a steady growth of urgency and hunger for reassurance." In critical times the American people have always turned to the White House for inspiration and answers. On this occasion they looked to the man who was the symbol of victory in World War II for a restoration of their shattered confidence. There was, as *Time* pointed out, "a sudden sharp disappointment that Americans had been outshone by the Red Moon." As a result, President Eisenhower faced "the most serious crisis" of his career, one that would not be over until "the U.S. no longer stood second best in the conquest of space."[17]

THE
SPUTNIK
CHALLENGE

CHAPTER ONE

Eisenhower returned from his Gettysburg weekend to find the White House engulfed in turmoil in the wake of *Sputnik*. The next week, according to one observer, was "one prolonged nightmare." "Any number of people—from the Pentagon, from State, and from the Hill—were dashing in and out of the President's office. Each new visitor had a longer face than the one before." One aide suggested to White House Chief of Staff Sherman Adams that the president offer to take a group of reporters on a tour of the nation's space facilities to reassure the American people and help dispel the "frightening mystery" surrounding the Soviet feat. The president himself appeared to be the calmest person in the White House, listening patiently to the conflicting advice and then at the end of the day, as his secretary noted, hitting "golf balls very late."[1]

On Monday morning Dr. Alan Waterman, head of the National Science Foundation, briefed the White House staff on *Sputnik*. Pointing out that there was no reason to doubt the Russians' claim that they had launched a 184-pound object into space, Waterman added, "Apparently a very successful job was done in placing the satellite in orbit." Secretary of State John Foster Dulles spent the first two days of the week conferring both with his brother, Central Intelligence Agency (CIA) Director Allen Dulles, and Press Secretary James Hagerty on the best way to explain this feat to the American people. Secretary Dulles, who first thought he should hold a press conference before Eisenhower did, finally deferred to Hagerty's plan for a presidential press conference on Wednesday, October 9.[2]

The president's most important meeting that week was on Tuesday morning, October 8. At 8:30 he and key members of the White House staff met with Waterman, Deputy Secretary of Defense Donald

3

Quarles, and John Hagan, the official in charge of Vanguard, the American satellite program. Quarles, who had overseen the satellite program for the Defense Department since its inception, presented Eisenhower with a detailed background memo on Vanguard and then, after a lengthy discussion of its implications, agreed to work with Alan Waterman on a statement for Eisenhower to issue when he met the press the next day.[3]

I

The Defense Department memo made it clear that Vanguard was the result of the administration's 1955 decision to separate the American satellite effort, undertaken as part of the International Geophysical Year program, from the development of military missiles. Following the White House announcement on July 29, 1955, that a scientific satellite would be launched as part of IGY sometime before the end of 1958, the Defense Department appointed a committee to decide which rockets to use. The committee ruled out both air force and army proposals on the grounds that they would rely on rocket launchers used for intermediate-range ballistic missiles (IRBM) and ICBM weapons. Instead it voted seven to two in favor of the navy Vanguard proposal: to use a navy Viking, a descendant of the original German V-2, as the first stage, an Aerobee rocket for the second stage, and a five-hundred-pound solid-fuel rocket, still to be developed, to place a twenty-pound nose cone with a small scientific package into orbit around the earth.

In the fall of 1955 Donald Quarles, then serving as assistant secretary of defense for research and development, approved the committee's choice, despite protests from army representatives that they could achieve an orbiting satellite a year earlier than the navy's Vanguard. Two considerations lay behind Quarles's decision. First, the administration wanted to give the highest priority to the development of both an IRBM and an ICBM; officials feared that using military components would slow down the much more vital missile program. But equally important was the administration's desire to make the satellite program an open one that could be shared with scientists from other nations as part of the IGY. This emphasis on openness, however, was not entirely without calculation. Since 1956 Eisenhower had approved U-2 flights over the Soviet Union, and he was hoping that satellites would provide a less provocative and more widely accepted way to continue that surveillance in the future. Thus, as the Defense Department pointed out, scientific satellites, "which would be clearly non-military and clearly inoffensive," might "help to establish the principle that outer space is international space."[4]

It was this search for a successor to the highly secret U-2 that convinced the administration that a scientific satellite would be preferable to a military one. A genuine risk was involved, however, in turning down a military satellite, which its advocates claimed could be developed much more quickly. The Soviets, who had also announced their intention of orbiting a satellite, might beat the United States into space.

The Vanguard program got under way in the fall of 1956 under the direction of Dr. John Hagan of the Naval Research Laboratory. It was plagued from the outset by inadequate funding and the lack of the same clear-cut priority given to military missiles. Initial plans called for six rockets to be launched in 1958, in hopes that one would succeed in putting a twenty-inch sphere filled with scientific instruments into orbit. In 1956 both Alan Waterman and I. I. Rabi, a distinguished physicist who headed a government scientific advisory committee, urged that the number of rockets be doubled in order to increase the chances for a successful orbit. On October 8, 1956, a year before *Sputnik*, Rabi warned prophetically that the failure of Vanguard to launch a satellite "would result in loss of U.S. scientific prestige that would be compounded by successful Soviet launching." But the Department of Defense, which was financing Vanguard from the secretary's emergency fund, turned down the request for six additional rockets on the grounds that it would hurt the military missile effort. Eisenhower concurred with this judgment, noting later, "Since no obvious requirement for a crash satellite program was apparent, there was no reason for interfering with the scientists and their projected time schedule."[5]

Without any sense of urgency and lacking a high priority, Vanguard followed a schedule designed to launch a scientific satellite sometime before the IGY ended in December 1958. On May 10, 1957, the National Security Council approved a timetable calling for flight tests of the three Vanguard stages in the fall of 1957, with the first fully instrumented satellite to be launched in March 1958. By the time of *Sputnik*, Vanguard was on schedule, with two successful tests of the first stage completed and plans for the first flight test of all three stages, but without a satellite, scheduled for early December.

The Defense Department memo of October 7 on Vanguard concluded with two recommendations. First, there should be no sudden change in the American satellite program as a result of *Sputnik*. Regrettably, there was no way to alter the fact that the Soviets were first into space, and there would be no gain now in trying to speed up Vanguard. "It appears sound," the memo argued, "to adhere to our program as presently planned." Second, the president should issue a public statement making it clear that the United States, unlike the Soviet Union, had chosen to divorce its satellite program from military missiles in order to cooperate with the international scientific community on the observance of the IGY. The president should point out that *Sputnik* added little to scientific knowledge because it lacked full instrumentation, compared with Vanguard. Equally important, he should argue that the Soviet satellite had "no military meaning" since the United States had chosen to develop its military missiles in an entirely separate program.[6]

After Deputy Secretary Quarles had briefed the president and his advisers on this history of Vanguard, he went on to point out that the army believed it could have launched a satellite a year ago. And, Quarles added, the army still thought that even now, if given approval and $13 million, it could launch a satellite a month before the navy's scheduled date of March 1958. The president, however, refused to be rushed into any sudden decision. He said he preferred not to depart from "the present orderly procedure to produce an earth satellite," but he did permit the Department of Defense to explore with the army the possibility of developing a backup to Vanguard. Eisenhower was firm on the line he wanted all within the administration to take publicly on *Sputnik*. The United States was determined to keep the satellite program "a scientific project and keep it free as much as possible from weaponry." The administration would adhere to the goal of orbiting a satellite before the end of the IGY and "intended to meet scientific requirements with a view toward permitting all scientists to share in information which the United States might eventually acquire."

Eisenhower did see one possible benefit from *Sputnik*. When Quarles commented that the Soviets might have "done us a good turn, unintentionally, in establishing the concept of freedom of international space," Ike asked the group "to look five years ahead" and then asked Quarles to brief them on the air force effort to develop a reconnaissance satellite. Despite the damage to public confidence done by *Sputnik*, the president was quick to grasp that it could well fulfill one of his principal goals: speed the day when an American satellite could take the place of the provocative U-2 overflights of the Soviet Union.[7]

By the end of the meeting, Eisenhower had decided how he would meet the *Sputnik* challenge. There would be no abrupt change in course, and he would defend the American decision to divorce the satellite effort from the military quest for an ICBM. When Defense Department spokesmen kept bringing up the possibility of an earlier army satellite launch, Ike reminded them of the deliberate separation of the two programs and his insistence that the satellite proceed "as a scientific effort." The last thing he wanted to tell the public, he stressed, was that we were in a race with the Russians in space. In a conference with Detlev Bronk of the National Academy of Sciences, Ike said he did not intend to "belittle the Russian accomplishment" in his public statements. He went on to state, however, that he did wish to "allay hysteria and alarm." Sherman Adams then asked Dr. Bronk if there was anything in *Sputnik* to cause any change in the American program. Bronk quickly said no, adding that "we cannot constantly change our program with every action by the Russians." He agreed with the president that American scientists had been given "adequate responsibility and opportunity to develop the satellite." Thus reassured, Eisenhower set out on the difficult mission of convincing the American people that, despite *Sputnik,* the nation's scientific effort in space was in sound shape.[8]

II

The president opened his press conference on October 9 with the release of a prepared statement that reflected the decisions he had reached the day before. Summarizing the history of the American satellite program, Eisenhower stressed the deliberate separation of Vanguard from the military missile effort. The United States, he insisted, in an attempt to cooperate with the IGY celebration, sought to "accent the scientific purposes of the satellite" while avoiding any "interference with top priority missile programs."

The president congratulated Soviet scientists for their achievement, but he reiterated that the American satellite program "has never been conducted as a race with other nations." Nor, he added, would there be any change in Vanguard as a result of the Soviet feat. The United States would adhere to its "well-designed and properly scheduled" program in order "to achieve the scientific purpose of which it was initiated." Accordingly, the first test vehicle would be launched on schedule in December, and the first fully instrumented satellite shot would take place in March 1958.[9]

In answering the reporters' questions that followed, Ike repeated his assertion that the administration had never viewed the United States as being in a race with the Soviets to be first in space. He played down the significance of *Sputnik,* referring disparagingly to a concentrated Russian effort that led only to putting "one small ball in the air." He suggested that it would be a long time before satellites could be used for reconnaissance of the earth, adding, "The value of that satellite going around the earth is still problematical." But when pressed, he did acknowledge that through *Sputnik* the Russians had "gained a great psychological advantage through the world," and that in hindsight perhaps the United States should have tried harder to be first in space. He admitted that American scientists were aware of the Soviet program and had informed him of the possible "great psychological advantage in world politics" the Russians might achieve with the first satellite, but that did not seem to him "to be a reason for just trying to grow hysterical about it."

Ike was even more defensive when the journalists asked him about the military implications of *Sputnik.* He emphasized the separation between the American satellite and military missile programs, saying that both the IRBM and ICBM had been given "top priority." He had given the Defense Department "to the limit of my ability the money that they have asked for, and that is all I can do." Pushed further, he said that the United States was currently spending more than $5 billion a year on missiles, adding, "Now that isn't any weak, pusillanimous effort; that is a lot of money."

The reporters, however, kept coming back to the implications of *Sputnik* for national security. Eisenhower was forced to admit that the Soviets, in launching a 184-pound satellite, had demonstrated they possessed rockets powerful enough to send warheads thousands of miles across the earth. But there was no evidence that they had solved the difficult problems of accuracy and reentry into the earth's atmosphere involved in developing a successful ICBM. Asked about Soviet leader Nikita Khrushchev's recent statement that *Sputnik* indicated that bombers would soon become obsolete, the president was quick to argue that there would be a long transition period; the change from bombers to missiles would be "evolutionary," not "revolutionary."

NBC correspondent Hazel Markel gave Ike a chance to close the press conference on a positive note by asking him, in view of the "great faith" the American people had in his military experience and judgment, whether he was "saying at this time with the Russian satellite whirling about the world, you are not more concerned nor overly concerned about our Nation's security." The president stumbled for a moment, saying he was always concerned about security, but then added, "So far as the satellite itself is concerned, that does not raise my apprehensions, not one iota." The military experts had assured him that the American missile program was in good shape, and the scientists felt that the satellite "involves no new discovery to science," so he felt safe in concluding that *Sputnik* by itself "imposes no additional threat to the United States.[10]

Eisenhower's low-key response to *Sputnik* completely failed to defuse the growing sense of public alarm. He had not given the kind of personal assurances that, because of his stature as a renowned military hero, would have carried great weight; rather, he seemed unsure and uncertain of what the Russian satellite signified, falling back again and again on what the scientists and other experts had told him. His repeated statements that the missile program was unaffected by *Sputnik* rang hollow, thereby raising rather than lowering national anxiety. The people had waited nearly a week for the president to reassure them, but instead of the confident statement they expected, he had offered what one observer called "a curiously uncertain, even fumbling, apologia." Another critic called the presidential display of complacency "incredible." Arthur Krock, usually supportive of Eisenhower, stated flatly that "he is not leading the country in a crisis," adding, "Only he can lead it and . . . he must meet this supreme obligation."[11]

III

Within the administration *Sputnik* created a sense of urgency that belied the president's public response. Those involved in the satellite program realized that in reality they were in a race with the Russians and that the only way to reassure the nation would be to place an object in orbit as soon as possible.

It was this consideration that led the president to include the date for the December launch of a Vanguard test vehicle in his public statement. The original plan had been simply to prove out the three rocket stages without attempting to put a satellite into orbit. Now, under orders from the White House, the navy informed John Hagan that it wanted a small, six-inch satellite included in the December test. When Secretary of the Navy Thomas Gates expressed concern over this new development, warning that there was at best only a "probability," not a "certainty," of success, Secretary of Defense Neil McElroy held firm on the December launch. "The Soviet's success with their satellite has changed the situation," he pointed out. "The psychological factors in this matter obviously received a new emphasis." The president, he concluded, was insistent on the new schedule, and therefore the navy had to move ahead with the December Vanguard shot "with deliberate speed."[12]

While the navy struggled to speed up Vanguard, the army took advantage of the post-*Sputnik* atmosphere to reopen its case for launching its own satellite. In 1955 the army had proposed using a modified Redstone missile as the first stage for Project Orbiter, its entry into the satellite competition. The Redstone was a land-based missile with a two-hundred-mile range developed from the German V-2 by a team of rocket experts headed by Wernher Von Braun at the Army Ballistic Missile Agency (ABMA) in Huntsville, Alabama; it had gone into production in 1953 and would become operational as the army's primary tactical nuclear launch vehicle in early 1958. The decision to keep the scientific satellite separate from the military missile program had led Quarles and his committee to reject Orbiter in favor of Vanguard.

General John Medaris, the officer in charge of the army missile program, refused to accept the Vanguard decision as final. He kept Orbiter alive at Huntsville, instructing Von Braun to develop it under the code name Jupiter-C as a way to test nose cones for the Army's IRBM, known as Jupiter. In fact, Jupiter-C was a modified Redstone, not a Jupiter IRBM, but the confusion over names enabled Medaris and Von Braun to build half a dozen Jupiter-C missiles as test vehicles without alerting the Pentagon to their true nature. The first Jupiter-C, essentially a Redstone first stage with two additional rockets consisting of bundles of solid-propellant engines developed by the Jet Propulsion Laboratory at Cal Tech, another army research agency, was fired on September 20, 1956. Carrying a Jupiter IRBM nose cone, it flew some three thousand miles and reached a height of six hundred miles, but the nose cone was not recovered. A second Jupiter-C went off course in May 1957, but a third, launched on August 8, 1957, performed perfectly, and the army recovered the Jupiter nose cone, which Von Braun termed "the first man-made object ever recovered from outer space." It was these three Jupiter-C shots that led Quarles to claim later that, if Project Orbiter had been approved in 1955, the army could have launched a satellite a year before *Sputnik*.

The successful test of the Jupiter IRBM nose cone prevented General Medaris from ordering any more Jupiter-C flights, but he carefully kept two fully assembled Jupiter-C missiles in Huntsville as possible backups for Vanguard. On October 4, 1957, the day the Soviets launched *Sputnik*, incoming Secretary of Defense Neil McElroy was touring the Huntsville facility. When Medaris and Von Braun learned of the Soviet satellite, they both immediately lobbied McElroy for permission to use Jupiter-C, rather than Vanguard, to launch a satellite, which they claimed could be quickly designed and provided by the Jet Propulsion Lab in California. "Vanguard will never make it," Medaris remembers Von Braun telling McElroy. "We have the hardware on the shelf. For God's sake turn us loose and let us do something. We can put up a satellite in sixty days." Medaris quickly broke in, saying the army would need ninety days but adding that, with permission to launch two Jupiter-C shots, "we have a 99 percent probability of success." McElroy was noncommittal, but Medaris was confident enough to instruct Von Braun to begin preparing the two Jupiter-Cs at Huntsville for a satellite launch.[13]

In the course of his October 8 deliberations with his scientific and military advisers, President Eisenhower agreed to Quarles's suggestion that the Defense Department explore the possibility of using the Jupiter-C missiles as a backup to Vanguard. On October 30 McElroy proposed exactly that, saying that the additional cost would be only $4 million. Ike quickly agreed, adding angrily that he had favored such a step eighteen months earlier, only to be dissuaded by the Defense Department with the argument that the scientific and military missile programs should be kept entirely separate.[14]

Despite a successful test of the first stage of Vanguard on October 24, the Defense Department gave the army official orders on November 8 to go ahead with work already under way to prepare two Jupiter-C missiles for a satellite launch in early 1958. Vanguard still had priority, but, if there were delays or failures in that program, then the army would get the chance to launch the nation's first satellite.[15]

This decision clearly contradicted the administration's claim that it was not in a race with the Soviets in space. Notwithstanding Eisenhower's complacent reaction to *Sputnik* at his October 9 press conference, he and his advisers were fully aware of how important it was to restore public confidence in American science and technology by putting a satellite into orbit as soon as possible. Thanks to the refusal of Medaris and Von Braun to take no for an answer, the president had an option that would prove invaluable.

IV

Eisenhower deliberately misled the American people on yet another aspect of Sputnik. At his October 9 press conference, he was being less than truthful when he played down the possible significance of *Sputnik* as the harbinger of a new age of satellite reconnaissance. As Quarles had noted in the White House meeting on October 8, the Soviets had accidentally helped the United States by setting a precedent for peaceful overflight of another nation from outer space.[16]

The American reconnaissance program was well established by the time of *Sputnik*. Studies commissioned by the air force and conducted by the Rand Corporation, culminating in Project Feedback in 1954, indicated not only that "an efficient satellite reconnaissance vehicle" was feasible but that its development was a matter of "vital strategic interest to the United States." Accordingly, that same year the air force began research program WS-117L to develop such a spy satellite. Early studies proved promising, and in October 1956 the air force awarded a contract to Lockheed, the corporation that had built the U-2, to develop a military satellite to photograph the Soviet Union from space. In fact, one reason the Defense Department preferred to have Vanguard proceed as a scientific program in cooperation with the IGY was to divert attention from the highly classified WS-117L.[17]

The air force satellite program consisted of three elements. One was Discoverer, an experimental effort to perfect, through trial and error, the best ways to use cameras on satellites and to recover the exposed film. Another, dubbed SAMOS (Satellite Missile Observations System), was a high-altitude satellite with wide-angle cameras to give broad coverage of the Soviet Union and to detect suspicious areas to be viewed by the more detailed Discoverer cameras. Finally, there was MIDAS (Missile Defense Alarm System), designed to detect the infrared signature of Soviet ICBM rocket exhausts and thus give the United States the earliest possible warning of a missile attack. The purpose of WS-117L was to develop this three-part system as a successor to the U-2 in the 1960s when, it was thought, the Russians would have the missile capability to shoot down high-altitude aircraft. No orbital tests were planned before 1960, and the development budget was set at a relatively low $13.9 million for fiscal year 1957 and $15.5 million for 1958.[18]

From the outset American officials were concerned with the legality of these future spy satellites. The concept of national sovereignty in a nation's air space was clearly established, but no one knew whether nations could also claim sovereignty beyond the atmosphere. When the Soviets launched *Sputnik,* they seemed to be acknowledging the concept that, due to the earth's rotation, no nation could claim control of the space above it. The most noteworthy thing about *Sputnik,* claimed one commentator, was that, "despite the wave of emotions stimulated worldwide by the event, not a single government anywhere in the world protested the fact that *Sputnik* had flown over their lands."[19]

The Eisenhower administration noted this development with great interest. In a cabinet meeting on October 18, Donald Quarles pointed out that one reason for being careful to insulate Vanguard from the American military missile program was "to keep it purely scientific and thus perhaps obviate or weaken Soviet protest on over-flights." In launching *Sputnik,* Quarles contended, "the Russians themselves . . . had now established the acceptability of over-flights." There was clearly a difference between satellites carrying only scientific instruments and those envisioned in WS-117L with cameras aimed at Soviet military installations, but at least *Sputnik* would make it more difficult for the Soviets to object to future American spy satellites. For that reason Eisenhower preferred to keep a cloak of secrecy about the highly classified WS-117L and play down the possible significance of satellites for military reconnaissance.[20]

V

The most important meeting Eisenhower held in the aftermath of *Sputnik* came on October 15, 1957, when he conferred with the Science Advisory Committee (SAC). This body, created by President Truman in 1951 and made part of the Office of Defense Mobilization, was chaired by I. I. Rabi of Columbia University, a Nobel Prize–winning physicist Eisenhower had come to know well during his Columbia presidency. Other members included Edwin H. Land, inventor of the Polaroid Land camera and one of the key advocates of the U-2 spy plane, Detlev Bronk, president of the National Academy of Sciences, and James Killian, president of MIT, who had headed an important 1954 scientific study that had resulted in the crash American effort to develop the IRBM and ICBM missiles.[21]

The president opened the morning meeting by expressing his puzzlement over the public reaction to *Sputnik.* "I can't understand why the American people have got so worked up over this thing," he confessed. "It's certainly not going to drop on their heads." He then asked these distinguished scientists the question that was on everyone's mind in the days that *Sputnik* was orbiting the earth: Did they believe that "American science is being outdistanced?"

Rabi spoke up immediately to suggest that, while he felt America was still ahead of Russia in science and technology, the current trend was in favor of the Soviet Union. He argued that the Russians were emphasizing science more heavily in the schools than Americans did and that, as a result, their people were gaining a greater degree of scientific literacy. Unless the United States speeded up its scientific programs, within ten years the Russians would be ahead.

Edwin Land broke in to argue that the key issue was a matter of the relationship of science to society. Americans had become too lazy and complacent, content to enjoy the fruits of science. The Russians, on the other hand, were "teaching their young people to enjoy science." Americans no longer felt "the thrill of scientific life," and, unless this trend was reversed, "Russian scientific culture will leave us behind as a decadent race." It was up to Eisenhower to use the shock of *Sputnik* to stress the importance of science to national life, to rekindle the spirit of scientific inquiry, to single out scientists for special attention, and to give science the very highest national priority. Land urged the President to use the furor over *Sputnik* to speak out so as to "inspire the country—setting our youth particularly on a whole variety of scientific adventures."

At first Ike demurred, saying that the Russian science program was very narrow, restricted only to a talented elite, with the Soviet leaders "ruthlessly spurning the rest." But he did see the need to speak out in behalf of science. He commented that he would "like to create a spirit—an attitude toward science similar to that held toward various kinds of athletics" in his youth. And he agreed the timing was crucial. "People are alarmed and thinking about science, and perhaps this alarm could be turned into a constructive result."

Rabi then came forward with a specific proposal to advance the cause of science in government: the appointment of a qualified individual to advise the president on scientific issues. Eisenhower was surrounded by experts on fiscal, economic, military, and diplomatic subjects, but he needed someone who could point out the technological aspects of government policies and decisions. James Killian immediately supported this idea, suggesting a presidential science adviser backed by a small committee of experts, on the order of the Council of Economic Advisers. Eisenhower seemed to like the suggestion, noting that such an adviser could help keep track of all decisions with a scientific dimension and make sure they did not get lost in the bureaucracy.

The discussion then turned to the problem of research and development in the Defense Department and the need to avoid such problems as duplication of effort and interservice rivalry in the quest for new weapons. "The need is more for leadership than money," Killian argued. Ike agreed and immediately asked one of his aides to arrange for the scientists to present their views to the new secretary of defense that very afternoon.

The discussion covered other topics, including the possibility of relaxing legislative restraints to permit more consultation with scientists from friendly nations in order, as Rabi said, to "bring resources of the free world together," but at the end Eisenhower again focused on the need to arouse the American people to the importance of science in national life. He spoke of giving special recognition to prominent scientists in public ceremonies and devoting his next press conference to an appeal to the American people to "take an interest and a concern in science, and not just leave the matter to the scientists." As the group broke up, several members came up to General Andrew Goodpaster, Ike's personal aide who was keeping minutes, "to express their enthusiasm and appreciation of the session they had had with the President."[22]

That afternoon, without even a break for lunch, the members of SAC went to the Pentagon to repeat their views to Secretary McElroy. Robert Cutler, Eisenhower's national security adviser, summarized the morning discussion. Rabi and Killian expressed their concern that Russia was "trending at present rate to superiority in science" and warned that in ten years the United States could find itself behind the Soviets. Land again stressed the need to strengthen respect for science and to search for ways to transform the United States "into a more scientific country." When McElroy commented that such a reversal would require more than just presidential initiative, Killian agreed but said *Sputnik* provided "a wonderful chance to change the trend."

The discussion soon turned to the problem of funding basic scientific research. Killian and Rabi complained of the difficulty scientists had in securing research support from the Pentagon unless they could show a direct relationship to weapons development. Unrestricted funds for basic research were required, Rabi claimed, pointing out that the $200 million the government spent in 1956 on scientific research was not enough. Donald Quarles spoke up to warn that Congress would approve research funds only for projects directly related to national security, but then he added, "Unless Sputnik has converted our people." McElroy was more optimistic, asking the scientists to make specific proposals for more research quickly, saying that the Defense Department was "responsive to change now." The meeting ended on a somber note as Herbert Scoville, a nuclear weapons specialist from the CIA, warned that, unless the United States acted quickly, the Russians would "in a few years have a capability to knock us out."[23]

Robert Cutler, presumably acting at the president's request, followed up right away on the major points raised by the scientists. On the afternoon of October 15, he gave Rabi a document summarizing the morning discussion. SAC, under Rabi's direction, was to draw up a "frame of reference" for the better supervision of scientific activities within the government, which should include "some mechanism personal to the President for keeping constantly in touch with scientific interests—possibly an adviser or Special Assistant." Cutler wanted Rabi to prepare this proposal by the first week in November. Somewhat later, Cutler continued, SAC should explore "some way spiritually to awaken the U.S. to the need of becoming a more scientific community." It was vital, he concluded, to prevent the Soviets from surpassing the United States in the quality of their "scientific endeavors."[24]

The views of the scientists on SAC had a profound effect on Dwight Eisenhower. In the weeks to come, he would refer to this discussion again and again. Though he felt confident about America's satellite and missile programs, he had become aware of the danger of falling behind the Soviet Union in science and technology through complacency and the human tendency to sit back and enjoy the fruits of material abundance. He was determined to do everything he could to follow Land's advice to elevate the role of science in education, government, and American society at large. Above all, he would try to turn what he called "the current wave of near-hysteria" over *Sputnik* into an opportunity for constructive change.[25]

VI

Many scientists shared SAC's belief that *Sputnik* showed that Americans were not giving science a high enough priority. Surveys by popular magazines brought forth statements that the United States had failed to realize the importance of satellites and the possibilities opened up by the exploration of space. The Luce publications, *Time* and *Life*, led the way. In a cover story entitled "Knowledge Is Power," *Time* said that, while the nation was still strong in most areas of science, it had fallen dangerously behind the Soviets in certain ones. The article pointed to two specific weaknesses, basic research and education. The United States was spending only one-tenth of the national income on the fundamental research that was vital for all future technological growth. Equally disturbing was the lack of emphasis on science in the high school curriculum. Only one in twenty-four high school students studied physics, while just one in four took algebra.[26]

Prominent scientists echoed these sentiments. Edward Teller complained of the lack of prestige accorded science in American life, noting what he termed "a tone deafness toward science in our society at large." He was particularly concerned by what he felt *Sputnik* revealed about education. "We have suffered a very serious defeat," he declared, "in a field where at least some of the most important engagements are carried out: in the classroom." George R. Price, a University of Minnesota physicist, worried about the danger of the Soviets both winning the race for the ICBM and ultimately surpassing the United States in science generally. Writing for *Life*, Price warned that we had "frittered away" our post–World War II lead over the Soviets in weaponry, to the point where "the time is near when we must decide to set a higher value upon liberty than upon luxury." At the rate we were going, he claimed, "we will probably continue to have the world's best TV comedians and baseball players, and in a few years Russia will have the world's best teachers and scientists." To reverse this trend, Price concluded, Americans would have to show more interest in "giving our children a good education than about keeping our property taxes low" and become "more concerned about who wins the Nobel Prize in physics than about who wins the World Series."[27]

Other scientists pleaded for a more balanced response. Physicist Donald Hughes, just back from a tour of Russia, denied that the Soviets were ahead in basic science. They had simply chosen certain areas for concentration, put huge resources into them, and made some remarkable gains, but often at the expense of other equally important areas of scientific endeavor. Eugene Rabinowitch, the editor of the *Bulletin of the Atomic Scientists,* noted that since 1917 only one Russian had won a Nobel Prize, compared to forty-seven American scientists. But Rabinowitch agreed that the lesson of *Sputnik* was clear: The United States had to give "science and learning the place on the national scale of values which alone can assure America a leading position in the scientific age." William C. Davidon, writing in the same journal, agreed, commenting, "We have catered to desires for undisturbed comfort rather than focusing on larger goals and developing our potentialities."[28]

The scientists, however, were not sure what the best solution would be. Several warned against relying solely on money to do the job. One zoologist claimed that the scientific establishment had already proved it could not allocate government support wisely. "Never has so much been spent," he claimed, "with so little return." And Norman Cousins cautioned against responding to *Sputnik* simply by spending more money for science. "Our scientists by themselves cannot give us security," he wrote. "The devices and weapons they can create may help to restore the national ego, but they are not enough to create a functioning peace." The problem, many agreed, went beyond money and weapons. What was needed, summed up Rabinowitch, was a "concerted national effort" to improve science education and to give science and technology a higher priority in national life.[29]

VII

Throughout the rest of October, Eisenhower groped for ways to encourage the American people to turn their concern over *Sputnik* into a positive program for scientific advancement. For a while his aides mulled over a proposal to outfit a railroad car with exhibits of rockets, space suits, and scientific instruments and send it around the nation to help arouse greater public awareness of the need to rally against "technological blackmail" by the Soviet Union. The president finally turned down the project, and he also rejected a proposal by a Los Angeles insurance executive for Ike to bring some sixty business leaders to the White House to be assured that *Sputnik* had not undermined the nation's security. Rather than rely on this elitist approach, Ike decided to speak directly to the American people.[30]

He set forth his basic theme in the course of some routine remarks to a NATO group on October 11. "We must have faith not to get hysterical," he warned, "and we must not get complacent." On October 22, at the beginning of an address on medical education prepared before *Sputnik,* Ike announced his plans for a series of talks on "many other serious causes in the minds of our fellow citizens." He would deal frankly with such issues as national defense and scientific achievement in order to "set out in proper perspective the truth and facts in these matters." Near the end of his speech, he departed from his text to comment on the prevailing mood of pessimism in the nation. Referring to those who served in World War II, he said, "I don't believe that there's a single one of them that ever saw a victory won by growing pessimistic and putting your chin on your chest. You have to get it up." His aides liked the anecdote, and from that time on the planned presidential speeches were always referred to in the White House as "chins-up" talks.[31]

Eisenhower was genuinely puzzled by the panic over *Sputnik.* He knew he had run a risk in not making sure that the United States was first in space, but, according to James Killian, the president had no idea that the American public was "so psychologically vulnerable." He began to wonder, Eisenhower told one correspondent, whether "we Americans have become too complacent, too fond of the good things in life, and too disinclined to make the sacrifices that are going to be necessary if we win the peace we so devoutly desire."[32]

Above all, Ike felt it was necessary to prepare the American people for the long haul. He opposed both "hasty and extraordinary effort under the impetus of sudden fear" and "unjustified complacency" as satisfactory responses to *Sputnik.* Instead he wanted the people to be ready to support programs that might last "for years, even decades." Agreeing with someone who had written to praise the president for meeting the crisis "with calmness and maturity," Eisenhower concluded: "We face, not a temporary emergency, such as war, but a long term responsibility." His problem, however, was how best to persuade the American people to back him in the long-term effort to find appropriate and constructive answers to the challenges posed by the Soviet satellite. That task would test Eisenhower's power of leadership as no other had since he took office in 1953.[33]

CHAPTER TWO

On October 9, 1957, the day that Eisenhower gave his first post-*Sputnik* press conference, two significant ceremonies took place in the White House Cabinet Room. In the first the president presented outgoing Secretary of Defense Charles E. Wilson with the Medal of Freedom, lauding him for doing so much "in strengthening the security of the United States and its allies against aggression." Then Eisenhower swore in Neil H. McElroy as Wilson's successor.[1]

The changing of the guard at the Pentagon came at an appropriate time. For nearly five years Wilson, a blunt, outspoken man with strong managerial skills but little tact, had tried to carry out the New Look defense policy that Eisenhower and Dulles had instituted in 1953. Appalled by the jump in defense spending from $13.5 billion annually to nearly $45 billion as a result of the Korean War and Truman's Cold War policies, Ike sought to reduce the military budget to around $35 billion by cutting back on conventional forces and placing great emphasis on nuclear striking power. With this reliance on what Dulles termed massive retaliation, Wilson was able to reduce defense spending to under $40 billion a year, but despite rigorous economies he could not quite reach the desired goal of $35 billion. And in the process of trimming the military budget, Wilson made many enemies, both within the armed services—especially in the army and navy, which took the brunt of the cuts—and in Congress, where his candor and cockiness angered many Democrats, notably Senators Henry M. Jackson of Washington and Stuart Symington of Missouri, who felt that the New Look had seriously weakened national security.[2]

McElroy seemed to be an ideal choice to head the Defense Department in the wake of *Sputnik*. Unlike Wilson, he was a modest, soft-spoken man whose background was in sales and marketing. A native of Cincinnati, he had attended Harvard and then worked his way up to the presidency of Procter and Gamble. He had no direct experience with defense issues or industrial production, but he knew how to ingratiate himself with others, how to persuade and to cajole, and, above all, how to present a program in the best possible light. He would rely heavily on Donald Quarles, who had mastered the relationship between technology and defense as an executive of Western Electric, for advice on technological issues; McElroy would concentrate on convincing Congress and the nation that the Pentagon was meeting the challenge posed by *Sputnik*. Best of all, he was in the fortunate position of reversing Wilson's economy efforts and could instead become the advocate of spending more on defense to win the missile race with the Soviet Union.[3]

McElroy, like Wilson, would soon discover that his role would be limited to carrying out the decisions made by President Eisenhower, who preferred to act as his own secretary of defense. From the time he took office in 1953, Ike was determined to cut back on the heavy defense burden he had inherited from Truman. Essential to his outlook was the belief that the Cold War was a long-term contest in which one of the gravest dangers facing the United States was weighing down and eventually destroying the nation's economy with excessive military spending. Together with his closest ally, Treasury Secretary George Humphrey, he had worked with Wilson to reduce the defense budget steadily to reach a level he felt would be manageable over the long haul.

Sputnik thus posed a serious threat to one of the president's most cherished goals. Fearful of a crisis response that would lead to large deficits, he was intent on trying to reassure the nation that the administration could handle the challenge without a crash spending program. "The President's burning concern, now," commented one White House aide, "is to keep the country from going hog wild—from embarking on foolish, costly schemes."[4]

Ike made his concerns clear at the first cabinet meeting McElroy attended, on October 11. When Budget Director Percival Brundage projected a figure of $74 billion for the fiscal year 1959 budget (July 1, 1958, to June 30, 1959), both Eisenhower and the new treasury secretary, Robert Anderson, became upset. Anderson, who had recently replaced Humphrey and shared his predecessor's belief in fiscal austerity, wanted to try to hold the 1959 budget down to $70 billion, warning that "we should not let Russia impair the soundness of our economy." Ike agreed, saying that "the Administration must continue to try to keep its fiscal house in order despite increased tensions with which we would have to learn to live for a long time."

But Eisenhower realized that there would have to be some accommodation to the pressures released by the furor over *Sputnik*. Every member of Congress "will press" for more defense spending, he warned, adding, "We'll ride the black horse this year." Those in the individual armed services would be equally aggressive, he cautioned McElroy, as they would try to force him to make "an alleged choice between security and a sound budget." In reality, Ike pointed out, "both were necessities and the proper balance must be struck." But the president realized that the administration would have to "push forward" in some areas, especially in new missile programs. Thus he was prepared to see the defense budget rise from $38 billion in 1958 to $39.5 in 1959, but he still hoped that enough offsetting economies could be found to keep the total budget close to Anderson's $70 billion target.[5]

The president was right about the impact of *Sputnik* on Congress. Senator Stuart Symington issued a public statement on October 15 taking issue with Eisenhower's October 9 press-conference effort to reassure the nation. Symington claimed that the Russians were several years ahead of the United States in the race for the ICBM and accused the administration of failing to spend all the funds Congress had appropriated for national defense. Citing a recent comment by Khrushchev to the effect that bombers were "obsolete," Symington asked Ike to call a special session of Congress, appoint a "missile Czar" to direct the American ICBM effort, and lift the ceiling on defense spending. Then *Sputnik* might become "a blessing in disguise" by arousing a sleeping nation to face the new peril.[6]

Vice-President Richard M. Nixon, always sensitive to political currents, had also anticipated the Democratic attack. At the October 11 cabinet meeting, he had spoken out in favor of increased defense spending, saying that as a result of *Sputnik* "the country will support it." A few days later he told Secretary of State Dulles that the administration needed to take the initiative on the missile issue, rather than simply become the target of a congressional investigation. Nixon had already begun gathering data to show that it was the Democrats under Truman who were responsible for America's lack of missile progress. If it came to a partisan fight, Nixon promised Dulles, "we can tear them to pieces."[7]

Eisenhower preferred a more conciliatory approach, however. On October 14 he met with McElroy to go over the military response to *Sputnik*. When the secretary asked if he could go beyond the ceiling of $38 billion in the 1958 defense budget, the president quickly agreed. Eisenhower went on to explain that he had not wanted to set a rigid ceiling on defense spending "but had done so on the repeated request of Secretary Wilson." The $38 billion figure, however, was intended not as an arbitrary limit but only as "a judgment as to a proper level."

In a press conference at the end of October, Eisenhower made public his decision to permit defense spending to go beyond $38 billion. He told a reporter that he had directed McElroy to exceed the ceiling for 1958 and that he was prepared to authorize more than $38 billion in defense spending for the 1959 budget.[8]

This concession, however, did not come easily to the president. At a cabinet meeting on October 18, he expressed confidence that, despite "all the talk of satellites and missiles, the United States with all its planes still retained the power of destroying Russia." But he recognized the need "for convincing the world—presently scared by Russia—that the United States is doing what it should." So he told the cabinet that it was no longer a question of "butter *and* guns, rather it is one of butter *or* guns." Telling them that they faced "the most difficult budget ever," he asked the cabinet members to continue trying for the $70 billion goal by having the country "do a little less 'buttering' and more 'gunning.'"[9]

Eisenhower's response to the budgetary decisions brought about by *Sputnik* was characteristic of his overall strategy in the Cold War. Convinced that the United States and Russia were locked in a contest that would last for decades, he refused to make an abrupt change in his priorities. Yet at the same time, he realized that the sense of national peril forced him to defer his hopes for a balanced budget and to take steps that would persuade the American people that *Sputnik* had not upset the military balance of power. Thus he was willing to grant modest increases in defense spending, but he was not prepared to order a crash program with its resulting deficits. He summed up his feelings on *Sputnik* and the budget most aptly when he told the cabinet, "I'd like to know what's on [the] other side of the moon, but I won't pay to find out this year."[10]

I

The American missile program was already well established by the time the Soviets launched the first *Sputnik* in 1957. In the mid-1950s the Eisenhower administration had decided to make a major commitment to the development of both ICBMs and IRBMs. As a result, six major missile programs were under way in October 1957, at a cost of more than $1 billion a year.

The initial American missile programs after World War II had proved disappointing. A cutback in defense spending by the Truman administration in 1949 had temporarily ended the early efforts to build on the German V-2 experience, and then the Korean War focused military spending in a different direction. Moreover, the air force displayed a strong bias in favor of manned bombers and a disposition to neglect missile development. When the ICBM program was revived in 1951, it was hampered by a relatively low budget and very unrealistic requirements for high accuracy and warhead size. The air force bureaucracy seemed to take the position, according to the historian who has studied this issue most closely, that, "if the missile projects were not funded, then the missiles would not be built."[11]

Two things happened in the early 1950s to change this situation. The first was the election of Eisenhower, which brought the appointment of a new group of top-level officials in the Pentagon. The man who emerged as the chief sponsor for the revival and speedup of the American ICBM program was Trevor Gardner, originally special assistant to Air Force Secretary Harold E. Talbott, and then later assistant secretary of the air force for research and development. Gardner, an engineer who had headed his own company, immediately challenged the air force's neglect of missiles and appointed a committee of distinguished scientists, headed by mathematician John von Neumann of Princeton University, which included Dr. Simon Ramo and Dr. Dean E. Wooldridge, who had recently left Hughes Aircraft Corporation to found their own aerospace company.

The other significant development came from the Castle series of thermonuclear tests in the Marshall Islands in the spring of 1954. The extremely heavy weight of an atomic warhead had been one of the major problems facing those designing an ICBM. The new hydrogen bomb warheads tested in the Castle series suddenly made the ICBM feasible; they were in the megaton range, nearly a thousand times more powerful than the original atomic bomb. It would now be possible to launch a relatively light nuclear missile over long distances and still destroy a target even if the warhead landed several miles away.[12]

In early 1954 the von Neumann committee anticipated the Castle findings in recommending that the air force redesign its ICBM program around the lighter but far more powerful hydrogen warhead and create a new agency to oversee the effort. The scientific panel predicted that the ICBM could be operational within six to eight years if the project were given the "highest national priority." A few days later, a separate Rand Corporation study reached similar conclusions, pointing out that, with a relaxation of the rigid air force requirements for an ICBM, coupled with increased funding, "an operational missile system of great value should be obtainable by 1960," five years ahead of the current schedule.

In March 1954 Air Force Secretary Talbott accepted these recommendations and ordered the acceleration of the ICBM program. Following the advice of the two studies, the air force relaxed the specifications for the ICBM, calling for a missile with a range of fifty-five hundred miles, an accuracy of five miles, and a one-megaton warhead. The goal was to achieve initial operational status by June 1958. Gardner failed in his efforts to have a new, separate agency oversee ICBM development, but he did secure the appointment of General Bernard Schriever to head a new Western Development Division within the air force's Air Research and Development Command. Based at Inglewood, California, Schriever would be close to both Convair, the builder of the ICBM, and Ramo-Wooldridge, which held the contract to design the new missile.[13]

Despite this breakthrough, both Gardner and Schriever felt hampered by continued resistance from the air force bureaucracy, which favored the new B-52 bomber and feared that Gardner would become the "czar" of a separate missile agency. To gain the freedom and resources they wanted, Gardner and Schriever finally turned to Congress. In the spring of 1955, they told two key members of the Joint Committee on Atomic Energy, Senators Clinton Anderson, its chairman, and Henry M. Jackson, who headed the subcommittee on military applications, of the bureaucratic obstacles they were facing and then warned that the Russians might well be moving ahead in the race for the ICBM.

Senators Jackson and Anderson responded by sending an urgent letter to President Eisenhower on June 30, 1955. In somber terms the two senators expressed their concern that, in light of the "peacetime" status of the American program and the likely high priority of the Russian effort, "the Soviet Union may now be ahead of us in the race for the ICBM." Anderson and Jackson warned that there was "no effective defense" against an ICBM, which they called "the ultimate weapon," and that Soviet possession could well lead to a "nuclear Pearl Harbor." Therefore they called on the president to put the ICBM on a "wartime footing" with a crash program, giving it the highest national priority. They also proposed a separate budget for the ICBM and the appointment of a presidential assistant with sole authority over its development, the "czar" so feared by the air force bureaucracy.[14]

President Eisenhower was impressed by this appeal. Two weeks later he called Gardner and Schriever to the White House to give a special briefing on the ICBM to the National Security Council (NSC). After due deliberation the president authorized the NSC to give the ICBM "the highest national priority," which would enable Gardner and Schriever to overcome any bureaucratic obstacles they faced. Eisenhower refused, however, to begin a crash program or to create a missile czar to oversee the effort. "I am convinced," he wrote to Senators Anderson and Jackson on September 13, 1955, "that in order to achieve maximum acceleration of this project, we should continue to build on the sound foundation that has been laid." But he assured the senators that he shared their determination to get an ICBM ahead of the Russians by concluding that "no other development program is now the subject of so urgent and emphatic a directive."[15]

Yet even as Eisenhower was responding to the growing political pressure for the ICBM, his scientific advisers were pushing equally hard for another expensive program, the IRBM. In March 1954 the president asked a panel of the Scientific Advisory Committee to study the problem of defending the United States against a surprise attack in the thermonuclear age. A Technological Capabilities Panel led by

MIT President James Killian studied the problem for nearly a year and then reported its findings to Eisenhower on February 14, 1955. The Killian report endorsed the ICBM program, calling progress on this weapon "satisfactory" but warning that it was unlikely to be available in large enough numbers to have military significance before 1965. To protect the United States against an earlier Soviet ICBM, the Killian panel stated, "it is important that the U.S. initiate a medium range ballistic missile program to increase the probability that the U.S. is first to achieve a ballistic missile capability." Therefore the report recommended developing both land-based and sea-based IRBMs with a range of around fifteen hundred miles.[16]

A bureaucratic tug-of-war soon broke out in the Pentagon. The Defense Department was willing to give the IRBM high priority, but with the understanding that there be "no interference to the valid requirements of the ICBM program." The State Department, however, insisted that the IRBM be given priority even over the ICBM. If the Soviets developed the first medium- or long-range missiles, then they would be able to wage nuclear blackmail, undermining the confidence of our allies in American technical superiority and persuading some of them to move toward a "third force" orientation. The earliest possible development of an American IRBM was thus vital in order to "strengthen free world confidence in the U.S. retaliatory power."

Informed by his scientific advisers that it would be possible to develop an IRBM more quickly than the ICBM, the president decided to reject the Pentagon's request. Instead he ordered the National Security Council to give both programs "highest national priority"; if any conflicts developed, they would be referred to the president for his personal decision. Ike was troubled, however, by the possible duplication of effort involved in giving priority to both the ICBM and the IRBM. Accordingly, on December 15, 1955, he told the Secretary of Defense, both by telephone and by a written memo, "that nothing in the way of rival requirements is to delay the earliest development of an effective ballistic missile with significant range—that is to say, at least 1000 to 1700 miles." To make it clear that he sided with the State Department's priority for the IRBM, Ike informed Secretary of Defense Wilson that he had amended the NSC Record of Action of December 1 to state that "priority will always be given to the development (in whichever program) of an effective missile with a range of at least 1000-1700 miles."[17]

Thus by the end of 1955, the president had not only approved a speedup in the ICBM program but given equally high priority to the IRBM. Indeed, he had made clear to Secretary Wilson that if there was any "mutual interference," it was the ICBM that would give way to the urgent need for a missile that could reach the Soviet Union from overseas American bases.[18] Most important, the groundwork for the American missile program had been fully established two years before the launch of *Sputnik*. Yet the belief that we were locked in a dangerous missile race with the Soviet Union helped create an atmosphere that would contribute heavily to the post-*Sputnik* sense of panic. The possibility that we had already lost the race for the ICBM to the Russians frightened the American people and obscured the very important foundations that the Eisenhower administration had already laid for American security in the missile age.

II

The American missile program grew rapidly between 1955 and 1957. The air force led the way with the ICBM. In November 1955 Secretary Wilson created a Ballistic Missiles Committee within the Defense Department to prevent any interference from the three services, while the air force set up its own Ballistic Missiles Committee to bypass the Air Staff, which still placed greater reliance on the Strategic Air Command and B-52 bombers. These arrangements permitted General Schriever and his Western Development Division to have direct access to the top civilian officials in the Pentagon and ensure that the president's grant of highest priority to the ICBM effort would be honored.

General Schriever gave primary attention to the development of the Atlas missile as the nation's first ICBM. It was originally conceived of as a huge, five-engine rocket, but the von Neumann committee, now reconstituted as the Atlas Scientific Advisory Committee, succeeded in scaling it down to a more modest size to carry the lighter but more powerful hydrogen warhead. The final configuration, designed by Ramo-Wooldridge and built by Convair, consisted of a 250,000-pound missile powered by three rocket engines with a thin-skinned, inflatable air frame carrying the huge tanks for the liquid fuel. With the earliest possible initial operational capability made the most urgent requirement, its designers sacrificed such possible features as a rigid frame, which would have permitted its deployment in underground silos, or multistage engines that would have fired in the atmosphere and thus provided greater total thrust. Instead they focused their efforts on the goal of an operational Atlas before the end of the decade.[19]

The crash program to build the Atlas led to several new departures in weapons procurement. To save time Schriever set up a systems approach, which meant that the various elements of the Atlas were designed and tested simultaneously as part of an overall weapons system. He also pioneereed the concept of concurrency, which permitted the various parts of the Atlas to go into production while still being tested and perfected. Concurrency continued even into the actual production of the missile itself, beginning with the building of a prototype on the assembly line and then changing various elements as a result of flight testing.[20]

In the spring of 1955, Schriever received permission to develop a second ICBM, the Titan, in order to test more sophisticated missile technology, both as a backup to the Atlas and for future weaponry. Freed from the time constraints on the Atlas, the Western Development Division designed the Titan as a two-stage missile, with the second stage engine igniting in the atmosphere. Titan also had a more advanced guidance system and a rigid frame which permitted it to be launched from an underground silo that would protect it from enemy attack.[21]

While the air force was developing the Atlas and Titan ICBMs, scientists began to explore the possibility of a much smaller and more efficient solid-fuel missile. Both the Atlas and the Titan required highly volatile liquid fuels kept at very low temperatures, which meant a considerable delay before they could be launched. A solid-fuel missile would weigh much less, since it would not require the heavy tanks and complex piping of a liquid-fuel missile, but there were enormous problems in developing a solid propellant that would burn evenly and permit the missile to maneuver in flight. But the savings in missile weight, overall cost, and weapons readiness were so great that in September 1957 the air force set up a special group to design a solid-fuel ICBM, first called simply Weapon System Q but soon dubbed Minuteman, because it would be ready for launch on only a minute's notice.[22]

By the fall of 1957, the air force was well along in the quest for the ICBM. The first Atlas test, in June 1957, came only thirty months after approval of the air frame design; despite the missile's destruction after only a minute of flight due to engine failure, the test provided a great deal of helpful information. The second flight test, on September 25, 1957, also proved unsuccessful but informative. Despite these failures, the Atlas program was on schedule, while the more advanced Titan promised a more sophisticated weapon for the 1960s. And the decision, made a month before *Sputnik,* to develop the Minuteman indicated that the United States was already thinking ahead to a second generation of ICBMs, which would provide the nation with a virtually invulnerable second-strike strategic weapon.[23]

III

The State Department's fear that the Soviets would perfect the world's first operational ballistic missiles led to an even greater effort to develop IRBMs. President Eisenhower had made clear that he considered the achievement of a missile with a range of between a thousand and seventeen hundred miles the most urgent task facing the nation. In his memoirs he expressed his belief at the time that "the political and psychological impact on the world of the early development of a reliable IRBM would be enormous, while its military value would, for the time being, be practically equal to that of the ICBM."[24]

This presidential concern led to an intensive effort to develop an IRBM in all three services and, much to Eisenhower's dismay, to extensive waste and duplication of effort. The air force led the way with its Thor. A spinoff from the Atlas, Thor was designed to carry a one-megaton warhead fifteen hundred miles from bases in friendly European countries. Since it shared many of the Atlas components but had only one engine, the air force hoped to have it operational at least a year earlier. Work on the Thor went ahead quickly, and after four failures the first successful flight test took place on September 20, 1957, just two weeks before *Sputnik*.[25]

Meanwhile, the army and the navy were racing to perfect their own IRBMs. This effort began as an interservice project in fall 1955. The army, which had relied on a team of German rocket scientists led by Wernher Von Braun at its Huntsville, Alabama, proving grounds to develop the two-hundred-mile Redstone nuclear missile, received permission to join with the navy to build an IRBM that could be launched from either land bases or specially designed ships.

Major General John D. Medaris was put in charge of the newly created Army Ballistic Missile Agency to oversee this effort. Von Braun and his team at Huntsville used many of the Redstone components in designing the new Jupiter IRBM, a sixty-foot-long liquid-fuel missile with a thrust of 150,000 pounds designed to deliver a one-megaton warhead at a target up to fifteen hundred miles away. The navy soon decided that such a missile was simply too heavy and cumbersome for shipboard launch and dropped out of the Jupiter program in fall 1956. At the same time, Secretary of Defense Wilson issued an order restricting the army to missiles with a range of no more than two hundred miles, thus ensuring that the Jupiter, even if perfected by the army, would be deployed by the air force.[26]

Medaris and Secretary of the Army Wilber Brucker fought tenaciously to preserve the Jupiter. Despite the president's concern over the cost of such interservice rivalry and duplication of resources, in January 1957 the army received Pentagon permission to go ahead with the development of the Jupiter. After three failures the army carried out the nation's first successful flight test of an IRBM when the Jupiter soared fourteen hundred miles into the Atlantic from the launch site at Cape Canaveral, Florida, on May 31, 1957. Despite a second successful test flight in July, the fate of the Jupiter remained uncertain. A Pentagon committee charged with choosing between Thor and Jupiter could not reach a decision in August 1957, and both programs were allowed to continue pending further review, although the outlook for the army's Jupiter seemed bleak.[27]

The navy appeared to have the most promising solution to the IRBM problem. In the original Jupiter program, the navy had planned to deploy the sea-launched IRBM from surface ships, since a submarine large enough to accommodate the sixty-foot Jupiter would have had to be the size of a cruiser. By early 1956 Rear Admiral William F. Raborn, in charge of the navy's Special Projects Office, had decided to explore the alternative of a smaller solid-fuel missile that could be launched from a submarine. Edward Teller helped persuade Raborn by informing him that by the early 1960s the Atomic Energy Commission (AEC) would have perfected much smaller nuclear warheads, which would make a twenty-eight-foot IRBM feasible.

When his staff began to make some significant breakthroughs on solid fuels, including the use of fiberglass casing to cut the weight substantially, Raborn decided to request that the navy drop out of the Jupiter program with the army and develop its own smaller solid-fuel missile, the Polaris. He convinced the cost-conscious Charles Wilson by pointing out that using submarines rather than surface ships would save the navy missile program nearly half a billion dollars. On December 8, 1956, Wilson issued an order permitting the navy to drop out of the joint Jupiter program and instead develop the Polaris on its own.[28]

The Polaris tended to lag behind both Thor and Jupiter, due to both its late start and its new technology. Raborn's group did not settle on the design for the missile envelope that would be placed on board each nuclear submarine until March 1957, and tests of the compressed air system that would propel the Polaris to the surface, where it could be ignited for flight, did not come for another year. Such problems as how to steer the solid-fuel missile in flight and what type of guidance system to employ still remained unresolved by the time of *Sputnik,* and flight testing was not due to begin until fall 1958. Yet the enormous strategic advantage of having a nuclear deterrent aboard submarines made the Polaris very attractive to the Eisenhower administration. Prodded by SAC chairman I. I. Rabi, Secretary Wilson decided to give Raborn additional funds in the spring of 1957 in order to speed up Polaris in hopes of achieving an initial operational capability by 1961, two years ahead of the original schedule. Justifying this expenditure to the president, Wilson quoted Rabi as saying that "a relatively small number of equipped, lighter-weight submarines could present the Soviets with a serious deterrent threat—a threat that would be difficult for Soviet intelligence to estimate."[29]

Thus by the fall of 1957, the 1954 recommendation by the Killian panel had led to three separate IRBM programs, all competing for a share of the $38 billion defense budget that Eisenhower and Wilson were trying so hard to maintain. Jupiter was furthest along in testing, and Thor had the advantage of being the first to enter into production due to Schriever's concurrency approach, while Polaris, still in the development stage, promised to become the most versatile addition to the nation's strategic arsenal.

IV

The decision to build three ICBMs and three IRBMs led to severe budgetary pressures and serious administrative problems. In the months before *Sputnik*, the Eisenhower administration tried to reduce both the heavy level of spending and the inevitable duplication of effort in the missile program.

The costs began to be felt in 1955, when spending jumped from $14 million in fiscal 1954 to $161 million (see Table 1). The 1956 total rose to $515 million; then, in 1957, with three IRBMs in development along with the Atlas and Titan ICBMs, missile spending climbed to well over $1 billion, where it was expected to remain for several years.[30]

Even this high level of expenditure did not please everyone. In February 1956 Trevor Gardner resigned to protest both the decision to permit the army and navy to go ahead with Jupiter and what he considered inadequate funding for the air force missile effort. Two months later Wilson responded to renewed congressional pressure for a missile czar by appointing Eger V. Murphree to the new post of special assistant to the secretary of defense for guided missiles. The tactful Murphree, whose background was in the oil industry, had relatively little power to settle the constant infighting between the services. In May 1957 Wilson replaced him with William Holaday, another oil company research director, and gave him somewhat broader authority. The new special assistant for guided missiles, however, soon proved unable to assert his control over the burgeoning missile program.[31]

President Eisenhower, concerned that the missile effort would raise defense spending beyond his $38 billion ceiling and annoyed at the overlapping service programs, finally decided to call a halt. On July 8, 1957, he ordered Secretary Wilson to begin a study of the "financial feasibility" of all existing missile programs and recommend to him no later than August 15 those that could be eliminated by October 1.

Wilson responded by cutting back on the army's Nike-Hercules antimissile program and eliminating an already obsolete air-breathing

TABLE 1: Cost of U.S.
Missile Programs

Fiscal Year	Dollar (in millions)
1953	3
1954	14
1955	161
1956	515
1957	1,380
1958	1,349

missile, the Navaho, projecting a savings of $220 million in fiscal 1958 from these moves. Additionally he made an across-the-board cut of $170 million in Defense Department spending for research and development. His August economy moves also included reducing overtime in several of the ballistic missile programs, giving Titan a lower priority than Atlas, limiting spending on Polaris to 95 percent of its 1958 budget, and halting all further production of Jupiter and Thor missiles pending the outcome of a decision of a committee headed by Holaday on which IRBM to build. As a result, Wilson felt confident that he could achieve Ike's goal of holding defense spending to the $38 billion limit in fiscal 1958.[32]

The timing was unfortunate. A few days after *Sputnik,* rumors of these reductions began to appear in the press. On October 17 Eisenhower raised the question of a ban on overtime with the new secretary of defense, Neil McElroy, and told him that if such an order was holding up the American missile program he should rescind it, "at least on a selective basis." Moving quickly, McElroy restored full overtime on Atlas and other missile programs on October 28 and also lifted the 10 percent across-the-board reduction in research and development. Wilson's reductions, while politically embarrassing, had little effect on the overall American missile program, which was already well established by October 1957.[33]

Indeed, just one day after *Sputnik* outgoing Defense Secretary Charles Wilson gave his final approval to plans for the initial operational capability (IOC) for the new American arsenal. As a result of decisions reached by President Eisenhower in spring of 1957, the United States planned to deploy forty Atlas and forty Titan ICBMs in squadrons of ten in three continental bases by 1962, with the first squadron tentatively scheduled to become operational in March 1959. In addition, Pentagon plans called for an IOC of sixty IRBMs, with the first to be deployed overseas in late 1958, along with an eventual fleet of six Polaris submarines, carrying a total of ninety-six missiles beginning in mid-1961. Thanks to the foresight of men like John von Neumann, Trevor Gardner, and James Killian, the Eisenhower administration had taken the necessary steps before *Sputnik* to provide for a large and balanced force of ballistic missiles. The program was still in the early stage of testing and development, however, and *Sputnik* appeared to confirm a growing fear that the Soviets were far ahead in the race for the ICBM.[34]

V

The United States had been carefully monitoring the Soviet missile program since the early 1950s. The CIA created an Office of Scientific Intelligence in 1952 and put a former army officer, Colonel Jack A. White, in charge. By 1954 White's office was predicting that the Soviets would be capable of launching an earth satellite by the end of 1957 but would not have an operational ICBM before 1960. The air force disagreed, warning that the Soviets might well have an operational ICBM by the end of the decade. In 1955, the year the Eisenhower administration decided to give the ICBM effort its highest priority, the air force joined with the CIA in a new Guided Missiles Intelligence Committee under Colonel White's direction to compare American and Soviet progress in the ensuing race for the ICBM.

American intelligence relied on two highly secret sources of information on the Soviet missile program. The first was a radar listening post at Kiyarbakir, Turkey, some six hundred miles from the main Russian test site at Kapustin Yar, not far from the city of Volvograd. Using antennae half the length of a football field, this radar could monitor a small but key portion of test flights, from the time a missile rose above the horizon until it entered outer space. The second source was the U-2, the American high altitude spy plane, which began overflying the Soviet Union in June 1956 and brought back regular reports on Russian bomber and missile development with pictures so sharp that one official claimed it was possible to "almost read the tail markings on the bombers." A government official later revealed that U-2 reconnaissance flights provided "information on airfields, aircraft, missiles, missile testing and training" as well as on submarine production and aircraft deployment.[35]

Interpreting the evidence from the Turkish radar and the U-2 flights was often problematic. Beginning in 1954, the air force, misled by fly-bys of Russian Bison bombers at the annual May Day parades in Moscow, had been contending that the Soviets were building up a huge fleet of heavy bombers that would surpass the number of American B-52s by the end of the 1950s, creating a "bomber gap." Congressional critics, led by Democratic Senator Stuart Symington, accepted these findings and pressed the Eisenhower administration hard for increased spending on bombers. By mid-1957, however, the CIA had sharply lowered its projections of future Soviet bomber strength on the basis of U-2 photos that showed very few heavy bombers present on Russian airfields.

With the demise of the bomber gap, the air force turned to evidence of nearly three hundred Russian missile tests over distances ranging from 75 to 950 miles to warn that the Soviets were well ahead of the United States in developing IRBMs, thus opening up a future "missile gap." The CIA tried to play down this danger, which threatened our European allies and the American overseas bases but not the continental United States. New evidence from U-2 overflights in spring 1957, however, showed a much more alarming development. The Soviets had built a second missile test site at Tyuratam, a remote region of southern Russia near the Aral Sea, that was designed to conduct ICBM tests over 3000 miles across Siberia to the Kamchatka peninsula.[36]

President Eisenhower learned of this ominous news at a National Security Council briefing in May 1957. Prior to the briefing, Ray Cline, in charge of preparing National Intelligence Estimates for the CIA, had given Allen Dulles this new information, but the CIA director had originally planned not to mention it to the NSC because it was "too technical." At the NSC session on May 10, however, as he was finishing his briefing, Dulles said that Cline would present some "disturbing new evidence about Soviet weapons." At the end of Cline's remarks, the president asked him if an ICBM launched from Kamchatka could reach the United States. Cline's reply, that it could hit Hawaii but not California, was hardly reassuring, but the president quickly turned the discussion to other issues.[37]

The CIA then began a regular surveillance of the Tyuratam testing grounds. By that time the Soviets were well along on the development of their first ICBM. Like the Americans, they had relied initially on German V-2 experts captured at the end of World War II for their early rocket designs. But by the 1950s Russian scientists and engineers had taken over from the German technicians. Basing their design on the large warhead required prior to the perfection of the hydrogen bomb, the Russians developed a huge rocket, later called the SS-6, with a thrust of more than 250,000 pounds. After successful static tests of the rocket engine in 1956, the Soviets prepared for the first flight test of the SS-6 at Tyuratam in summer 1957.[38]

The Eisenhower administration, therefore, was not surprised when the Kremlin announced on August 26 that it had conducted the first successful flight test of its ICBM over an undisclosed range. In fact, according to one report, an American U-2 "actually looked down on the first Soviet ICBM on its launcher," while the Turkish radar monitored the three-thousand-mile flight to Kamchatka. News of the Soviet ICBM created great concern in the American press, however; the *New York Times* stated that, if the report were true, "the Communists would have won what has been considered a crucial race." In a news conference in early September, the president tried to allay this fear. He pointed out the difficulties involved in perfecting an ICBM, such as resolving problems of guidance and reentry, and argued that for the foreseeable future bombers, not missiles, would be "the best means of delivering an explosive charge." He did add, however, that he had given the American ICBM effort "highest priority."[39]

A second successful Soviet ICBM test flight in early September, coupled with the second Atlas failure later that month, contributed to the growing feeling that the United States was falling behind in missile development. The launch of *Sputnik* on October 4 led the CIA to conclude that the Russians had developed a rocket powerful enough to hurl a two-thousand-pound warhead at a target five thousand miles

away. Thus *Sputnik* forced the administration to begin a careful reconsideration of where the United States stood in regard to the Soviet
Union in the race for the first operational ICBM.[40]

On October 22, 1957, Allen Dulles convened a board of scientific
consultants to advise him on the state of the Soviet missile program.
These experts, who had been consulted regularly by the CIA since
1954, concluded after an examination of all the available intelligence
data that the United States was two to three years behind the Soviets in
developing the ICBM. Based on the extensive test flights of shorter-
range missiles, the powerful thrust of the rocket that launched
Sputnik, and the two successful flights of the Soviet ICBM, the CIA
consultants reported that "the USSR can have some (a dozen) operational missiles by the end of 1958." They called for a "most determined and concentrated US effort" to catch up, warning that "the
country is in a period of grave national emergency."[41]

In early November the CIA issued a new National Intelligence Estimate (NIE). The previous one, dated March 12, 1957, had estimated
that it would be 1961 before the Soviets would have an operational
ICBM. The new estimate advanced the timetable for the Russian
ICBM to 1959 and predicted Soviet deployment of IRBMs with a
range of a thousand miles before the end of 1958. The November
NIE predicted that the Soviets would have ten ICBMs operational by
1959, one hundred by 1960, and five hundred by 1962, compared
with only twenty-four American ICBMs by 1960 and sixty-five by
1961. The air force considered this estimate to be too conservative,
contending that the Russians might well have a thousand ICBMs by
1962. The CIA had tempered its figures on the basis of the bomber
gap experience, but even so it accepted the underlying air force premise that the Soviets, having failed to go all out for bombers, were likely
to seek supremacy in the delivery of nuclear weapons with a huge
arsenal of ICBMs.[42]

The most frightening implication of the CIA estimate was the future vulnerability of American bomber forces. The air force was in
the process of replacing outmoded turboprop B-36s with B-52 jet
bombers at its eleven Strategic Air Command bases in the continental
United States. In addition, there were twenty-eight wings of B-47
medium bombers in American bases overseas. With reaction times
ranging from thirty minutes for the B-47s overseas to more than two
hours for the B-52s in the United States, it was conceivable that by
1959 the Russians would have the capacity to knock out the overseas
deterrent with IRBMs and launch an equally deadly ICBM attack on
the remaining B-52s in the United States. This was a worst-case
analysis, which assumed not only that the Soviets would be able to
coordinate such a concerted strike but that they would succeed in
solving the difficult problems of guidance and reentry for long-range
missiles. But the very possibility of an enemy attack that could wipe

out SAC, the entire American nuclear deterrent, in one swift blow compelled the Eisenhower administration to reconsider its budgetary and strategic priorities.[43]

VI

The president's first response to the strategic crisis posed by Sputnik was to speed up earlier plans for the initial deployment of American IRBMs overseas. In January 1957 the United States had proposed deploying the first IRBMs to be ready in British bases, where their fifteen-hundred-mile range would reach as far as Moscow. At the Bermuda Conference in March 1957, designed to heal the breach in Anglo-American relations after Suez, Eisenhower and Prime Minister Harold Macmillan signed an agreement providing for the placement of American IRBMs in bases in England, to be manned by British personnel but with the nuclear warheads under American control. Since the IRBMs were still undergoing testing and development, no date was set for their actual deployment.[44]

A few days after the launch of *Sputnik,* Macmillan sent a message to Eisenhower expressing his concern and calling for joint efforts by the United States and the NATO allies "to meet the Soviet challenge on every front, military, political, economic and ideological." A week later, the president asked Secretary of State Dulles to arrange a visit by Macmillan and British Foreign Secretary Selwyn Lloyd to begin planning a coordinated Western response to *Sputnik*. Macmillan accepted eagerly, for he was intent on securing Ike's agreement to amend the McMahon Act of 1946, which forbade sharing nuclear secrets with American allies. Eisenhower and Dulles, meanwhile, were equally determined to nail down the Bermuda agreement on British-based IRBMs and to make plans for deploying additional IRBMs in other NATO countries.

During the three days Macmillan and Lloyd were in Washington, the American and British negotiators quickly worked out the deal that the president and prime minister announced on October 25. For his part, Eisenhower agreed to seek amendments to the McMahon Act in order to permit "an enlarged Atlantic effort in scientific research and development in support of greater collective security." The British agreed to create a joint committee headed by Sir Richard Powell, permanent secretary of the Ministry of Defense, and Donald Quarles, the American deputy secretary of defense, to "make recommendations on missiles and rocketry." The press correctly interpreted the job of this committee to be doing everything possible to expedite the deployment of American IRBMs in Britain.[45]

The most important result of the meeting with Macmillan became clear at the end of October, when NATO announced that Eisenhower and other heads of government would attend the alliance's next regu-

lar meeting, scheduled for December in Paris. The president and the
prime minister had conferred with the new NATO secretary-general,
Paul-Henri Spaak of Belgium, and he had agreed to this arrangement. In preparing for Macmillan's visit, Dulles and Eisenhower had
decided that their primary goal was to "close up the IRBM agreement
with Britain and then to extend it to other countries." By going to the
NATO session himself, Eisenhower hoped to persuade several of the
European allies to follow England's example and agree to accept additional American IRBM bases.[46]

The meeting with Macmillan buoyed Ike's spirits. The prime minister, noting that the president was under severe political attack for the
first time, commented that Ike "seemed much better than at Bermuda." "He was brisk, confident, and seemed more sure of himself,"
Macmillan observed. Eisenhower's aides were delighted with the positive public response to the sense of Western solidarity engendered by
the conference with Macmillan; Press Secretary James Hagerty agreed
with Dulles that "the meeting was wonderful." More significant was
the sense of relief felt in the Pentagon. The United States, faced with
the ominous Soviet lead in the race for the ICBM, could at least
counter with the deployment of Thor and Jupiter IRBMs in Europe to
maintain the nuclear balance until the Atlas and Titan intercontinental missiles were finally ready.[47]

VII

The delivery of a long-awaited report on America's nuclear defenses
in early November intensified the post-*Sputnik* sense of urgency
within the Eisenhower administration. On April 4, 1957, the president
had appointed a panel known as the Gaither committee to study and
evaluate a recommendation by the Federal Civil Defense Administration that the United States spend $40 billion to build blast and fallout
shelters to protect the American people in case of nuclear attack.
H. Rowan Gaither, a San Francisco lawyer who was head of both the
Ford Foundation and the Rand Corporation, was appointed chairman. In a White House meeting on July 16, Eisenhower made clear
his own reservations about spending so much on civil defense and
impressed on Gaither the importance of limiting his panel's study,
specifically ruling out any "detailed examination of national security
policies and programs" with an eye to suggesting changes.

Gaither appointed an advisory panel and four technical groups of
experts to gather information and prepare studies for the full committee, formally known as the Security Resources Panel, to use in its
final report, due in October. Members of the advisory committee included such prominent figures as General James Doolittle, chairman
of the National Advisory Committee for Aeronautics (NACA), Frank
Stanton of CBS, Ernest Lawrence of the University of California, and

two leading figures from the American legal and banking community who had held prominent positions within the Truman administration in the early days of the Cold War, Robert A. Lovett and John J. McCloy. Among the influential men serving on the technical panels were I. I. Rabi of Columbia University, James Killian of M.I.T, and Herman Kahn of the Rand Corporation. All in all, there were some sixty-five members of the various panels supporting the Gaither committee; they were drawn from government agencies, including the CIA, as well as outside organizations such as Rand and the Institute for Defense Analysis. Nearly all these people held "definite opinions of the problems of American military policy," and many believed that the Eisenhower administration had been risking national security in its efforts to contain defense spending in order to balance the budget. Service on the Gaither committee provided them with a golden opportunity to reverse what they felt was an increasingly dangerous situation.[48]

When Rowan Gaither became ill during the summer of 1957, leadership of the committee passed to two experienced government advisers, Robert C. Sprague of the Sprague Electric Company, who had served on Killian's 1955 panel, which had called for building the IRBM as well as the ICBM, and William C. Foster of Olin-Mattison Chemical Company, a former deputy secretary of defense. Sprague quickly became the driving force within the Gaither committee, and by the time it reconvened in September he was determined to broaden its mandate, despite the president's warning. Instead of focusing on passive civil defense, Sprague decided to examine the alternative of improving the nation's deterrent as its best chance of preventing a nuclear attack.

This new emphasis on active rather than passive nuclear defense measures provided an opportunity for Albert Wohlstetter, one of the ablest of the Rand Corporation experts on national security, to put forward his ideas. In September 1956 he had completed Staff Report R-290 for Rand, in which he warned that in the missile age the B-52 bombers that were America's main deterrent would be vulnerable to a Soviet first strike. Claiming that just 150 Soviet ICBMs could wipe out our B-52s, his report called for an extensive program of dispersing American bombers at many more bases and building hardened shelters to protect them against a sneak attack. Although not made public, Staff Report R-290 was widely known in the Pentagon, though apparently not in the White House. When called on by the Gaither committee for advice, Wohlstetter argued strongly for the views in his classified report and succeeded in convincing Sprague to shift the focus of the study to the vulnerability of the nation's deterrent. When the Gaither committee assembled in September in the old War-State-Navy building next door to the White House to study the panel reports, nearly all their time was spent on examining the question of how to guard the nation against a surprise nuclear attack in the missile age. It was a frightening experience, which William Foster compared to "spending ten hours a day staring straight into hell."[49]

By the end of the month, the Gaither committee, convinced that the administration did not appreciate the full extent of the threat to national security, prepared to issue its final report with a "real sense of urgency." Sprague delegated the drafting to another member of the group, James Phinney Baxter, a historian and president of Williams College. Baxter turned over the actual writing to Paul Nitze, who had been added to the panel in September. Nitze, a Democrat who had headed the State Department's Policy Planning Staff under Dean Acheson in the Truman administration, was an outspoken Cold Warrior. Best known as the author of NSC-68, which had outlined the Soviet threat in 1949 in ominous terms and called for a vast increase in defense spending, Nitze quickly began to set forth the need for another quantum leap in the defense budget in bold and unequivocal language. The Soviet launch of *Sputnik* on October 4 confirmed the feelings of the Gaither committee that the United States was lagging dangerously behind the Soviet Union in the missile race and permitted Nitze to add an even more urgent tone to the recommendations for a sweeping overhaul of national security policy.[50]

The Gaither committee presented its findings to the president at two meetings in early November. At the first, on November 4, a small group including Sprague, Foster, Stanton, McCloy, and Lovett presented the essence of their findings to Eisenhower orally. Disturbed by what he heard, the president asked them to check their figures before presenting the written report to the National Security Council. Three days later, Sprague and Foster presented the Gaither committee report to the full NSC at one of the largest meetings of that body ever held. In addition to the president and his top advisers, those assembled included the Joint Chiefs of Staff, the three service secretaries, and many of their key aides. Since most of those present had already read the report, all eyes were on the president to see how he would react to this alarming document, with its implicit criticism of his national security policies.[51]

There was little in the Gaither report that Eisenhower could have found encouraging. Noting that the committee had originally been asked simply to evaluate civil defense proposals, the report stated that the group had decided it was more important to explore the nation's "active" nuclear defenses and especially to compare Soviet and American strategic forces. "The evidence clearly indicates an increasing threat which may become critical in 1959 or early 1960." Citing Russia's rapid economic growth and willingness to spend heavily for defense, the report warned that the Soviet threat would grow in the future due to their "dynamic development and exploitation of their military technology." The Soviets have "probably surpassed us in

ICBM development," the report continued, and both the American people and SAC would soon be vulnerable to attack because of "an early Russian ICBM capability."

The Gaither report gave a relatively low priority to a nationwide system of fallout shelters to provide some protection to the population in case of enemy attack. Even this minimal protection would cost $25 billion over the next five years, while a more extensive program of shelters to protect against blast would be prohibitively expensive. Therefore, the report concluded, it was more imperative to spend $18 billion over the same period to upgrade and protect the Strategic Air Command bombers and accelerate the American missile program.[52]

The specific recommendations included proposals to lessen SAC vulnerability by keeping on alert five hundred bombers that could respond with only a few minutes' warning, dispersing B-52s more widely around the country and even to civilian airfields, developing a warning system to give between seven and twenty-two minutes' advance notice of a missile attack, and building shelters for B-52s that could withstand blasts up to two hundred pounds per square inch. The report also called for a massive increase in the planned size of the American missile force. The air force should quadruple the number of IRBMs to be based overseas, going from the programmed 60 Thors and Jupiters to 240, and plan for 600 Atlas and Titan ICBMs rather than the original 80, while the navy should aim at 18 rather than 6 Polaris submarines. At the same time, the timetable for the initial deployment of these weapons should be moved forward. "Every effort should be made to have a significant number of IRBMs operational overseas by late 1958," the report urged, "and ICBMS operational in the ZI (continental United States) by late 1959."[53]

The final section of the Gaither report dealt with the difficult issue of financing these recommendations. In addition to more centralized direction of missile development, which would cut costs by eliminating duplication, it called for a total increase of more than $40 billion in defense spending over the next five to eight years. The offensive measures alone, which were given highest priority, would add from $3 to $5 billion a year to the defense budget. Despite this enormous outlay, the report contended, the "demands of such a program on the nation's economic resources would not pose significant problems" and were "well within our economic capabilities." The report said that current defense spending represented only 8.5 percent of the gross national product (GNP) compared with 41 percent during World War II and 14 percent in the Korean War. The cost of the entire proposed program would represent no greater percentage of the GNP than Korean War spending, and it would be considerably less without the fallout shelters. It might mean raising taxes and slowing spending on highways and "other postponable public works," but the authors of the report were convinced that the American people would make the sacrifices necessary "to ensure our survival as a nation."[54]

It is hardly surprising that President Eisenhower did not share the Gaither committee's confidence that the American economy could withstand these additional costs. At the private briefing on November 4, he challenged the view of Lovett and McCloy that the United States could afford such heavy expenditures, expressing a "nagging fear that the American people would not be willing to pay the bill." He was particularly disturbed by the way the experts casually talked about spending billions of dollars. At a luncheon for the Gaither committee staff on November 6, he commented that few seemed to understand just how big a sum a billion dollars represented. "Why," he exclaimed, "it's a stack of ten-dollar bills as high as the Washington Monument." The president was particularly outraged by the proposal to spend $25 billion for fallout shelters, asking his staff how he could justify that expenditure "as a deterrent to war."

The president was equally certain that the Gaither report exaggerated the danger facing the nation, although he agreed on the necessity of dispersing and protecting our bombers and speeding up the missile program. Discounting the claim that we were behind the Russians in missile development, he told the Gaither committee on November 4 that for the next five years aircraft, not missiles, would still be the main nuclear delivery system. "We are not behind now," he added, "but we must make great exertions in order not to fall behind." Above all, he rejected both the alarmist tone of the Gaither report and the call for a crisis response. "The crux" of the problem, he said on November 4, was "how to keep up interest and support without hysteria." As he later told his aides: "We must neither panic nor become complacent. We should decide what needs to be done, and do it—avoiding extremes." His major concern was with the long haul, and his guiding principle, as he explained in his memoirs, was his determination not to "turn the nation into a garrison state."[55]

The president made his refusal to panic clear at the large NSC meeting on November 7. He listened to the presentation intently, balancing a copy of the report on his knee as he followed the briefing. He expressed some concern about the economic costs involved and then let Secretary of State Dulles, who worried about the effect of hasty action on our allies, speak out strongly against the recommendations. At the end of the session Eisenhower simply asked the various government agencies to study the recommendations of the Security Resources Panel and report back with any measures they felt should be implemented.[56]

Robert Sprague was keenly disappointed in the president's apparent rejection of the report. Deeply impressed by Wohlstetter's concern for the vulnerability of the deterrent, during a visit to SAC headquarters in Omaha Sprague had not been satisfied by General Curtis LeMay's assurances that the B-52s were a dependable striking force. Accordingly, on September 16 Sprague returned to Omaha with Foster and two other members of the Gaither committee and asked LeMay to order a practice alert. In the next six hours, not a single B-52 became airborne. LeMay was not upset, claiming that it took more than six hours to load and fuel B-52s. When Sprague asked what would happen if the Russians launched a surprise attack, LeMay first said it was beyond their capability, then pointed out that the practice alert was taking place at a time of low international tension. During a crisis, or at any time American intelligence detected any sign of a possible Soviet strike, LeMay would have the American B-52s in a high state of readiness. Asked what he would do if the Russians began massing their bombers for an attack, the general replied, "I'm going to knock the shit out of them before they take off the ground." When Sprague asked if this were national policy, LeMay said no: "It's my policy."

Sprague carefully kept this information to himself, but at a White House luncheon on November 6 he asked Air Force Secretary James Douglas if he were aware that virtually no American bombers could get airborne if the Russians attacked without warning. Douglas at first denied this but, after speaking briefly with LeMay, who was present, fell silent. After the formal NSC briefing on the Gaither report on November 7, Sprague met with Eisenhower and reported on the results of the September practice alert, claiming that the fact that it took more than six hours to get a single B-52 in the air proved how vulnerable the American deterrent had become. The president was not impressed, telling Sprague that attacks rarely came as a "bolt from the blue" but rather only after a gradual escalation in international tension, which would enable SAC to go on alert status. Sprague came away from this meeting dejected, convinced that the president did not understand the danger facing the country. In a letter to Ike a week later, Sprague said it was misleading to refer to the present era as a "time of nuclear stalemate," when in reality it could be "more accurately described as a period of possible annihilation."[57]

The president was more impressed by the Gaither report than Sprague realized. He had been checking into the readiness of SAC even before he received the report, and in early 1958 he instituted a new alert policy that kept a few B-52s in the air at all times and permitted 250 bombers to become airborne within six hours. He was also prepared to act on the recommendations for greater dispersal of bombers, development of an early warning system, and an increase in the size of the American missile forces, as well as a speedup in their deployment. But he was not willing to accept the entire Gaither report "as a master blueprint for action." "The President," he believed, "unlike a panel which concentrates on a single problem, must always strive to see the totality of the national and international situation." It was his responsibility, he continued, to "take into account conflicting purposes, responding to legitimate needs but assigning priorities and keeping plans and costs within bounds."[58]

VIII

Eisenhower's insistence on a moderate and balanced response to the Gaither report and the crisis in national security touched off by *Sputnik* was based on more than just his aversion to heavy defense spending. Since 1956 American U-2 planes had regularly been overflying the Soviet Union, giving him a clear picture of the pace and nature of the Russian ICBM program. He had known about the two tests of the Soviet ICBM as soon as they had taken place, and the CIA had even given him advance warning of *Sputnik*. The reconnaissance flights brought back pictures of a strip of Russian territory 125 miles wide by some 3,000 miles long with images clear enough to make a newspaper headline legible. The data gathered by the U-2 flights made it clear that the Soviets were still in the early stage of testing their ICBM and had not yet made any preparations for their deployment. They were no more than a few months ahead of the United States in the race for the ICBM, and thus there was no grave peril to the American nuclear deterrent.[59]

The Gaither committee had been given access to large quantities of intelligence on the Soviet Union, but not to the closely held U-2 data. In early November Dulles advised the president to inform the American people that "the United States has the capability of photographing the Soviet Union from a very high altitude without interference." Although such a disclosure would have silenced his critics and relieved him of intense public pressure to increase defense spending, Eisenhower refused to jeopardize a program that had given the United States so much useful information already and promised to be even more helpful in the future. Indeed, after *Sputnik* he went out of his way to reduce the number of American overflights of the Soviet Union, indicating to aides that he preferred to "lie low" in the present "tense international circumstances" lest a mishap on a U-2 flight provoke a major crisis.[60]

This may well have been one of the wisest as well as most courageous decisions of his entire presidency. Keeping quiet about the U-2 robbed him of his most telling response to his critics in Congress and the press, as well as within the Pentagon; as Barry Goldwater later observed, "Ike took the heat, grinned, and kept his mouth shut." In the weeks following *Sputnik,* it must have been painful for Eisenhower to listen to all those who clamored for massive increases in defense spending and accelerated missile programs, knowing as he did they were not necessary. But at the same time, he knew it was vitally important to keep the U-2 confidential so that he could continue to monitor Soviet missile development and thus make appropriate adjustments in the American IRBM and ICBM programs.[61]

Sputnik thus confronted Eisenhower with difficult choices as commander-in-chief. He knew that he had already committed the nation to a large and expensive missile program, one whose potential for excessive duplication and waste worried him. But he also was aware that the American people were deeply concerned about the Soviet challenge to American strategic superiority and that they deserved to receive as much reassurance as he could possibly offer them. He felt he had carefully calculated a formula that would balance the equally important goals of nuclear safety and fiscal responsibility. His task now would be to persuade the American people that he understood the significance of *Sputnik* and was taking the proper steps to meet this challenge to both national security and American world prestige.

CHAPTER THREE

On Sunday, November 3, 1957, the Soviet Union again stunned the world by sending up *Sputnik II*. Weighing 1,121 pounds, the second Soviet earth satellite dwarfed the six-inch American *Vanguard*, which was still in the development stage. Scientists estimated that the rocket used to launch *Sputnik II* had a thrust of at least 500,000 pounds, more than enough to power an ICBM some five thousand miles across the earth's surface. Many agreed with Stuart Symington, who claimed that the most recent Russian feat showed that they had the capacity to launch an ICBM and that the United States was "at least two years" behind the Soviet Union in the race for this weapon.

But it was the dog named Laika aboard the Soviet satellite that most impressed the American people. The fact that the Russians could launch a space vehicle large enough for a dog suggested that they were already planning manned space flights in the future. Some commentators dwelt on the humorous aspects—one called *Sputnik II* "a case of the dog wagging the world"—but others warned of more ominous implications. The assistant director of the Smithsonian Astrophysical Observatory worried publicly that "the Russians will beat us to the moon. I would not be surprised," he predicted, "if the Russians reach the moon within a week."[1]

The Soviets made the most of their spectacular accomplishment. Timed to coincide with the fortieth anniversary of the Bolshevik Revolution, *Sputnik II* enabled Khrushchev to boast, as he watched a somber parade of Russian tanks, rockets, and missiles in Red Square, "Our satellites are circling the earth waiting for American satellites to join them and form a commonwealth of Sputniks."[2]

The White House was conspicuously silent in the face of this new evidence of Soviet scientific prowess. Eisenhower mentioned *Sputnik*

II while talking to John Foster Dulles on the telephone on the Sunday
it was launched. The secretary of state dismissed orbiting a dog as "a
real circus performance" but added that "the weight of this thing" had
to be taken seriously. Alan Waterman, the director of the National
Science Foundation, gave the offical administration response, telling
reporters that the Russians deserved credit for a "difficult engineering
accomplishment." Vanguard director John Hagan tried to be more
casual, saying that "they now have two gadgets in the air." Reassured
by his brother, CIA chief Allen Dulles, who told him the second
Sputnik had much less impact on world opinion than the first, Secretary Dulles tried to play down its military significance. It merely
showed what we already knew, he told a press conference on November 5, that the Soviet had rockets powerful enough to launch an
ICBM. But they still had to solve the problem of reentry, and there
was no evidence that they had an operational ICBM.[3]

Few Americans were ready to accept such glib reassurances. Henry
Luce's publications led the way in challenging the administration's
complacent reaction. *Life,* which devoted one-third of an entire issue
to the challenge posed by *Sputnik II,* called the first week in November
"one which showed the world might be at a turning point." The editors went on to warn that "the Soviets had burst upon the world as the
infinitely sinister front runners in the sophisticated and perilous science of space." *Time* was equally militant. It quoted a Los Angeles
resident as suggesting to a State Department official that "maybe you
should reserve a large share for the U.S. when you're dishing out the
aid to backward countries." Citing a need for a national reawakening,
Time demanded "a greater sense of urgency than Washington has thus
far displayed."[4]

Others echoed their dissatisfaction with the Eisenhower administration's sluggish response. The editors of the *New Republic* bemoaned
the fact that in Washington "complacency and star-gazing are still
accepted behavior." *Newsweek,* warning that "the Western world finds
itself mortally in danger from the East," pleaded for "a supreme scientific and financial effort" to catch up. The most outspoken criticism of
all came in a full-page advertisement in the *New York Times* by American Aviation Publications. The editor of a leading aerospace trade
journal called upon the administration to overtake the Soviets by embarking on a program to send men into space. "We must put man on
the moon and on our two nearest planets," he argued. "The United
States must show the way. If she does not, Russia will." The ad ended
by focusing responsibility directly on Dwight Eisenhower: "You don't
have to be a scientist, Mr. President, to solve this problem. You must
be a leader."[5]

The launch of *Sputnik II* did more than anything else to bring the
issue of presidential leadership to a climax. The clearest sign of the
growing public doubt came in the polls; Gallup's showed that Eisen-

hower's popularity had dropped twenty-two points from a post-reelection high of 79 percent in January 1957 to 57 percent by early November. The president himself felt bewildered by the series of events that had confronted him ever since the Suez crisis a year before. "When I wake up in the morning," he wrote to his brother Arthur, "I sometimes wonder just what new problem can possibly be laid on my desk during the day to come; there always seems to be an even more complex one than I could have imagined." Now, as he realized that he was in danger of losing the confidence of the American people, he would have to rise above self-pity and demonstrate the leadership that would restore the nation's faith, not just in him, but in itself.[6]

I

Eisenhower took the first step toward meeting the challenge posed by *Sputnik II* by advancing the timetable for his planned "chins-up" talks to the American people. On Monday, November 4, he decided to give the first reassurance speech from the Oval Office on the following Thursday, rather than a week later in Oklahoma City, as the White House had announced earlier. He also informed his staff that he would focus on the issue of national security rather than the broader topic of science and society, which would be left for the second speech, in Oklahoma City the next week.[7]

For the next three days, the president worked intensively on what he knew would be one of the most important addresses he would ever make. On Tuesday he told speechwriter Arthur Larson to drop out the sections of the draft speech that dealt with education and to concentrate instead on national defense issues. While he wanted to stress national security, he reminded Larson that more was involved than "materialistic" considerations: "We are defending priceless spiritual values." And he was determined to banish complacency and end on a firmly optimistic note. "In every point brought up," he advised Larson, "there should be the expression of complete conviction that the American people can meet every one of these problems and these threats if we turn our minds to it."

Eisenhower played an active role in the speechwriting process, going over successive drafts with Larson and actor Robert Montgomery, who worked with him on his television presentation. A perfectionist, the president kept making last-minute changes in a long session with Larson and Montgomery on Thursday afternoon as the deadline for that evening's speech drew closer. His secretary's diary entry for the day reflected the growing sense of tension in the White House; "*one* of the most dreadful days," she commented.[8]

"I am going to lay the facts before you—the rough and the smooth," Eisenhower told a nationwide radio and television audience on the evening of November 7, 1957. He admitted that the Russians had scored an important victory with *Sputnik* and that they were "building up types of power that could, if we were attacked, damage us seriously." But despite these advances, he and his most trusted scientific and military advisers were convinced that "as of today the over-all military strength of the free world is distinctly greater than that of the communist countries."

The president then spoke of the great retaliatory power that the United States already possessed. "Long-range ballistic missiles, as they exist today, do not cancel the destructive and deterrent power of our Strategic Air Force." Nor, he continued, were we lagging behind with new weapons. His administration was spending more than $5 billion a year on defense research and development, with more than $1 billion a year going into missiles alone. The air force, he went on, had tested IRBMs and ICBMs at distances up to thirty-five hundred miles, and the army had recovered a nose cone from a Jupiter IRBM intact. The television cameras showed the Jupiter nose cone as the president pointed out that this meant we had solved the critical reentry problem.

Eisenhower then announced two important steps he was taking to ensure continued American progress in science and technology. First, he planned to ask Congress to relax existing laws to permit greater technological cooperation with our allies in the belief that "most great scientific advances of the world have been the product of free international exchange of ideas." His second move would be to appoint James Killian to the new post of special assistant to the president for science and technology and to ask the secretary of defense to appoint a guided missiles director in order to put all the missile programs under a single manager.

Despite his recognition of the urgency of the situation facing the nation, Eisenhower closed with a note of caution, advising against going off "in all directions at once" and stressing the need to "clearly identify the exact and critical needs that have to be met." The nation had to be selective, discriminating between "what we must have and what we would like to have." Only by setting priorities and sticking to them could we achieve the desired goal of "both a sound defense and a sound economy." Then he ended with a reminder that what the world needed "even more than a giant leap into outer space" was "a giant step toward peace." He would only be content "when the scientist can give his full attention, not to human destruction, but to human happiness and fulfillment."[9]

Public reaction to the President's efforts at national reassurance ranged from biting criticism to lukewarm praise. Journals that were calling for heroic action thought Ike had not done enough. *Life* cited critical comments by Adlai Stevenson and banker Ferdinand Eberstadt to conclude that at best Eisenhower had only taken "a faltering step forward." The editors of the highly partisan *New Republic* were more outspoken, accusing the president of continued complacency and claiming that he was "treating Sputnik like a common cold, instead of a dangerous disease." One columnist called the speech "another tranquillity pill" and said many in Washington were now referring to the White House as "the tomb of the well-known soldier." The *Nation*, which felt that concern over *Sputnik* bordered on hysteria, praised Ike for proposing the sharing of scientific ideas with our allies but bemoaned the continued stress on a missile race with the Soviets. Only the editors of *Time* were willing to give Ike the benefit of the doubt, claiming that he had made a "turnabout" on defense spending that "set the U.S. on a new course." The speech, they concluded, "helped revive the President's prestige when it was sinking fast."[10]

The media's critical response to Eisenhower's efforts to restore national confidence may well have understated the real impact of his speech. Samuel Lubell, who conducted extensive interviews with individual Americans across the country after *Sputnik II*, was struck by how closely the comments followed the lead of the president rather than those of scientists, other politicians, and editorial writers. "In talking about Sputnik," Lubell found, "most people tended to paraphrase what Eisenhower himself had said." The people Lubell spoke with did not look elsewhere for guidance, nor were they, with only a few exceptions, "demanding more action than he was."[11]

The president's only regret was that he could not be absolutely candid with the American people. Secretary Dulles had urged him to reveal that U-2 flights gave him solid evidence that the United States was not behind the Soviet Union in the missile race, but Eisenhower had already "reluctantly" ruled out compromising that valuable intelligence source. When his critics continued to claim that he was too complacent, however, he must have regretted his decision. He hinted at his feelings in a letter to an old friend, saying in regard to the arms race, "You can understand there are many things that I don't dare to allude to publicly, yet some of them would do much to allay the fears of our own people." Like a good soldier, Ike was willing to take the political heat, sure that he was doing the right thing for the nation.[12]

II

The appointment of MIT President James Killian was the most important step that Eisenhower took following *Sputnik II*. The idea of creating the position of a presidential science adviser stemmed from the meeting Ike had with the Office of Defense Mobilization (ODM) Science Advisory Committee on October 15. A week later, White House Chief of Staff Sherman Adams invited Killian, who had made the original proposal, to come to Washington to consult with him and other key aides about this post. Killian carefully sought ideas and guidance from several leading scientists involved in advising on government affairs, including I. I. Rabi, Edwin Land, and James Fisk of the Bell Telephone Laboratories. During the course of a long meeting with White House aides on October 23 and a breakfast session with the president the next day, he spelled out a two-part program. First, Eisenhower would appoint a special assistant for science and technology to oversee all scientific aspects of current government policies and to make available to the White House the broadest possible range of scientific opinion. Second, to help carry out this latter objective, Killian proposed shifting the present Science Advisory Committee from the ODM to the White House, increasing it in size to make it more representative of the entire scientific community, and arranging for periodic meetings between this body of eminent scientists and the president. Killian stressed that the science adviser should not have any specific administrative tasks but rather a broad mandate to oversee all government science activities and be permitted to attend all cabinet and National Security Council meetings.[13]

At the end of their meeting, Eisenhower asked Killian to take on this new post. Killian hesitated, because of both personal considerations related to his wife's health and the need to secure an extended leave of absence from MIT. He soon resolved these problems and returned to Washington in early November for a final round of talks with Adams, Secretary of State Dulles, and the president. He told Eisenhower on November 4 that he would take the post for a year, explaining his desire not to give up the MIT presidency permanently. In discussing the new assignment, the president agreed that Killian would be free to consult with all government bodies, including the Joint Chiefs of Staff. Eisenhower felt that it was particularly important for his new science adviser to give him advice on matters that "affect national security," and he also agreed that Killian should have the "authority to carry out actions or give orders." At the end of their conversation, the president emphasized that he wanted Killian not only to provide him with insight into scientific issues but also to give a "greater sense of direction" to all those in the government involved in the missile and space efforts.[14]

Killian was an ideal choice for the new position. By background and training, he was a scientific administrator rather than a research scientist. A graduate of MIT, he had become an assistant to the university's distinguished leader, Karl Compton, during World War II. Both in that role and as editor of MIT's *Technology Review*, he had been exposed to a wide range of scientific and technical information. President of MIT since 1949, he had insisted on emphasizing the importance of the humanities in the training of engineers. He was no stranger to government scientific programs, having served on the ODM Science Advisory Committee and the President's Board of Consultants on Foreign Intelligence Activities as well as heading the important Technical Capabilities Panel in 1955, which had resulted in the speedup of the nation's missile programs two years before *Sputnik*.

The presidential assistant's personal qualifications for his new assignment were equally impressive. A native of South Carolina, he spoke in a soft drawl. Always calm and methodical in his approach to difficult problems, he had a cherubic face that disguised a tough mind and a steely resolve; one colleague described him as "disarmingly pleasant." He was sensitive enough to bureaucratic rivalries to tread carefully in dealing with various government agencies, yet confident enough of Ike's trust to insist on knowing everything of importance taking place in the missile and space programs.[15]

Most important of all, he shared the President's underlying view of *Sputnik*. He realized that, while the Soviet satellite launch indicated that Russia was probably ahead of the United States in the development of the ICBM, this feat was the result of a deliberate political decision. He was certain that it did not mean that the Soviet Union had surpassed the United States in science and technology, yet he understood how upset many Americans were and how much they needed reassurance on this point. His major concern, however, was that the United States would overreact to the challenge posed by *Sputnik*, thereby creating undue "strains and distortions" on "the fabric of American life." "I was fearful," he commented, "that it might heat up the cold war, accelerate the arms race, and encourage technological excess." This point of view, which dovetailed with Eisenhower's own determination to hold to a steady course and not bankrupt the nation with a panicky response, helps explain why the two men quickly developed such a warm and close relationship.

Killian understood clearly the political realities behind his appointment, calling it later "a calculated political act to fend off attacks" by associating the nation's scientific community with the Eisenhower administration. In announcing his acceptance of the post on November 7, Killian stressed his belief that "American science and engineering possess tremendous strength and vitality." He then promised to "move as rapidly as possible to marshall the best scientific and engineering judgment and creative talent in the U.S." in support of "national policy-making."[16]

The appointment won nearly universal praise. *Life* called Killian a "superexpediter" who would create "a sense of urgency without despair." Other commentators noted the high regard most scientists had for Killian and pointed out how effective he was likely to be in bringing the views of the scientific community to bear on national policy. Among the hundreds of letters the White House received about his appointment, there was not a single one critical of Killian's selection.[17]

The only dissent came from Congress, where many expressed disappointment that the President had not appointed a "czar" to take charge of the nation's lagging missile effort. Democratic senators were most vocal. John Kennedy praised Killian but regretted that he was not given broader authority; Henry Jackson felt that the administration needed a "full-time boss" for the missile program. Even some Republicans joined in the clamor for someone to direct the race for the ICBM. "He can be called director, coordinator or czar," Senator Styles Bridges of New Hampshire declared. "I don't care what his title is, so long as he has the authority to get the job done." Most of this criticism was directed not at Killian but at William Holaday, who was given the new title of director of guided missiles within the Pentagon. Holaday, a former oil company executive, had already been coordinating missile programs as a special assistant to the secretary of defense, and critics saw the new post as purely cosmetic. Killian made it clear that he had no intention of becoming a "missile czar," seeing his role instead as that of "an adviser and catalyzer." He worried more that press accounts billing him as a "miracle worker" would create jealousy among other White House aides. As one of thirty-three advisers on the White House staff, he knew that his effectiveness would ultimately depend on establishing a close personal relationship with Ike, and he made this his first priority.[18]

Killian's concept of his role fitted in perfectly with the prevailing White House view. On November 15, the day he was sworn in, National Security Adviser Robert Cutler advised staff secretary Andrew Goodpaster that the public must perceive Killian as not just another presidential assistant but rather "as a powerful voice speaking for the President." Accordingly, he was given a choice suite of offices in the Executive Office Building next to the White House, along with a deputy, three staff assistants, and four secretaries. To bolster his authority within the bureaucracy, Eisenhower wrote a formal letter of appointment, drafted by Killian, spelling out the duties of the new office, which included advising the president on "scientific and technical matters" as well as trying "to anticipate future trends." "It is the intent of the President," the letter continued, "that the Special Assistant for Science and Technology will have full access to all plans, programs, and activities involving science and technology in the Government, including the Department of Defense, AEC, and CIA." Armed with this broad authority, Killian was expected to provide "a greater sense of direction to all who are concerned in our nation's scientific and technical efforts."[19]

Killian's appointment marked a major step forward for American science. For the first time, a man who spoke for the nation's leading scientists was given a position of unquestioned national authority. "Science has never before been given that kind of attention at that level," noted *Time*. In fact, Eisenhower had relied heavily on the advice of the nation's leading scientists from the time he entered the White House, calling on such well-known figures as Edward Teller, I. I. Rabi, Edwin Land, and Killian himself for ideas and advice on a wide range of national security issues. But with Killian's appointment Eisenhower, who normally preferred to exercise his leadership quietly, out of public view, elevated the role of scientists to a prominent position as part of his larger effort to restore the nation's confidence. In this case, a shrewd public relations move also proved to be sound public policy.[20]

Killian's first action, carrying out his October 24 proposal, was to create the President's Science Advisory Committee (PSAC), which under his chairmanship would be the conduit between Eisenhower and the scientific community, by moving the existing Science Advisory Committee from the ODM to the White House and increasing its membership from twelve to seventeen. The new additions were five distinguished scientists and public figures: Harvard chemist George Kistiakowsky, University of California physicist Herbert York, Nobel Prize–winning Harvard physicist Edward Purcell, Cal Tech physicist Robert F. Bacher, and World War II hero General James H. Doolittle, vice-president of Shell Oil. I. I. Rabi stepped down as chairman but continued as a PSAC member, while Bacher and James Fisk of the Bell Labs agreed to serve as vice-chairmen. Killian was careful to invite Alan Waterman, director of the National Science Foundation and a man on whom Eisenhower had relied for technical advice in the past, to attend PSAC meetings; Detlev Bronk, whom Eisenhower had often consulted as head of the National Academy of Science, was one of the original committee members.[21]

The new arrangement worked very well. Killian proved to be adept in his role of middleman between science and government. "He seemed to know precisely what questions to ask the scientists," observed Herbert York, "and how to organize their efforts to produce valid answers and usable advice quickly." Equally important, Killian had the ability to put the often abstract and complex ideas of the scientists into language that political leaders could understand and act upon. Eisenhower had no reason to regret his choice. Indeed, he soon came to depend very heavily on his science adviser to guide him through the complexities of the new space age. "I shall never cease to be grateful," he told Killian later, "for the patience with which you initiated me into the rudiments of this new science."[22]

With characteristic modesty, Killian gave most of the credit for the productive relationship between the PSAC and the Eisenhower administration to the scientists themselves. "They were a collegium of scholars, intellectuals all," he wrote, "but their experience had tempered or kept in bounds any excessive sense of elitism or intellectual arrogance." The president grew so fond of this group who stood with him during the darkest days of the *Sputnik* crisis that he came to refer to them as "my scientists." In 1968, as he lay near death at Walter Reed Hospital, he asked Killian about several of them and then added, "You know, Jim, this bunch of scientists was one of the few groups that I encountered in Washington who seemed to be there to help the country and not help themselves."[23]

III

Eisenhower's second "chins-up" speech was designed to address the issue of science and society, especially the implications of the two *Sputniks* for American education. As the president worked on his remarks, an intense and prolonged debate developed over the country's system of public education. As Columbia University President Grayson Kirk noted: "The subject of education has moved out of the quiet of the classroom into the arena of bitter controversy."[24]

In fact, *Sputnik* served as a catalyst that brought a long-developing drive for educational reform into the spotlight. Since the early 1950s, academic critics of progressive education had been attacking the educational establishment for what they considered too much emphasis on life adjustment and not enough on traditional subjects such as English, history, math, science, and foreign languages. Led by historian Arthur Bestor, these critics wanted to take control of the public schools away from the colleges of education and stress the training of teachers with solid knowledge of the subjects they taught. Paul Woodring summed up the attack on progressive education when he wrote in 1957, "Just as war is too important to be left to the generals, education is too important to be left to the educators. It must concern us all."[25]

Public outcry now focused on the schools as a main reason why the United States was falling behind the Soviet Union. Speakers bemoaned the fact that in American schools too much time was taken up with "clubs, student newspapers, marching bands and drum majorettes." Others warned that the elder generation's preoccupation with acquiring big cars and watching television fostered a feeling that learning was unimportant. "Many a bright student finds only boredom in a class where the intellectual level is pitched to the duller students," observed Grayson Kirk. Scholars called for more high school courses in history, math, and foreign languages to replace "things like 'how to have a successful date' and 'how can my home be made democratic.'"

The most widely expressed concern, however, dealt with the training of scientists and engineers. Former President Herbert Hoover bemoaned the fact that "the greatest enemy of all mankind, the Communists, are turning out twice or possibly three times as many" scientists and engineers as the United States. Senator Henry Jackson claimed that the Soviet Union "turns out more scientifically trained people than any Western nation and is accelerating the output at a higher rate than any nation." And an aide to Senate Majority Leader Lyndon Johnson reported that the Russians had more than twice as many high school science and math teachers as we did—350,000 to 140,000. The consensus reached by most commentators was that *Sputnik* was no fluke but rather the result of a deliberate Russian decision to give science the highest possible priority in their educational system.[26]

Health, Education, and Welfare (HEW) Secretary Marion Folsom confirmed this trend in a report released in early November, "Education in Russia," The study pointed out that, over the ten years of the primary and secondary curriculum, Russian students took five years of physics, four of chemistry, and five of math beyond arithmetic. In contrast, only one in three American students had taken chemistry, and just one in four physics. As a result, the Soviets were producing nearly 225,000 scientists and engineers a year. "This system of education gives little freedom of choice to the individual," commented *U.S. News & World Report.* "But it produced the scientists and engineers who built and launched *Sputniks I* and *II.*"[27]

The most influential support for an overhaul of American education as a result of *Sputnik* came from Admiral Hyman Rickover, highly regarded as the "father" of the nuclear submarine. Citing Sputnik as a "catalyst" for long-overdue school reforms, Rickover hoped it would "do in matters of the intellect what Pearl Harbor did in matters industrial and military." Denouncing current high school courses as soft and undemanding, he proposed creating a Council of Scholars to set up a nationwide curriculum based on the study of science, math, and foreign languages and making only graduates of schools with this rigorous course of study eligible for college admission. Defending this proposal for radical change, Rickover insisted: "We must sweep clean the temple of learning and bring back quality."[28]

Not all observers agreed with this bleak comparison of American and Soviet education. A Russian-born engineer at MIT claimed that most of the Russians were being narrowly trained as technicians, not as genuine scientists. Moreover, the system was hopelessly elitist, with only one-third of the youth attending high school and just a tiny fraction going on to college. The editor of *Science* saw greater strength in the Soviet educational system, but he cautioned against adopting a hasty crash program in response, calling instead for long-overdue basic reforms in American schools "from grade level to college." In particular, he favored federal scholarships to permit bright students to meet high college costs. Others warned of the danger of mimicking the Russians by overstressing science, saying that then the American educational system might be "reduced to a satellite of the Russian system, spinning in an orbit dictated by Russian scientists."[29]

As this debate continued, three issues stood out clearly. First, most Americans felt that an overhaul of the schools was long overdue, one that shifted the focus from cultural adjustment to serious training in basic subjects. But on the second point, whether to focus almost exclusively on science and math, there was considerable disagreement, with many arguing for a well-rounded approach that included the humanities. Finally, there was strong division of sentiment over whether the *Sputnik* crisis should lead to extending federal funding and control into an area traditionally in local and state hands. Proposals for federal scholarships and national curriculum standards raised questions that would force the Eisenhower administration to decide how far it wanted to go in playing a leading role in fostering educational reform. Whatever the outcome of the debate, most who took part could agree with John Dunning, dean of engineering at Columbia University, who said of *Sputnik*, "In winning a propaganda victory, the Russians may have given us the warning and the chance we needed to reestablish our technological supremacy and vindicate our traditional freedom."[30]

The Scientific Advisory Committee echoed these comments in offering suggestions for Eisenhower's address scheduled for Oklahoma City on November 13. The scientists urged the president to go beyond the military implications of *Sputnik* to point out the importance of both science education and the basic research that underlay all technological advance. They saw an opportunity for the president to use the Soviet challenge so that American youth would become "inspired to venture into the unknown and into fields of new discovery and undreamt of technical accomplishment."[31]

Eisenhower chose a more restrained approach. Aware of the continuing public fear of the military implications of *Sputnik* as well as the qualms of experts expressed privately in the Gaither report, he began by reiterating his confidence in America's defenses. Citing Khrushchev's new boasts of Soviet superiority and his older claim, "We will bury you," Ike responded, "In a bit of American vernacular, 'Oh Yeah?'" Explaining that he was personally conducting a "critical reexamination of our entire defense position," the president spelled out some of the steps he had already taken to protect the American deterrent, including improved warning times of enemy attack, dispersal of SAC bombers, and increased spending on long-range missiles. But, he added, while he would not hesitate to spend whatever sums necessary to protect the nation, he still strove for a balanced budget in his devotion to "keeping our economy, and therefore our total security, strong and sound."

The body of his speech dealt with two closely related problems facing the nation—basic research and science education. He was vague on the first, saying simply it was important to continue investing in laboratories and other scientific efforts to ensure "future discoveries even more startling than nuclear fission."

Eisenhower was more specific on education. He acknowledged that the Russians were turning out scientists and engineers at a faster rate than we were and said we needed "thousands more" in the next ten years. He called this need "the most critical problem of all," claiming that training scientists and engineers was even more important than speeding up missile production. Then he listed possible ways the federal government could help achieve this goal, including identifying high school students with scientific potential, giving grants for training teachers and equipping labs in the schools, and providing graduate fellowships designed "to increase the output of qualified teachers."

In making these proposals, Eisenhower carefully qualified his remarks to avoid taking sides in the ongoing public debate. Thus while he stressed the need for more engineers and scientists, he pointed out it was important to educate an entire generation so that American youth would be "equipped to live in the age of intercontinental ballistic missiles." The teaching of the humanities and the social sciences was just as important as instruction in math and science in producing "leaders who can meet intricate human problems with wisdom and courage." And, the president emphasized, the challenge went beyond federal action. He asked every school board and every citizen to examine the local curriculum and improve it to meet "the stern demands of the era we are entering." The federal government would do all it could, but the states and local school boards would have to act as well. "The task," he asserted, "is a cooperative one."[32]

Eisenhower's words were well received. *Time* praised his remarks and noted that his response to Khrushchev's boasts drew an especially favorable reaction from his audience. The editors of the *New Republic* agreed with Ike that, just as there was more to national security than money, so "there is much more to education than science." They hoped that the president's words would lead to "a general educational revival," not just "an accelerated race with the Russians to see who can produce the greatest number of technicians in the next generation."[33]

Even before he delivered the Oklahoma City speech, the President had directed HEW Secretary Marion Folsom to begin preparing educational legislation. Eisenhower wanted a new approach to the long-deadlocked issue of federal aid to the schools, one that departed from past controversies and met the challenge posed by *Sputnik*.

Harry Truman had first put federal aid to education on the congressional agenda in 1949 as part of his Fair Deal. Democratic proposals for grants to states to assist in meeting educational costs quickly became enmeshed in two difficult issues: the traditional belief that funding and control of the schools was a local matter, and the problem of whether to include private and parochial schools. In the 1950s the onset of the baby boom and the difficulty cities, states, and local school boards were having in financing the building of new schools to meet the ever-increasing flow of pupils—estimated to peak at 44 million elementary and secondary students by the mid-1960s—shifted the focus to federal funds for school construction. Eisenhower backed a limited program to assist states and local communities in meeting the needs for new schools, but Democratic proposals for much more sweeping programs, coupled with growing southern fears that federal funding of education would force rapid desegregation after the *Brown* decision in 1954, doomed this legislation. As recently as July 1957, Congress had failed by a handful of votes to pass a $400 million school construction bill.[34]

On November 6 the President met with Folsom and several of his deputies, including Eliot Richardson, who had been serving as an assistant secretary of HEW since January and had been exploring alternative legislative approaches. When the HEW secretary began to outline a new school construction bill, Eisenhower interrupted to make clear that he was opposed. He stressed budgetary concerns and suggested that the federal government concentrate on a more limited approach to give matching funds to states to equip more labs for science courses. Saying that he doubted Congress would pass a school construction bill, he told Folsom "it was necessary to get something new and in the present public mood." Ike went on to repeat the concerns that scientists such as Land and Rabi had expressed to him at the October 15 meeting. "Our greatest danger today," Ike concluded, "is failure to educate scientists for the future." Accordingly, he asked HEW to draw up a new legislative proposal to meet this critical national need.[35]

Secretary Folsom presented a five-part HEW program, largely drafted by Richardson, to the cabinet in two meetings in mid-November and early December 1957. First, citing studies that showed that as many as half of those in the top 25 percent of their high school classes did not attend college, he proposed a federal scholarship program to encourage the brightest high school graduates to go on to college. Funded by the federal government but administered by the states, the scholarships would go to twenty thousand students a year, or eighty thousand over a four-year span. The next three sections called for matching federal grants for the training of science and math teachers, and for the teaching of foreign languages and for equipping science labs in the nation's schools. Finally, Folsom outlined plans for graduate fellowships to train teachers and researchers in both the sciences and foreign area studies. Calling graduate education "a critical bottleneck," Folsom said the United States needed to double the current output of nine thousand Ph.D.s a year.

Cabinet comments were generally favorable, but the president and several others worried about stretching the nation's resources too thinly. Ike wondered why the program had to include the social sciences and humanities; he would prefer to limit the college scholarships to those enrolled in science and engineering programs. Commerce Secretary Sinclair Weeks and conservative Secretary of Agriculture Ezra Taft Benson also had doubts. Weeks wanted to limit federal aid to subjects deemed "essential" to national security, while

Benson objected to the government entering into a new field, asking, "Where will it end?" Others came to the defense of the HEW proposals. Jim Killian, recalling his MIT experience, stressed the need to include the humanities both to have a well-rounded program and to make it attractive to the entire educational community. Secretary of State John Foster Dulles agreed, warning against too "materialistic" an approach and citing the danger in viewing this as a contest with the Russians in which we sacrificed the values we were striving to protect.

Despite some misgivings about the breadth of the HEW legislation, the president liked the overall approach. He was particularly pleased with the total cost, estimated at $300 million over four years with a limit of $100 million in the first year. When objections developed within the cabinet, he kept repeating, "I see some need for federal money." But he was adamant about holding down the costs, telling Folsom he was "dead set" against a 75–25 matching grant formula, insisting instead that the federal share be limited to 50 percent. And he stressed again and again that this support was conditioned on the temporary nature of the federal program, geared as it was to meet an emergency. The program must be designed so that the federal government "could withdraw once the need is met."[36]

Eisenhower's support for this limited program of government aid to education became clear in a meeting on December 4 with Republican congressional leaders. After Folsom outlined the program, GOP congressmen began to pick it apart. House Republican leader Charles Halleck of Indiana spoke disparagingly of a recent Purdue graduate he had hired who knew little except "aesthetic dancing," and he warned that such an elitist program of supporting only the brightest high school graduates would be "bad politically." Senator Styles Bridges of New Hampshire warned of likely opposition in Congress, comparing the proposed legislation to "opening Pandora's box" and expressing doubt that the Russians "were so damn far ahead." The president responded by citing the advice he had gotten from some of the nation's most eminent scientists on October 15. The real crisis facing the nation, they had convinced him, was not the satellite orbiting the earth in 1957 but the possibility that in ten years the Soviets would far surpass the United States in science and technology. Unless we act now, Ike asserted, we could be "irretrievably behind" in another decade. The only solution, he concluded, lay in "starting to straighten out the matter now, not on a crash program but on a reasonable and timely basis."[37]

It is clear that within two months after *Sputnik* Eisenhower had framed his basic response. In education, as in the missile and satellite programs, he rejected both hasty and expensive efforts that overestimated the danger facing the nation and would unbalance the budget. He preferred to settle down for the long haul, building on programs under way and only adding new ones that promised to meet the long-run problems confronting the nation. Persuaded by the scientists that we were lagging behind the Soviets in both basic research and the training of scientists and engineers, he was prepared to back a modest effort to remedy these deficiencies rather than undertake a sweeping reform of American education. He summed up his views best when he told the GOP congressional leaders that he favored "a reasonable program" that focused on science education. The problem, he told them, was real but not insurmountable. "Russians aren't 14 ft. high," an aide recorded him saying, "and [their] brains aren't [the] size of bushel baskets."[38]

IV

The *Sputnik* crisis had begun to take its toll on President Eisenhower; the long hours of working out the American response and preparing the "chins-up" speeches left him tired and irritable. In mid-November, after the Oklahoma City address, he left Washington for a week of relaxation at his favorite resort, the Masters golf course at Augusta, Georgia. But back in Washington on Friday, November 22, he spent the day in long cabinet and NSC meetings and then worked until midnight on the text of his third speech, scheduled for Cleveland in late November.

This address was never delivered. On Monday, November 25, the president went to the airport to greet the king of Morocco, for whom there would be a state dinner that night at the White House. After lunch Ike complained of feeling dizzy, then suddenly discovered he could not speak coherently. Some words came out jumbled; others he could not utter at all, to his growing frustration. His secretary, Ann Whitman, called White House doctor Howard Snider, who quickly ordered the president to lie down, suspecting a slight stroke that affected speech patterns but apparently nothing else. Vice-President Nixon agreed to stand in for Eisenhower at the state dinner that evening, and the White House issued a brief statement saying that the president had suffered a chill at the airport. The most puzzled person of all was Ike, who rose from his nap feeling fine and protested strongly when his wife and doctor explained that he could not attend the evening function.[39]

The next day, as the president continued to have trouble speaking yet felt fine, his advisers were in a turmoil. White House Chief of Staff Sherman Adams conferred regularly with Secretary of State Dulles and Vice-President Nixon. Their initial concern centered on the NATO conference forthcoming in December. Ike had planned to attend to gain NATO agreement to the plan to base IRBMs in Europe as a way to protect against any early deployment of Soviet ICBMs. The three men contacted Press Secretary James Hagerty, already in Paris to set up the advance preparations for the president's trip. They all agreed that the NATO trip was now out of the question, and Dulles expressed the fear that the world reaction would be "terrific" if it proved that the stroke was serious. A Paris newspaper expressed a widely held view when it commented: "It is the whole free world that is sick in bed with Ike, and waiting for his recovery."[40]

The president proved to be more resilient than his aides dared hope. By Wednesday, November 27, his speech had cleared up, though he continued to speak quite slowly and distinctly as he recovered from what he termed "that cerebral thing." He awoke from a good night's sleep, showered and shaved himself, and told Dulles he was in "fine spirits." While Dulles, Adams, and Nixon worried about how to handle the NATO trip, Ike announced that he planned to attend next week's cabinet and congressional meetings and had no intention of calling off the Paris visit. He went to church on Thursday to celebrate Thanksgiving and then left for a long weekend at Gettysburg. His aides tried to talk him into staying for ten days to conserve his energy for the NATO talks, but he insisted on returning to Washington to conduct the cabinet meeting and a bipartisan session with congressional leaders.

Back in the White House, the president brushed aside all suggestions of limiting his schedule and insisted impatiently that he was determined to make the Paris trip. On Monday, a week after his stroke, his aides asked him simply to open the cabinet meeting and then leave, but he stayed two hours and afterwards worked through the afternoon in the Oval Office. According to Ann Whitman, he "seemed chipper and entirely sure of himself when he left to go over to the house. He set his hat at a jaunty angle . . . and walked firmly home, not nearly, seemingly, as tired as he had every right to be." Two days later, he ended any further discussion about going to the NATO conference when he directed his speechwriters to draft "something sentimental" for his remarks on arrival in Paris and then said he was "going to the farm and paint."[41]

The president had made a remarkable recovery from his third bout with illness in only two years. Many had feared that the constant tension and sense of crisis that had begun with the Suez incident in 1956 and continued though the Little Rock desegregation episode and the two *Sputniks* in the fall of 1957 had sapped his last reserves. He had begun to complain of the unending problems he faced and seemed to have lost his usual buoyancy by mid-November. But the stroke forced him to make a choice: either face up to the national crisis with renewed leadership or simply give up. When his wife asked him to cut down on his schedule and ease his burdens, he refused, saying, "If I cannot attend to my duties, I am simply going to give up this job. Now that is all there is to it." He could not go on being president in name only; he decided he would make the full effort required to overcome the crisis in confidence facing the nation and his presidency.[42]

Friendly observers were delighted at the speed with which Ike seemed to come back from the stroke. The editors of *U.S. News & World Report* commented about his "dramatic comeback," while the Luce publications described him as "chipper" and "bouncing back with a vigor that astonished his staff." Somehow the stroke, while making Ike grumpier and more irritable, also gave him a new resolve to meet the challenge of *Sputnik*. The apathy that some had detected in the president after his reelection was now gone. He got to his desk every morning by eight and often worked until six, taking only a break for a brief after-lunch nap at his doctor's orders. "Cabinet members and members of the White House staff were in and out of the White House," commented one aide, "in a revolving-door sequence reminiscent of the brisk first months of 1953." The stroke and the two days when he had trouble speaking appeared to have jolted him out of the complacency that marked his initial reaction to *Sputnik*. The "chins-up" speeches may not have energized the country, but perhaps in giving them Eisenhower realized that more than words were necessary to reassure a troubled nation. With a new sense of purpose, he set out to offer the American people the leadership that they so desperately wanted him to provide.[43]

CHAPTER FOUR

On the Monday Ike suffered his stroke, November 25, 1957, Lyndon B. Johnson gaveled open Senate hearings on the impact of *Sputnik.* The first witness, scientist Edward Teller, spoke in ominous terms of the implications of *Sputnik,* saying it indicated the Soviets were beginning to take the lead in science and technology. A *New Republic* columnist praised Teller for stripping off layers of U.S. complacency "like a man peeling an onion," then noted a striking contrast: "At one end of Pennsylvania Avenue a physicist proclaiming Moscow is two years ahead of us, at the other end a sick President." At the White House, Eisenhower responded by telling AEC Chairman Lewis Strauss, a staunch backer of Teller, how much he was distressed by scientists who "tried to be experts in military and political matters."[1]

In the next few weeks, the president would find it much easier to recover from his stroke than to escape the political fallout from the Soviet space spectacular. For more than five years, Eisenhower's personal popularity had stymied the Democrats. Only two years after his election in 1952, they regained control of Congress, but Ike's claims of peace and prosperity had easily earned him a second term in the White House in 1956. A coalition of northern Republicans and southern Democrats had blocked all efforts at liberal reform legislation. But Eisenhower was now suddenly vulnerable. Southerners were unhappy over the way he had used force to uphold court-ordered school desegregation in Little Rock in September; the *Sputnik* launch the next month brought his greatest asset, expert judgment on the nation's Cold War military requirements, into question. Those Democrats, like Missouri Senator Stuart Symington, who had repeatedly charged Eisenhower with risking national security to balance the budget saw a chance both to increase defense spending and damage Eisenhower

61

politically. Sensing "a political turn in their direction," noted the editors of *U.S. News & World Report,* the Democrats "are not in the mood to help the White House out of any holes, at home or abroad, unless they get credit publicly and are suitably rewarded."[2]

The Senate hearings thus opened a new phase in Eisenhower's campaign to contain the post-*Sputnik* hysteria. He had to contend with serious partisan opposition in his efforts to persuade the American people that his administration had the situation under control. His determination to resist calls for increased spending to meet the Soviet challenge would face its sternest test yet. But there was more at stake than just the goal of a balanced budget. His own prestige was now on the line. In fighting for what he believed was a proper response to *Sputnik,* he risked his reputation as the prudent and trustworthy president who had helped the American people regain a sense of tranquility and well-being after the trials of Korea and McCarthyism.

I

Lyndon B. Johnson was responsible for the first challenge facing the recuperating president. Over the weekend following the October 4 *Sputnik* launch, he arranged with Senator Richard Russell of Georgia, chairman of the Senate Armed Services Committee, to have the Defense Preparedness Subcommittee that LBJ chaired undertake an inquiry into why the Soviets had been the first into space. Russell backed Johnson, his protégé, as a way to head off Stuart Symington, who had urged a sweeping investigation by the full Armed Services Committee aimed at revealing how Eisenhower had allowed his concern for budgetary cuts to imperil the nation. Russell feared that a probe dominated by Symington would open the Democrats to the charge of playing politics with national security; he commented later that the Missouri senator "would raise a lot of Hell, but it would not be in the national interest."[3]

Johnson moved quickly to establish a bipartisan tone for his inquiry. Working closely with the White House staff, he arranged for his aides in Washington to examine all the relevant materials on satellite and missile programs. He conferred by telephone with Secretary of Defense McElroy and a leading Republican on his subcommittee, Senator Styles Bridges of New Hampshire. Following the advice of George Reedy, LBJ set forth lofty goals when he announced plans for the subcommittee hearings on November 4. There would be no partisan attempt "to fix blame or put anyone on trial"; instead, the inquiry would try to stimulate "bold, new thinking in defense and foreign policy."[4]

The Eisenhower administration tried to be as cooperative as possible in working with Johnson to avert a partisan quarrel over *Sputnik.* Secretary of State Dulles called LBJ repeatedly at his Texas ranch to keep him advised of diplomatic developments related to his investigation, including an abortive move to involve Adlai Stevenson, the defeated Democratic presidential candidate, as an adviser for the NATO meeting in Paris. Bryce Harlow, the White House aide in charge of congressional relations, cooperated with Johnson to contain Symington. When the Missouri senator sent the White House requests for a special session of Congress on *Sputnik,* Harlow forwarded them to Johnson along with a copy of Eisenhower's letter turning down Symington's appeal. And during the weeks of preparation for the Senate hearings, newly appointed presidential science adviser James Killian met with members of the subcommittee staff to help them "conduct this hearing in an impartial and constructive manner."[5]

The White House, however, did not ignore the political danger inherent in Johnson's forthcoming hearings. Less than two weeks after *Sputnik,* Eisenhower ordered a full-scale review of all missile and satellite decisions stretching back into the Truman administration. Bryce Harlow took charge of this project, paying special attention to the lack of progress under the Democrats after World War II. One of his researchers soon discovered that a Truman administration cutback of $75 million in research funding led to the elimination of the early Atlas ICBM program in 1949. And, the assistant informed Harlow, "Stu Symington, as first AF Sec, had to approve said action." Harlow passed on this information to the Republican National Committee, and soon Congressman Gerald Ford was publicly accusing Symington of being responsible for the current Soviet ICBM lead because he had killed the Atlas when he was secretary of the air force.[6]

Before the end of the year, Harlow had compiled a fourteen-page history of the American missile effort, which he distributed to Republican members of Congress. Citing the 1949 Atlas decision, this document accused the Truman administration of putting the United States at a great disadvantage vis-à-vis the Russians in missile development. "For eight years we slept while the Russians advanced." Then in 1953 Eisenhower revived the moribund American ICBM effort, which quickly "surged ahead with great speed." Pointing to the billions spent on IRBMs and ICBMs in the 1950s under Ike, the Republican document claimed that the Democrats were responsible for less than 1 percent of the total missile budget.[7]

Eisenhower was apparently aware of Harlow's discoveries when he met with Senator Johnson on November 6. The majority leader, intent on stressing his concern for a genuinely bipartisan investigation, claimed that he was resisting calls for a special session of Congress. Eisenhower endorsed a bipartisan approach, saying that the Republicans "would not be first to throw the stone." He added that he had instructed Defense Secretary McElroy to give Johnson and Bridges a thorough briefing, but he stressed the need for discretion. Without mentioning Symington by name, the president commented afterwards that "there are some members of the Committee with whom he cannot be that frank, a matter Johnson well realizes."

Although Eisenhower knew that LBJ had his own agenda, he accepted Johnson's promise to avoid partisanship at face value. In dictating notes of the meeting, he told his secretary that he believed LBJ was "aware" that the Democrats "are also vulnerable" on the missile issue. "He said all the right things," the president commented. "I think today he is being honest."[8]

The main reason for this confidence was Ike's realization that he and Johnson shared a common interest in containing Stuart Symington. The majority leader, realizing that the Missouri senator was a leading contender for the 1960 Democratic nomination he himself prized, carefully blocked Symington's efforts to expand the hearings into a full-scale probe into the state of the nation's defenses. Rather than focus on such issues as the need for dispersal of American B-52 bombers and the level of defense spending, issues on which Symington was an expert, LBJ preferred to use the hearings to show how the United States had fallen behind the Soviets in the new areas of space and missiles and then suggest how we could redeem ourselves. Accordingly, he decided to begin with scientists rather than military men and to control the hearings by having his staff conduct the questioning, with senators limited to just ten minutes with each witness. Above all, he insisted that the hearings do nothing to embarrass the "one man who can give the orders that will produce the missiles. That man is the President of the United States."[9]

There was a shrewdness to Johnson's strategy that transcended his need to outflank Symington. Ignoring advice from those who saw the hearings as a perfect chance to attack the president, he realized that the public would quickly react against what he termed "ward-heeler" tactics. This was a time when a high-minded approach would not only serve the national interest but be good politics as well. By letting prominent scientists and public figures testify to the Soviet success in space and missiles, inevitably putting administration witnesses on the defensive, LBJ would be able to discredit the party in power without attacking Eisenhower personally. Moreover, by refraining from partisan charges the Democrats would avoid the inevitable GOP counterattack on the Truman record. To Eisenhower's ultimate dismay, the hearings would turn out to be what Rowland Evans and Robert Novak called a "minor masterpiece" that met Lyndon Johnson's fundamental aim as majority leader, being "damaging to the Republicans and beneficial to the Democrats."[10]

II

Three well-known public figures dominated the opening week of the preparedness subcommittee hearings. Edward Teller, the "father of the H-bomb," Vannevar Bush, the man who mobilized American scientists in World War II, and James Doolittle, who led the famous 1942 raid on Tokyo, offered testimony strikingly similar to what the Science Advisory Committee had told Eisenhower privately in mid-October. All three viewed *Sputnik* as a sign that the Soviet Union had made dramatic gains in science and technology and might soon surpass the United States in this vital area.

Each emphasized a different aspect of the problem. Teller concentrated on missiles, claiming that the United States had waited too long before developing its missile program, thereby allowing the Russians to get a head start. *Sputnik* showed that they had developed the powerful rocket boosters needed for an ICBM, but there was no evidence that they had solved the key problems of guidance and reentry. The United States enjoyed a lead in nuclear weapons technology and, with a determined effort, could still win the missile race. Vannevar Bush made a broader assessment, stressing the need for greater emphasis on basic scientific research rather than crash weapons programs. In particular, he bemoaned the interservice rivalry, which he felt hampered the American missile program. Doolittle, in contrast, emphasized the need to "overhaul our own educational program," claiming that the Russians were training far more scientists and engineers. Blaming American society rather than the Eisenhower administration, he called for upgrading science in the schools and for awarding scientists greater recognition for their achievements.[11]

One common theme ran through the testimony of all three of these distinguished witnesses: *Sputnik* posed a fateful challenge for the United States. The problem was not simply getting an American satellite into space, something they assumed would soon be done. Rather it was a question of making new commitments to give far higher priority, both in money and national attention, to science and technology. "We have been complacent and we have been smug," Bush warned. "We must develop a sense of urgency," Doolittle urged; "we must be willing to work harder and sacrifice more." The goal was not just to survive through more and better weapons but to explore the wonders of space and the secrets it might unlock, from mastery of the weather to greater knowledge of the universe. Above all, they warned that we were in a race in which the Russians were clearly ahead. Like Pearl Harbor, there was a silver lining in *Sputnik;* it could rouse us to our peril before it was too late. "I think the primary thing that needs to happen to us here in this country," concluded Vannevar Bush, "is that we wake up to the fact that we are in a tough, competitive race."[12]

The administration's two main witnesses during the first week of testimony, Secretary of Defense Neil McElroy and his deputy, Donald Quarles, tried to persuade the senators that they had the situation well in hand. McElroy, asked about a mid-November statement in which he conceded the Russians were ahead in the missile race, tried to hedge. Claiming that there were too many unknowns, he stated that he did not have "positive knowledge" of whether we were ahead or behind the Russians in IRBMs and ICBMs. Quarles was more emphatic, declaring that "it is a neck-and-neck kind of situation." When it came to overall national security, including bombers as well as missiles, McElroy was more definite. Pressed on this point by Stuart Symington, he asserted his belief that the United States was "still distinctly ahead of the U.S.S.R."[13]

The staff and members of the preparedness subcommittee quickly revealed their skepticism. Edwin L. Weisl, the subcommittee's counsel, and individual senators hammered away on two points where the administration was vulnerable. The first was the interservice rivalry and apparent bureaucratic confusion mentioned by Bush. The hearings stressed the duplication of effort involved with the three IRBM programs—Thor, Jupiter, and Polaris—as well as the decision to separate Vanguard from the military missile programs that promised much quicker results. Johnson and Symington were especially critical of Holaday, the guided missile director, pointing out his lack of clear authority and asking why the administration did not apppoint a "missile czar" to end the waste and duplication.

The subcommittee was equally intent on showing how Eisenhower's budget ceiling had limited the American missile effort. McElroy and Quarles admitted that the president had set a ceiling of $38 billion on defense spending, but both preferrred to call it a "guideline" and claimed that it did not prevent them from using money from low priority items to ensure that missiles got all the funds they needed. But Senator Harry Byrd of Virginia scored heavily when he got McElroy to confirm that Congress had appropriated $1.5 billion more for defense in the past four years than the administration had requested. "I think it is important," Byrd declared, "in endeavoring to ascertain the cause of the fact that it is admitted that we are lagging in the missile-development field . . . to make it clear that these appropriations were made by Congress." In other words, the Republican president, not the Democratic Congress, was to blame for the looming missile gap.[14]

The most serious blow the administration suffered during the hearings came on November 26 and 27, when CIA Director Allen Dulles and nuclear arms expert Herbert Scoville testified on Soviet capabilities in closed sessions. Dulles admitted that the Soviet rate of economic growth was double that of the United States and confirmed Doolittle's warning that the Russians were training more scientists and engineers than we were. In fact, Dulles estimated that they already outstripped us in scientific personnel, 1.5 million to 1.3 million. Scoville had even more ominous figures for Soviet missile development; he said intelligence on Russian tests indicated that the Soviets already had an operational missile with a 750-mile range. He predicted that they would deploy a 1,000-mile IRBM in 1958, with ICBMs fully operational by 1960. The CIA estimated that they would have two hundred ICBMs in place by 1960 and as many as five hundred by 1962. Dulles concluded the briefing on an even more frightening note. Pointing out that the Russians were developing cruise missiles with a range of five hundred miles, he forecast the possibility of Soviet submarines armed with nuclear-tipped cruise missiles threatening the American coastline by the early 1960s.[15]

Although the CIA testimony remained secret, Senator Johnson did tell the press that Dulles had given them some somber news, including the fact that Russia "is now outstripping the U.S. in developing a scientific and technological manpower pool." Senator Symington was more blunt, calling the CIA report "a sad and shocking story," while GOP Senator Styles Bridges admitted to receiving "very unpleasant information."[16]

After a two-week delay, the hearings resumed for another week in mid-December. Most of the witnesses were military men, and the inquiry focused on much more specific issues. William Holaday, the director of guided missiles, confirmed the prevailing view of his incompetence, admitting at one point that he was not "an expert" on missiles. General James Gavin, who had recently resigned as director of the army's research and development program, gave the most sensational testimony. In addition to calling for the breakup of the Joint Chiefs of Staff and the appointment of a missile czar, he claimed that the army could have launched a satellite long before *Sputnik*. He and General Curtis LeMay, head of the Strategic Air Command, reinforced the senator's complaints that Eisenhower's insistence on economy was endangering national security. LeMay even claimed that SAC was nearly grounded near the end of the 1957 fiscal year by a shortage of funds to buy fuel.[17]

As the hearings began to degenerate into a military sour grapes session, Johnson adjourned them for the Christmas holidays. The first week's testimony had put the administration on the defensive by suggesting that the Republicans had let the United States fall behind the Soviets in the missile race because of false economy and poor planning. *Time* aptly claimed that the preparedness subcommittee had revealed to the nation that "the Pentagon is wreathed in fog and confusion." But the increasingly partisan tone began to make the Senators appear to be playing politics with *Sputnik*. Senator Symington was the worst offender. Despite a press release on December 5 denying any political motive, the Missouri senator told a New Orleans audience that *Sputnik* was a "technical Pearl Harbor" that destroyed the administration's contention that we enjoyed a qualitative if not quantitative lead over the Soviet Union. "This premise of our military planning was blasted on October 4," Symington declared. "We no longer have such supremacy."[18]

By December a reaction began to develop to this kind of rhetoric. When Minnesota Senator Hubert Humphrey joined Symington and Tennessee's Estes Kefauver in calling for a new Department of Science and Technology, *Reporter* magazine asked these liberal Democrats, "Why not a Department of Common Sense?" And the editors of the *Nation,* still skeptical of the post-*Sputnik* "semi-hysteria," suggested that it was time to stop listening to "those who simply repeat what everyone is saying" and instead seek "a restatement of goals and objectives." "We need a new program for peace," they wrote, "not an intensification of Cold War military policies."[19]

It is unlikely that Eisenhower ever read these comforting words, but he nevertheless remained firm in his determination not to be swept away by the growing pressure for action. At the same time, he realized that he needed to do more than simply give the American people verbal reassurances. He had to act in two areas, defense spending and a space launch. Unless he could convince Congress and the people that he would not endanger the nation to balance the budget and that he would deliver on his promise to launch an American satellite into space, he faced a bleak winter.

III

The key decisions on defense spending came while the preparedness subcommittee was airing its charges of inadequate funding and unnecessary duplication of effort in the missile program. The president had already announced that he would no longer insist on a defense ceiling of $38 billion, but he continued to resist the efforts of the individual services to pad the budget for their pet programs. On several occasions he asked Secretary of Defense McElroy to prepare a unified budget rather than simply add up the requests made by the army, navy, and air force. It soon became clear, after the services submitted requests for additonal funding totaling nearly $5 billion, that the president and the National Security Council would have to make the final allocations.[20]

There were two primary considerations: additions to the fiscal year 1958 budget, which ran through the summer of 1958, and approval of the 1959 budget. The president had already agreed to substantial additions to the current defense budget of $38 billion to allow for acceleration of both the ICBM and IRBM programs, expansion of the satellite reconnaisance effort, and dispersal and increased alert time for the nation's primary nuclear deterrent, B-52 bombers. After deliberations throughout November and early December 1957, Ike finally agreed to ask Congress for over $1 billion in additional 1958 defense spending.

The major struggle came over the size of the increase in the 1959 military budget. On November 11 the president reluctantly agreed to raise the original level from $38 billion to $39.5 billion. "If the budget were carefully prepared," an aide noted him telling McElroy, "he thought we could defend a budget that stays below $40 billion." But once again he urged the Defense Department to evaluate the claims of the three services and present a unified budget to the NSC.[21]

Over the next three weeks, the budget debate centered on missiles. The Gaither report had called for a vast expansion in the ICBM program, proposing that the planned number of Atlas and Titan missiles operational in the early 1960s be raised from eighty to six hundred. The administration finally settled on a much more modest increase, setting a goal of ninety Atlas and forty Titan missiles for 1962 at a cost of less than $200 million in additional funding each year. The major new expenditure would go instead to the IRBM program. Worried that the Soviets might have operational ICBMs by 1959, the administration planned to place as many IRBMs in European bases as possible to prevent a missile gap that would endanger American security before the Atlas and Titan ICBMs could be deployed. Thus much of the additional spending in both 1958 and 1959, on the order of $600 million a year, was earmarked for the stopgap IRBMs. Some of this was allocated to the navy's Polaris, which was still in an early stage of development, but most went to the more advanced Jupiter and Thor programs.

Eisenhower continually questioned the Defense Department's insistence on expanding the IRBM effort from a planned 80 missiles by 1962 to a projected 240. He told McElroy that the amount requested for IRBMs in 1959 was so large that people would say that "nothing had been done during the last five years." Scientists told him, the president added, that "there was a limit to the amount of money that could be wisely spent." McElroy replied that the fear of a missile gap required the deployment of IRBMs in several European countries; we had to be able to show our allies at the forthcoming NATO conference that we were serious about using IRBMs to counter the Soviet ICBM threat.[22]

Not only did the president finally agree to the large sums required for these missiles, but he grudgingly permitted McElroy to announce plans for the production of both the army Jupiter and the air force Thor. The need to produce as many IRBMs as quickly as possible overcame the original plan to choose between these competing weapons before going into production. The Thor was closer to production status, but the Jupiter, made almost by hand by Wernher Von Braun's team at Huntsville, had more impressive test results.

McElroy announced the decision to go ahead with both missiles when he testified before LBJ's preparedness subcommittee in late November. Although the president had given his general agreement earlier, the announcement came after a spirited White House debate while Eisenhower was recovering from his stroke. McElroy was candid in admitting that the primary purpose of announcing the production of both Jupiters and Thors was "psychological—to stiffen the confidence and allay the concern particularly of our own people." When Secretary of State Dulles argued that American bombers were a sufficient deterrent and that the Europeans were not demanding that the IRBMs be deployed quickly, other White House aides made it clear that the primary consideration was domestic and bureaucratic politics. Wilton Persons pointed out that "there is great pressure from the Congress to do this or something like it," a point reinforced by both McElroy and Vice-President Nixon. The secretary of defense also argued that it was vital to keep the services happy and prevent them from lobbying directly with Congress. Jim Killian summed up the decision to go with both the Jupiter and Thor as "important" to restrain interservice rivalry and to reassure the American people.[23]

Eisenhower was finally placed in the uncomfortable position of defending budget increases that he felt were primarily designed to build public confidence rather than meet strictly military needs. When former Treasury Secretary George Humphrey wrote him a stern letter complaining about going above the $38 billion defense ceiling, Ike replied that an inflation rate that totaled 6 percent over two years alone justified the increases. "Since 6 percent of 38 billion is more than 2 billion, you can see what a bloody fight I have been waging in the current sessions." In meetings with congressional leaders in early December, the president defended his defense program by explaining the need for apparent duplication of effort, pointing out that you could not tell in advance which program would prove most effective. He saw his decison to increase defense spending by about $2 billion a year as a reasonable response, one designed "not to panic but rather to carry on a steady program." In giving his final approval to the increases to McElroy, Ike said he was devoting a great deal of thought to "what is the figure that will create confidence." He finally concluded that "about two-thirds of the supplementary funds are more to stabilize public opinion than to meet [a] real need for acceleration."[24]

Difficult as the budgetary decisions were for Eisenhower, they reflected a careful weighing of both the external danger and the political impact of *Sputnik*. The president realized the need to protect the deterrent even though U-2 flights suggested that the Soviets were far from deploying ICBMs. He approved new funding to disperse B-52 bombers, still the nation's primary nuclear delivery system, and he accepted the inevitable waste and duplication involved in putting both the Jupiter and Thor IRBMs into production. As much as he disliked excessive government spending and the possibility of an unbalanced budget, he recognized the importance of restoring public confidence and meeting the Democratic challenge to his leadership. As a result, he was willing to spend more than was militarily justified in order to prevent a panicky overreaction that might well endanger not only the health of the economy but his presidency as well.

IV

Eisenhower had much greater difficulty in fulfilling his October 9 commitment to put an American satellite into orbit in December. This rash promise ignored the fact that the December launch would be the first of the complete Vanguard; only the first stage had undergone a successful flight test. Yet on October 16 Eisenhower had instructed his aides to make sure that the December launch went off on schedule; he did not want any delays while the scientists tried to perfect their handiwork.[25]

As the time for the launch approached, the nation's press gathered at Cape Canaveral in Florida to report on the first American probe into space—a grapefruit-sized ball on top of the three-stage Vanguard rocket. The Defense Department closed the launch area, but more than a hundred reporters and TV cameramen gathered along a nearby beach where they could observe the launch pad. Government spokesmen held hourly press briefings after the countdown began on December 5, but a series of delays ensued. Finally, just before noon on Friday, December 6, Vanguard's first-stage engine ignited. "A ball of flame followed," a reporter observed, "a brilliant orange in color, bright as a welder's arc. The ball of flame hovered above the launching stand for a few seconds, then disappeared amid great clouds of black smoke." After only going a few feet in the air, Vanguard fell back on the pad with a roar; a broken fuel line killed the rocket engine and led to a spectacular explosion.[26]

The Vanguard fiasco was a national humiliation. The American people, hoping for a successful launch that would end the Russian monopoly in space, felt they had been betrayed. Headline writers had a field day; Flopnik, Dudnik, Kaputnik became familiar synonyms for the Vanguard failure. Editorials spoke of the damage done to American scientific prestige and blamed the administration for transforming a delicate experiment into a public relations stunt. "We managed so successfully to focus the eyes of the world on the effort," commented the editors of the *Nation*, "that, when it exploded, the whole world was watching." Lyndon Johnson voiced a widely shared feeling when he noted, "I shrink a little inside whenever the U.S. announces a great event and it blows up in our face." Even *Time*, usually supportive of the administration, began to express doubts about the president's leadership. Claiming that Vanguard showed the need for "a general overhaul of old habits of thought and judgment," the editors warned

Ike that the nation "will tolerate nothing less than a day-to-day leadership more strenuous than at any previous time during his term in office."[27]

Belatedly the administration tried to limit the damage. Worried that many would conclude, as *U.S. News & World Report* did, that the "same shortcomings" might plague the American missile programs, officials tried to isolate the Vanguard issue. Hurried telephone calls among Secretary of State Dulles, Vice-President Nixon, and White House Press Secretary Hagerty finally led to a Pentagon statement that no military rockets were used for Vanguard and therefore "this incident has no bearing on our programs for the development of intermediate range and intercontinental ballistic missiles, which are continuing to make fine progress." But despite this effort, Dulles confessed that he had seldom been "as despondent as this moment re Vanguard," and Nixon admitted that "we failed to recognize the psychological importance" of space satellites.[28]

James Killian took charge of the effort to prevent future embarrassment. Replying to a senator who complained about the advance publicity for the Vanguard launch, he promised that in the future the administration would try to avoid releasing specific dates for tests. But he pointed out that, since no military secrets were involved, it was hard to keep the media from observing the launches at Cape Canaveral. He explained to the president that the Defense Department would try to make "improper observation and eavesdropping" more difficult but admitted that the press had developed such "effective audio-visual monitoring techniques" that it was impossible to conduct major firings "without their knowledge."

The real problem, as Killian observed to Eisenhower, was the inherent difficulty facing scientists and engineers as they "worked on the border of the unknown" and had to learn through testing what "could not have been anticipated in advance." Scientists were already "under enough tension and pressure in conducting the tests"; they needed to be protected from the "glare of publicity." Killian refrained from reminding Eisenhower that the president's own statements had focused national attention on the December Vanguard launch.[29]

The truth was that the United States was still a long way from duplicating the Soviet feat in launching *Sputnik.* Members of Killian's President's Science Advisory Committee felt that Vanguard was so complicated that the odds for a successful launch sometime in 1958 were only 50–50 and that the army's *Explorer,* scheduled for a late January attempt, offered a better chance for success. The president's decision to keep the military missile program separate from a civilian space launch continued to hamper the American satellite effort. In that regard, Eisenhower had no one but himself to blame for the continuing public outcry.[30]

V

The main American diplomatic response to *Sputnik* helped take some of the sting out of the Vanguard failure. On December 15, 1957, President Eisenhower led the American delegation to Paris for the NATO conference. John Foster Dulles was the moving force behind this initiative. He felt it was essential for the United States to reassure worried Western Europeans by placing American IRBMs in European bases. The British had already agreed to accept sixty IRBMs; Dulles pressed hard for the Pentagon to increase the projected number of Thors and Jupiters so that he and Eisenhower could make a broader commitment at the Paris conference.

After the president's stroke in late November, it seemed unlikely that he could attend the NATO conference. But Ike recovered quickly and insisted on attending the meeting, later claiming that he would have resigned if the doctors had forbidden him from traveling. The whole idea of having heads of government take part in this NATO meeting was to allow Eisenhower to reassure Europeans personally that the United States was still strong and would defend the NATO countries even at the risk of a Soviet ICBM attack against the United States.[31]

The president appeared robust in public. At the opening session, he spoke boldly about the need to dispel "the shadows that are being cast upon the free world. We are here to take store of our great assets," he declared, "in men, in minds, and in materials." Eisenhower and Dulles were able to carry out their primary objective at Paris: The United States succeeded in gaining agreement in principle for the basing of intermediate-range nuclear missiles in Europe to defend NATO. Pointing to the "present Soviet policies in the field of nuclear weapons," the final communiqué stated that the NATO Council agreed that "intermediate range ballistic missiles will have to be put at the disposal of the Supreme Allied Commander in Europe."[32]

The NATO conference was a major victory for the Eisenhower administration. Despite Soviet threats of retaliation against any country that received the American missiles, the European allies accepted the IRBMs as proof of U.S. determination not to be awed by the apparent Soviet lead in ICBM development. Neither Germany nor the Scandinavian NATO members volunteered to take any IRBMs, but eventually Italy and Turkey would join England in providing bases for these American missiles. The Europeans understood the underlying significance of both Ike's personal involvement and the offer of IRBMs. A French newspaper summed it up best with the succinct headline "IRBM PLUS NATO EQUALS ICBM."[33]

The trip to Paris also helped reassure the American people about Eisenhower's health and vigor. He withstood the grueling trip well, traveling for miles through Paris in an open car and spending eight to ten hours a day at the negotiating sessions. He was, as *Time* noted, "the Ike that Europe remembered."

Yet once home, Eisenhower made a tactical error that undercut much of the gain from the NATO conference. Appearing with Secretary of State Dulles for a thirty-minute television report on the Paris meeting, Ike spoke only briefly, letting Dulles ramble on for more than twenty minutes in a tedious summary of the negotiations. "Here was the President of the United States," noted the editors of the *New Republic*, "looking bored and self-conscious, cast in a subordinate role to an underling." A Republican newspaper commented even more savagely on "the spectacle of two tired, aging men talking about the gravely compromised half-measures which bind and separate America from its European allies."[34]

Even the substance of the Paris agreements did not evoke too much confidence. Although Dulles boasted to Lyndon Johnson that the administration "will get missiles where we need them," the reality was that the United States had yet to produce a single operational IRBM. The first Thors and Jupiters were not expected to come off the production lines until late 1958. At best, as Lawrence Loeb has noted, the IRBMs "were valuable as instruments of propaganda." More than three months after the launch of *Sputnik*, Eisenhower still could not point to any substantial American achievements in either missiles or satellites to balance the Soviet feat.[35]

VI

The traditional year-end summing up of the state of the nation and the world offered little comfort to the beleaguered Eisenhower administration. *Time* magazine put Nikita Khrushchev on its cover as Man of the Year. The editors justified their choice by contrasting the Vanguard failure with the two *Sputnik* successes. "In 1957," they wrote, "the U.S. had been challenged and bested in the very area of technological achievement that had made it the world's greatest power." Acccording to the *New Republic*, 1957 was the year "when Americans were stunned, chastened and confused into a mood of salutary humiliation after five years of unparalleled complacency." Even the editors of the conservative *U.S. News & World Report* were forced to admit that *Sputnik* had let to a sharp decline in Eisenhower's popularity and given "a sudden boost in prestige to Russia." "All at once," they wrote, "life had become more uncertain."[36]

The most somber comment of all came from political scientist Hans J. Morgenthau, who saw *Sputnik* as a devastating "national failure" that might well signal the beginning of a permanent decline in American power. While Morgenthau admitted there was no single scapegoat, he laid most of the blame on "the absence of consistent and informed Presidential leadership." He claimed that it was a "virtual certainty" that the Soviets would have an operational ICBM before the United States, and he criticized the decision to base IRBMs in Europe for making us too dependent on our NATO allies. Asserting that only a heroic attempt to rebuild American military power could restore the nation's world prestige, he called for a defense effort "comparable to that following Pearl Harbor."[37]

These pessimistic appraisals reflected Eisenhower's failure to convince the nation that his administration had the situation under control. Three successful test flights at Cape Canaveral in mid-December indicated that the American missile program was in much better shape than critics realized. The army's Jupiter flew over a limited test range, and the air force Thor completed a twelve-hundred-mile flight, landing within two miles of its target. Reporting on these developments to Eisenhower, James Killian predicted that full-scale production of both IRBMs would begin very soon. He was even more pleased with the first successful Atlas test flight over a limited, five-hundred-mile range. Speaking for the entire President's Science Advisory Committee, Killian concluded, "We are confident that the U.S. has ample technical competence in our ballistic technical groups to achieve satisfactory operational missile systems at an early date."

Killian admitted that the outlook for satellites was bleaker. He did not favor putting greater effort into Vanguard, which his group felt had only a fifty–fifty chance of success, but he did recommend more resources for Jupiter-C, the army's Explorer program. Above all, he stressed the need to look beyond the early missiles to the development of a second generation of more sophisticated and advanced weapons relying on solid-fuel propellants. These efforts must be "vigorously and imaginatively pursued," he argued. "We attach great importance to boldness in our planning for these future missiles and the initiation and successful carrying through of fundamental and exploratory work."[38]

Killian's report reflected the paradox surrounding the Eisenhower administration's missile program. Due in large part to Killian's 1955 report, the administration had begun a major effort at developing both IRBMs and ICBMs long before *Sputnik*. Yet the president's insistence on separating the satellite program from the military missile effort, based primarily on his desire to develop a space reconnaissance vehicle to replace the U-2, allowed the Soviets to score a major propaganda victory with *Sputnik*. Although Eisenhower himself was certain that the Soviets had not opened a potential missile gap, he failed to anticipate the widespread public anxiety triggered by the satellite.

The result was at best a mixed record of presidential leadership. On the one hand, Eisenhower had carefully weighed the danger to national security and had concluded that the efforts begun long before *Sputnik* were adequate to meet the Soviet challenge in missiles and space. Yet his restrained attempts to reassure the American people were undercut by the continuing Soviet space spectaculars and the highly publicized Vanguard failure. The added burdens of the November stroke and the shrewd way that Lyndon Johnson led the Democratic critique at the preparedness subcommittee hearings created the impression that Eisenhower was no longer capable of leading the nation.

In 1958 the president faced the challenge of proving both his ability to lead and the soundness of his measured response to *Sputnik*. The long honeymoon was over. For five years Eisenhower had presided over a period of peace and prosperity, basking in public gratitude for ending the Korean War and letting the nation enjoy great material abundance. Now he suddenly had to convince a skeptical nation not only that he understood the new problems facing the country but that he possessed the energy and vision needed to restore the United States to its accustomed position of world primacy.

CHAPTER FIVE

The new year found the Eisenhower administration in a beleaguered position. Despite the successful missile tests in December 1957, the American people still waited for the United States to match the Russians by launching its first satellite into orbit. At the same time, an economic recession that had deepened throughout the fall added a new sense of anxiety. More ominous were the growing leaks about the Gaither report that suggested Americn defenses were in much worse shape than Eisenhower would admit. Finally, the Democrats were looking ahead to the next session of Congress to gain political advantage by claiming that the Eisenhower administration had failed to meet the challenge posed by *Sputnik* in education, space exploration, and, above all, national security.

The steadily worsening economic decline put the administration on the defensive. The economy had begun to slow in August, and all through the fall a steady drop in personal income, a decline in production, and rising unemployment rates had begun to create a realization that the United States was in the early stages of at least a mild recession. The fact that production fell much less than personal income helped relieve economists but did not prevent growing public concern. The increased government spending on defense and missiles occasioned by *Sputnik* promised to halt the decline, but even these expenditures, much lower than the Democrats advocated, would not lead to an improved economic performance for several more months.[1]

The leak of the highlights of the still secret Gaither report greatly intensified the public's growing anxiety over national security. On December 20 reporter Chalmers Roberts published a summary of the Gaither recommendations in the *Washington Post*. Roberts described the report in ominous terms, claiming that the experts saw the United States "in the gravest danger in its history" and moving toward the "status of a second-rate power." He repeated the panel's call for $8 billion annual increases in defense spending for a speeded-up missile program, for dispersal and protection of the nation's bombers, and for greatly expanded scientific research and development. Warning that the nation faced "cataclysmic peril" in the future, Roberts claimed the Gaither report "strips away the complacency and lays bare the highly unpleasant realities" confronting the United States in its rivalry with the Soviet Union.[2]

The Roberts article was part of a determined effort by members of the Gaither panel, notably William Foster and Paul Nitze, to pressure the administration into making their report public. Eisenhower, who felt that the report vastly overestimated the Soviet danger, refused even to consider its release, contending that it would be inappropriate for him to make public the confidential advice he had sought for his own private use. But when Lyndon Johnson repeatedly asked that the report be given to his preparedness subcommittee as part of its investigation, the president did allow his science adviser, James Killian, to brief the subcommittee staff on the report off the record. On December 27, 1957, Killian met with Edwin Weisl, the subcommittee's counsel, and told him that virtually everything in the report had already come out in the public hearings. Weisl failed in his effort to have the Gaither report released to the subcommittee, but Killian did agree to allow some information in the report to be shared with the senators in a closed session.[3]

The public concern intensified in early January 1958 with the release of a Rockefeller Brothers Fund report on national security. The result of a study by a blue-ribbon panel that included Henry Luce and Edward Teller, this public document warned that the United States was on the verge of losing its military lead over the Soviet Union. "Unless present trends are reversed," the Rockefeller panel warned, "the world balance of power will shift in favor of the Soviet bloc." Calling for the streamlining of the Pentagon, dispersal of Strategic Air Command bases, and a stepped-up missile effort (all echoing the Gaither report), the study recommended increasing the defense budget by $3 billion annually for the next five years.[4]

The public outcry touched off by the publicity surrounding the Gaither and Rockefeller reports played directly into the hands of the Democratic party. No one realized this more fully than Majority Leader Lyndon Johnson, who had been conducting his preparedness subcommittee hearings skillfully, avoiding direct partisan attacks on the administration while presenting evidence that strongly suggested American defense was being handicapped by interservice squabbling and Eisenhower's own stubborn refusal to spend the money needed to protect America from the new dangers revealed by *Sputnik*. Posing as one concerned only with what was best for the country at a time of grave national crisis, Johnson was in the perfect position to use the next session of Congress to score a major political victory for the Democratic party as well as advance his own presidential ambitions.

On the eve of the opening of what reporters dubbed the "Sputnik Congress," LBJ decided to put the president on the defensive with a well-publicized speech to the Democratic caucus. Speaking on January 7, just two days before Eisenhower's State of the Union address, Johnson sought to seize the initiative on the vital issue of space. Blaming the administration's desire for a balanced budget for crippling the nation's satellite program, LBJ emphasized what was at stake. "Control of space means control of the world," he declared, warning that for the Soviets to gain mastery of space, "the ultimate position," would be more dangerous than "any ultimate weapon." The only possible American response, he claimed, would be to seize "the ultimate position" ahead of the Soviets; "our national goal and the goal of all free men must be to win and hold that position."[5]

Critics debated how effective Johnson's bold move had been. Some portrayed him as a "space cadet" who overreacted to the Soviet scientific feat. The *Nation* argued that "the phrase 'control of the world' grated harshly on many ears; it did not enchant, it appalled." But *U.S. News & World Report* printed the text of his speech next to the president's State of the Union address, highlighting Johnson's statement that "total control over the earth lies somewhere out in space." *Life* featured LBJ on its cover and commented, "Never before had the Democrats, Senate Majority Leader Lyndon Johnson included, dared to mount so bold a challenge to a uniquely popular President."[6]

Later in January, after the preparedness subcommittee hearings ended, Johnson sent Eisenhower a copy of the body's public statement, which expressed "deep foreboding" over the increased risk of nuclear war. Stating bluntly that the "Soviet Union had led the world into outer space," the subcommittee statement made seventeen specific recommendations, including proposals for the dispersal of American bombers, the development of huge rockets for space exploration, and the acceleration of all existing intermediate-range and intercontinental ballistic missile programs. "We are engaged in a race for survival and we intend to win that race," Johnson's statement concluded.[7]

I

As the Democrats launched their partisan charges, President Eisenhower realized that he faced the sternest challenge of his political career. He spent the entire first week of January preparing what he knew would be a carefully examined State of the Union address. He did not lack advice. At a cabinet meeting, Secretary of State Dulles urged the president to reassure the people regarding national defense. Stressing that we had the bombers to deliver a deadly nuclear strike, Dulles favored playing down the missile issue.

Congressional Republicans, on the other hand, called for a more vigorous approach. House Minority Leader Charles Halleck suggested that Ike deliver a "ringing pronouncement," a speech filled with the "old 4th of July spirit" that would inspire the trust and confidence of the American people. Senator Leverett Saltonstall preferred a more substantive approach. Pointing out that LBJ's hearings had revealed the way interservice rivalry and inadequate funding had hampered the missile program, Saltonstall wanted the president to appoint a missile czar and to recommend large increases in defense spending.

Eisenhower responded skeptically to many of these proposals. He kept reminding his associates that the real challenge facing the nation was a long-term one, which could not be met with a quick fix such as a one-shot increase of $10 billion in defense spending. "It was possible to do almost anything you wanted for one year," Ike explained, "but when it was a matter of trying to carry on for thirty or forty years, that was entirely different." He made it clear that he would not do anything that would run the risk of ruining the American economy. At the same time, Eisenhower admitted that he may have been "guilty of understatement" in his response to the *Sputnik* crisis. The problem was how to call upon the American people to make sacrifices—"to put on hair shirt and sackcloth"—without frightening them to death.[8]

As the time for his speech approached, Ike went over the text line by line on January 6 with speechwriter Arthur Larson, Press Secretary Jim Hagerty, and UN Ambassador Henry Cabot Lodge. The next day he worked for another three and a half hours on the final draft, only taking time out to confer with former Secretary of Defense Charles Wilson on the Pentagon section. Even on the morning of January 9, the day he was to speak to Congress, he made last-minute changes in the text.[9]

The result was a forty-five-minute address that dealt broadly with the challenge facing the nation. Never referring specifically to *Sputnik,* he nevertheless acknowledged that "many Americans are troubled about recent world developments." While he felt "honest men" might differ "in their appraisal of . . . the dangers that confront us," he agreed that "these dangers are real." He then outlined three broad responses that he felt would ensure the nation's safety in a troubled and turbulent world.

First, he made the case for moderate increases in defense spending without admitting that the national security was at risk. Expressing full confidence in America's deterrent forces, he claimed that any attacker faced "the prospect of virtual annihilation of his country." But he did admit that the Soviets were "waging total cold war" and that the United States was "probably somewhat behind" in the ICBM race. He then called on Congress to approve his request for an additional $1.3 billion in the 1958 budget and several billion more in 1959 for the Pentagon. The extra funds, he explained, would speed the output of Thor and Jupiter IRBMs already in production and accelerate the development of the Polaris and Atlas missiles.

The president put even greater emphasis on a second area, defense reorganization. Pointing out that the new technology cut across the traditional dividing lines between the three armed services, he spoke out in favor of giving more authority to the secretary of defense. The new weapons "defy classification according to branch of service," he argued; it would be far better to consolidate all development and deployment of missiles and satellites in the Defense Department itself. Saying that he would present detailed plans for these changes to Congress later, Eisenhower made it clear that he intended to "end interservice disputes" that had hampered the missile program by giving the secretary of defense the authority to impose "clear organization and decisive central direction."

Finally, the president spoke out eloquently on the need to "improve our resources" in education and scientific research by spending over $1 billion in this area over the next four years. He referred to the plans being developed within the Department of Health, Education, and Welfare for both federal college scholarships and graduate fellowships in science and foreign language study. In addition, he was recommending a fivefold increase in National Science Foundation programs to improve the teaching of science in the nation's schools. At the same time, however, he warned against excessive reliance on federal aid to education, saying that the effort to improve education must be a joint endeavor involving state and local bodies, and, above all, parents and students. "With this kind of all-inclusive campaign," Eisenhower predicted, "I have no doubt that we can create the intellectual capital we need for the years ahead, invest it in the right places—and do this, not as regimented pawns, but as free men and women!"

The president closed his address with a plea to both the Soviet Union and the American people. He called upon the Russian leaders to join him in new efforts at disarmament and world peace. But, aware of the dim prospects for any sudden end to the Cold War, Eisenhower placed greater stress on asking the American people to make the sacrifices that the new burdens in defense and education would place on the federal budget. Only by cutting back on nonessentials, he warned, could we afford to pay for the additional weapons and the educational advances he had outlined. Pointing out that the entire world was watching "to see how wisely and decisively" the United States would meet the challenge facing the nation, Eisenhower closed by affirming his belief that "the response of Congress and of the American people will make this time of test a time of honor."[10]

A packed congressional audience applauded vigorously throughout the speech and gave Eisenhower a standing ovation at the end. Democrats as well as Republicans were generous in their praise. Speaker Sam Rayburn of Texas called the address "the strongest the President has ever presented to the Congress," while Senator Prescott Bush, a Connecticut Republican, hailed it as "the best speech of his career." The Luce publications were also enthusiastic. *Time* praised the president's words for their balance, saying that he was providing the kind of leadership the nation wanted. *Life* expressed some reservations about the lack of emphasis on space exploration but agreed that the speech was "generally a success." The editors felt that Ike had once again shown that he was the "'artist of the possible' whose special genius is to unite the country rather than divide it." They predicted that Ike's leadership would lead to a revival of American self-confidence "which is essential to the self-confidence of the entire free world."[11]

The mood in the White House was equally optimistic. Ann Whitman, the president's private secretary, commented that Eisenhower had come back to the Oval Office "in fine spirits." She found the applause "heartening" and felt that the "whole performance" had given Ike "a great lift." The next day, she noted the new air of confidence that pervaded the executive offices. "The hump has been crossed," she wrote in her diary. "Everything is all right again." Vice-President Nixon agreed, telling Foster Dulles that everywhere he went he was getting favorable reactions to the State of the Union speech. People felt that Eisenhower "had once again asserted his leadership," but Nixon warned about the danger of complacency, adding, "We should not lose the ball again to the other side."[12]

Encouraging as this initial reaction was, Eisenhower still faced the difficult task of persuading Congress and the nation to support his three-point program of a moderate increase in defense spending, a thorough reorganization of the Pentagon, and limited federal aid to education. Democrats were certain to call for more expensive efforts in both defense and education, while resisting any attempt to limit congressional control over the competing armed services. Eisenhower was aware of the contest that lay ahead. He told one admirer that he intended to resist measures "that are hysterically proposed and as quickly abandoned." Instead, as he had explained earlier to legislative leaders, he was prepared to take a stand for long-term solutions and reject any quick fixes. His success in dealing with the *Sputnik* crisis would depend on how well he could maintain this resolve throughout the long congressional session that lay ahead.[13]

II

The president laid out his proposals for increased defense spending in the annual budget message to Congress on January 13, 1958. He reiterated his request for an additional $1.3 billion for the Pentagon for the 1958 budget, with more than half going to increased missile development and production, and much of the rest for dispersal of the nation's main deterrent, B-52 bombers, and for the highly secret military reconnaissance satellite. The lion's share of this additional spending would go to the air force, much to the dismay of army leaders, who suffered a reduction from twenty-seven divisions at the height of the Korean War to just fifteen by 1958.

The most startling aspect of Eisenhower's 1959 budget request was the high percentage devoted to defense. The president proposed a national budget of $73.9 billion, with more than half, $40.3 billion, devoted to the military. Defense spending would thus increase by $2.7 billion over the original 1958 budget; the combined increases in the 1958 and 1959 sums came to almost $4 billion. The result was a deficit of $400 million for 1958 with even a larger figure likely for 1959, which *Time* aptly called "red ink brought on by Red Sputniks." Missiles accounted for most of these increases; the ICBM and IRBM spending went up from $3 billion in 1957 to $5.3 billion in 1959. Secretary of Defense McElroy noted that 75 percent of the $15 billion requested for weapons procurement went for items that did not even exist before 1955.[14]

The president justified his reluctant request for increased defense spending with the hope that this "expresses the way the American people will want to respond to the promises and dangers of the dawning age of space conquest." Not all commentators agreed. The *New Republic* feared that the increased military funding would come at the expense of such domestic programs as housing and welfare, thereby forcing the states to take up the slack. The editors of the *Nation* felt that the American people were far more worried "about cold cash than the cold war" as the economy continued to decline. But *Time* and *U.S. News & World Report* were enthusiastic over what they felt were long-overdue efforts to meet the *Sputnik* crisis.[15]

The budget message simply confirmed the decision that Eisenhower had made in December to increase American spending for missiles. The additional Pentagon funds would allow the dual deployment of the Thor and Jupiter IRBMs, with the first squadrons scheduled to become operational in Europe before the end of 1958, and speed up the Polaris submarine missile as well as both the Atlas and Titan ICBMs. A National Security Council meeting on January 22 confirmed this decision. Where earlier the Atlas alone had the highest priority, the president now instructed McElroy to give the three IRBMs—Thor, Jupiter, and Polaris—the same status, along with the reconnaissance satellite as well as the Vanguard and Jupiter-C scientific satellites. If any serious conflicts in priorities developed, McElroy would resolve them in the Defense Department or, as a last resort, refer them to the president for resolution.[16]

Eisenhower's decision to speed up the missile programs made the Gaither report largely irrelevant. While the president's increases in military spending did not aproach the $8 billion a year the panel had proposed, he had adopted many of the specific suggestions in the November report. Thus the administration was now committed to developing no fewer than three different IRBMs on a crash basis to protect against any possible Soviet lead in producing an ICBM. The Titan was being given the same status as the Atlas ICBM, and the air force was also going ahead with the solid-fuel Minuteman for the 1960s. The president was never likely to approve the massive fallout shelter program suggested by the Gaither report, but he had already moved to disperse the B-52 bomber fleet and had instructed an unwilling air force to begin considering ways to harden missile sites to protect against a Soviet first strike.[17]

Prominent members of the Gaither committee, unaware of the impact of their findings, continued to press for the publication of their report, or at least of its major recommendations. Eisenhower had James Killian carefully defuse this campaign, reminding the members of the panel that they could not speak publicly or even privately to Congress about their confidential recommendations to the president. And the White House finally responded publicly to Lyndon Johnson's repeated requests to have the Gaither report released to his preparedness subcommittee. "I consider it improper and unwise for me to violate the confidence of the advisory relationship," Eisenhower informed Johnson, ". . . or to make public the highly secret facts contained in their reports." In private the president was indignant at the Democrats for their constant pressure for even more defense spending than he had grudgingly authorized. Modern weapons, he complained, were "just so damn costly." It was folly, he burst out, to believe that "money is the cure"; it was "just not right."[18]

From a later perspective, it is clear that Eisenhower had correctly assessed the military danger to the United States in the wake of *Sputnik*. As political scientist Edgar M. Bottome pointed out in 1971, it would have been impossible for the Soviets to have launched a sneak attack against the United States in the late 1950s. The United States had more than four thousand nuclear delivery vehicles spread out at nearly sixty bases at home and abroad. "The problem of destroying all of these delivery vehicles at the same moment in order to prevent retaliation," Bottome argued, "was extremely difficult, if not impossible." The Soviets would have had to launch a simultaneous attack on some twenty-five hundred American aircraft at fifty-nine bases ranging in distance from five hundred to five thousand miles from the borders of the Soviet Union.[19]

The real question was not whether the United States was vulnerable to an enemy first strike in early 1958, but whether the Soviets might be far enough ahead in the ICBM race to make such a threat credible within a few years. Eisenhower felt that the programs he had initiated in 1955 to develop both IRBMs and ICBMs had progressed far enough by October 1957 to safeguard the nation's security for the indefinite future. But, stung by public criticism and urged on by groups like the Gaither panel, he had significantly increased the level of funding in order to accelerate these programs and guard against any future missile gap. Convinced in his own mind that he had done more than enough to protect the nation, and reassured by U-2 photos that showed no early Soviet ICBM deployment, the president still had not persuaded the American people that there was nothing to fear from the military consequences of *Sputnik*. In that sense, however prudent Eisenhower's policies were from a national security standpoint, they nonetheless failed to meet the political test of restoring a shaken nation's confidence in itself.

III

In contrast to his reluctance in seeking higher levels of defense spending, Eisenhower was personally committed to the goal of defense reorganization. Long before *Sputnik* he had sought to lessen interservice rivalry and strengthen the role of the president and secretary of defense in directing the armed forces. In 1953 he had tried to streamline the Defense Department, but after meeting stern resistance in Congress he had to settle for modest changes that gave more authority to the secretary of defense and the chairman of the Joint Chiefs of Staff over the individual services.[20]

The public outcry over *Sputnik* created a new opportunity for more sweeping changes in defense organization. Johnson's preparedness subcommittee hearings had brought home to the nation the high cost of interservice rivalry, which had led to not one but three IRBMs—the army's Jupiter, the air force's Thor, and the navy's Polaris. The attempt by each service to have its own missiles had led to waste, inefficiency, and, some argued, a possibly dangerous Soviet lead in this vital new area of weaponry. "Many blame the U.S. missile lag on arguments over which service should develop which missile," commented *U.S. News & World Report*. *Time* expressed the same concern that "interservice rivalry" had handicapped the American missile effort. "Some hard decisions must be made," the editors concluded, "and they must be made in the Pentagon and the White House."[21]

Eisenhower was in full agreement. In early January he asked Ann Whitman to look back through the files to see how many times he had lectured the Joint Chiefs on the danger of interservice rivalry. She found five separate occasions. The most memorable was on March 30, 1956, when Ike had told them to stop "quarreling over missiles" and reminded them that "each Chief should subordinate his position as champion of one particular service" to a concern for overall national policy. What the president wanted above all else was for the four members of the Joint Chiefs to stop acting as the spokesmen for their own branches and instead give broad, disinterested advice to the secretary of defense and the White House.[22]

The first time Eisenhower turned to this issue after *Sputnik* was on November 4, 1957. Over breakfast Nelson Rockefeller, chairman of the Advisory Committee on Government Reorganization, briefed the president and Budget Director Percival Brundage on tentative plans for defense reorganization. The recommendations included the creation of unified commands (units of several different services serving together for a particular mission) under the supervision of the Defense Department and the Joint Chiefs rather than any one service and a proposal to give the secretary of defense full authority over all research and development of new weapons. Ike responded with great enthusiasm. He told Rockefeller that he believed that shifting "operational responsibilities" out of the services to the Joint Chiefs of Staff would lead to "a marked decrease in inter-service rivalry." He also liked the idea of a unified research and development effort in the Pentagon, suggesting that one official in the Defense Department be placed in charge of all such projects, including the various service missile programs.[23]

Two days later, however, Ike found the Joint Chiefs as resistant as ever to change. When he outlined Rockefeller's proposals, Generals Nathan Twining, the Joint Chiefs chairman, and Thomas White, air force chief of staff, took exception, saying that each service had different needs and therefore had to develop its own weapons. When Ike replied that the *Sputnik* crisis showed the need to rise above "narrow service considerations," Admiral Arleigh Burke, the chief of naval operations, chimed in with his dissent. The president pointed out that the armed services would have to meet him halfway; he planned to cut back on domestic programs to fund the expanded military demands of the missile age. The trouble was that Congress and the American people "now believe the services are more interested in the struggle with each other than against an outside foe." The only way he could persuade Congress to provide the additional funds, he warned, would be to have the military agree on a plan for defense reorganization to end waste and duplication.[24]

Rockefeller and Brundage submitted a revised draft plan for defense reorganization to Eisenhower on November 12. It included the earlier proposal for unified commands that would limit the three services to support and logistical roles. The most striking feature was a section giving the secretary of defense complete control over all funding for military research and development. The secretary could then make allocations to the various services or keep some of the money within the Defense Department for special weapons projects. Such a departure, they argued, would "terminate any unwarranted competition among the services and achieve the optimum over-all results."[25]

Eisenhower received similar advice from James Killian and the new President's Science Advisory Committee. On November 6 this body sent the president a memorandum deploring the "wasteful" and "damaging" impact of interservice rivalry on the missile program and calling for a new policy of central direction "to give focus and purposefulness to military technology." On December 30, Killian informed Eisenhower that the PSAC felt that "modernization of organization is the single most important factor in improving our defense technology."

In early 1958 Killian sent Secretary of Defense McElroy a memorandum stressing the need for "central planning" in defense research. He suggested creating the new post of deputy secretary of defense for science and technology charged both with supervising weapons development in all three services and heading a new Pentagon agency to undertake research in areas beyond the scope of any one service. Such an arrangement, Killian argued, "can strike deep roots into our civilian scientific community" and take advantage of "new discoveries which may be profoundly influential in the new weapons technology."[26]

By the end of 1957, Eisenhower was convinced of the need to revamp the Defense Department to permit unified commands, increase the authority of the secretary of defense, and create a central office to oversee all Pentagon research and development along the lines proposed by Killian and the PSAC. However, he feared going ahead with such sweeping plans without the approval of the defense establishment. If the admirals and the generals testified against a presidential defense reorganization plan before congressional committees, it would be doomed to defeat. Ike therefore informed Rockefeller and Brundage not to make public their draft plans. Instead Eisenhower would try to get the Pentagon to take the lead.[27]

Neil McElroy was the key to the president's new approach. With some reluctance, the secretary agreed to have the Defense Department come up with a plan of reorganization, asking only that he be given time to persuade the military leaders of the need for change. McElroy then appointed a blue-ribbon committee of leading private citizens, including Admiral Arthur Radford and General Omar Bradley, both former Joint Chiefs chairmen. Charles Coolidge, a highly regarded Boston lawyer, agreed to serve as chairman.

Eisenhower chafed at the delay that followed as the new committee proceeded with due deliberation. He tried to focus national attention on the need for defense reorganization in his State of the Union address, but he could only speak in broad terms of the need to replace "inter-service disputes" with "decisive central direction." At a press conference on January 15, 1958 (the first Ike had held since his stroke the previous November), reporters found his answer to a question about defense reorganization vague and unresponsive. Pushed harder, Eisenhower fell back on the procedural issue, explaining that he had to wait for "a consensus reached with the Congress [and] with the people that have the job of operating the services." "I am certainly hopeful," he added lamely, "that it goes in the direction of what I believe."[28]

Privately Eisenhower was furious over what he felt were the parochial interests of the service spokesmen who appeared before LBJ's preparedness subcommittee. On January 11 the president expressed to an air force group his anger over a recent statement by General Bernard Schriever, head of the air force's Atlas and Titan ICBM programs, denouncing a proposal for a unified Pentagon space agency. Five days later, Ike fumed to his secretary about what he called the "revolt of the generals." One of the president's aides suggested that, "if someone had been sent to Alaska at the first sign of such a thing, it would have been stopped." When Republican congressional leaders asked Ike about the slow progress on defense reorganization, he said he would do all he could to urge McElroy to move more quickly. Then he vented his frustration by adding, "I've got three more years—if I live. But we're talking of [a] job for 15 years." And he added, ruefully, "I know more about this than any other person in the world! I think I do!"[29]

The president tried to do what he could. He met privately with General Omar Bradley, who expressed his strong support for unified commands, and with Secretary McElroy, who the president said was "coming around" on the issue of defense reorganization, but "not completely." Finally, Eisenhower took Nelson Rockefeller's advice and attended a meeting of the Pentagon committee headed by Charles Coolidge on January 25. The results were disappointing. Although he came mainly to listen, the president soon found himself saying more than he had intended. The committee was too absorbed with details and apparently intent on making only small, incremental changes. Ike spoke out forcefully on the need to respond to the public's criticism of interservice rivalry. He was especially hard on the Joint Chiefs, asking them to stop going to Congress to plead for their individual services but to act instead as a unified advisory body to the president. He reiterated Killian's proposal for centralized control over research and development and then shocked the group by arguing that Congress should appropriate all research funds to the secretary of defense, who in turn would have "the power of decision as to where any particular activity would be carried on."[30]

Three days later, Eisenhower told Republican congressional leaders that he was fed up with the Coolidge committee's "cautious approach." If the Pentagon could not come up with a satisfactory reorganization plan, the president told the legislators, he would act on his own. "I will just have to take the bull by the horns—call in the leaders of the Senate and House, including Democrats, in an effort to try to get their support," Eisenhower recalls saying in his memoirs.[31]

As the president must have known, it was not a very believable threat. Congress had traditionally been opposed to defense reorganization, especially measures designed to increase the power of the executive branch. Members of the Armed Services Committee preferred to work with the Joint Chiefs of Staff divided, each chief coming before Congress to plead the case for his own service. The idea of appropriating funds for new weapons to the secretary of defense went against the whole concept of the power of the purse and the allocation of military spending to the states and districts represented by the most influential members of Congress.

Eisenhower was caught in a dilemma. He had been trying hard to persuade Congress and the American people that the Soviet launch of *Sputnik* had not endangered the nation's defenses. Yet his only chance of winning sweeping defense reorganization was to appeal to the sense of national peril resulting from the apparent Soviet advantage in science and technology. His best chance of streamlining the Defense Department would be through a Pentagon program, not through a personal appeal from the White House. Despite his frustration with the Coolidge committee, he had no choice but to wait for McElroy to work out the best possible compromise with the generals and the admirals.

IV

Educational reform proved to be the most controversial of all the areas in which Eisenhower sought to respond to the *Sputnik* crisis. Nearly everyone agreed that American schools were long overdue for a thorough overhaul, but there was wide divergence over the general nature of the problem and the appropriate remedy. In addition, the federal bureaucracy was at odds over the best possible approach.

The National Science Foundation (NSF) sought healthy increases in its budget to expand existing programs to improve the quality of science teaching in the nation's schools. Long before *Sputnik* the NSF had been sponsoring summer workshops and intensive training programs for high school math and science teachers. Director Alan Waterman had been particularly interested in recruiting leading university scientists to help prepare new curricular materials for high school science and math courses. On November 20 Waterman sent the president copies of a new high school physics text designed by an NSF committee that included two Nobel Prize winners. Eight schools had begun teaching the new course in the fall of 1957; NSF hoped to train ten thousand teachers so that the innovative physics course could be used in schools across the country by 1960.

James Killian, as the new presidential science adviser, became the focus for efforts to have the NSF rather than HEW supervise and administer all new science education programs. John Stambaugh, a presidential consultant on education, pointed out that for seven years the NSF had proved itself by running summer institutes and working with colleges and universities on improving high school science teaching. Warning that HEW was likely to work through state education departments, Stambaugh argued that developing more scientists "is the job of scientists, working with the National Science Foundation," not of educational bureaucrats. Lee DuBridge, the president of Cal Tech, gave Killian similar advice, stressing that at all levels "the primary requirement is for more and better teachers." Sympathetic to these pleas from the scientific community, Killian urged Eisenhower to expand the NSF's role in science education as a way of meeting the *Sputnik* crisis.[32]

At the same time, the president was committed to supporting the broad program of federal aid to education that HEW had been preparing since November 1957. On December 30 Secretary Marion Folsom came to Eisenhower's farm in Gettysburg to present the revised HEW program. Scaled down to meet Eisenhower's budgetary ceiling of $1 billion over four years, the HEW plan called for college scholarships for talented high school graduates in all fields, with special emphasis on science and engineering, graduate fellowships to train future college teachers, and matching programs to help states improve the teaching of math, science, and foreign languages. With the president's approval, Folsom released details of the administration's educational program to the press later that day.[33]

Eisenhower was not very enthusiastic about the HEW program. While he told Folsom that he had "no quarrel" with the various provisions, he did not have any great sense of urgency, commenting, "I can't understand the United States being as panicky as they really are." He went on to express his belief that all high school students should concentrate on math, one foreign language, and English. The most important point to get across to the American people, he told Folsom, is "that a football player is no more important than a person who does well in mathematics or a good well-balanced student."[34]

Milton Eisenhower, president of Johns Hopkins University, reinforced his brother's doubts. He felt that the federal scholarships were probably "politically necessary" but that what colleges really needed were much larger federal subsidies to cover the costs of instruction. Milton criticized the HEW proposal to pay higher salaries to math and science teachers, warning that it would destroy the morale of all other teachers and "throw the entire school system into turmoil." He particularly opposed the effort to upgrade science teaching at the high school level; it would be far better, he argued, to concentrate on such fundamentals as math, English, and foreign language in the schools and save science courses for college instruction. The best way to reform the schools, Milton Eisenhower contended, was to have the nation's leading colleges announce that they would not admit students in the 1960s unless they had proper training in the fundamentals. "Then the secondary schools would have to come along," he concluded.[35]

Following Killian's advice, Eisenhower decided to back both approaches to the educational problem. In his budget presentation in mid-January and a special message on education on January 28, 1958, the president outlined a dual program. First, he was requesting $140 billion for the National Science Foundation for 1959, a threefold increase in its funding. Some of this new money was to raise the level of support for basic research, but the major share would be used to expand the NSF's promising efforts to improve the quality of science teaching with new textbooks, new course outlines, and summer institutes for high school teachers. At the same time, he asked for nearly $1 billion in increased funding for HEW to allow for forty thousand scholarships over the next four years to encourage high-aptitude high school graduates to attend college, for graduate fellowhips to increase the future supply of college teachers, for matching funds to improve teaching of science and math in the high schools as well as to provide laboratory equipment and supplies, and for special centers at selected universities to promote foreign language instruction.

In both messages Eisenhower showed his ambivalence toward federal aid to education. He stressed the "emergency" nature of his request in light of the need to meet the Soviet challenge by producing "a growing supply of highly trained manpower—scientists, engineers, teachers and technicians." Expressing his belief that "responsibility for education" should be "kept close to the people it serves" and be "sustained by a rich variety of public, private and individual resources," he saw the new federal role as purely temporary in nature. Once the crisis was over, the states and local agencies should once again assume full responsibility. In his memoirs he said he went along with the proposals of his advisers reluctantly, adding, "I disliked the use of federal funds to pay for the normal operation of schools."

The president was especially bothered by the apparent need to stress science and engineering over the humanities. Reflecting views expressed by both his brother Milton and James Killian, Eisenhower tried to caution against a purely technological response to the Soviet feat. "Specialized programs," he warned, "must not be allowed to upset the important balance needed in a well-rounded educational program which must insure progress in the teaching of all areas of learning." So even in justifying federal aid to education in terms of a crisis situation, he spoke of giving "special, but by no means exclusive, weight to science and engineering." In his memoirs Eisenhower once again revealed his true feelings by quoting a telegram he had received shortly after *Sputnik* from James Conant, the former president of Harvard University. What the nation needed, Conant told Eisenhower, was "not more engineers and scientists, but a people who will not panic and political leaders of wisdom, courage and devotion . . . not more Einsteins, but more Washingtons and Madisons."[36]

Critics quickly perceived the grudging nature of Eisenhower's federal aid to education program. Most commentators described the administration proposal as modest, stressing the annual limit of ten thousand college scholarships and the $1 billion budgetary ceiling over four years. Noting that there were over twenty thousand high schools in the nation, they called for a much larger number of federal grants. Educational organizations proposed raising the number of scholarships to at least twenty-five thousand a year, while the Democrats introduced legislation recommending forty thousand annually over a six-year period. *Time* and *Life* both chided the administration for its cautious approach, claiming that the *Sputnik* furor deserved a more ambitious response. The editors of the *New Republic* were more blunt, calling upon the Democrats in Congress to frame "a more realistic program for education." "It seems clear," they wrote, "that the preference for dollars-over-minds which dominated the nation's thinking for so long a time before Sputnik is still very much with us."[37]

Those who had been calling for educational reform before *Sputnik* greeted Eisenhower's program with guarded optimism. They especially applauded the idea of college scholarships and the call for greater stress on fundamentals in the schools. But some feared that a panicky nation would place too much stress on technology at the expense of the liberal arts. Thus Stringfellow Barr, president of St. John's College, spoke of the "horror" he felt over "the talk of crash programs in mathematics and science when there were so much more important reasons for teaching these subjects." Arthur Bestor, a University of Illinois historian in the forefront of the reform movement, warned that "the educationalists" would use the new federal funds to teach science and math at the expense of history and English. Yet he shared Barr's desire to "exploit the rise of the Red Moons to get our education house in order" and to "finance it seriously for the first time."

Max Ascoli, editor of the *Reporter,* singled out the most sensitive aspect of federal aid to education. While he welcomed the new funds that would permit long-overdue reforms, he warned against the danger of federal control supplanting local supervision of the nation's schools. Yet he also cited Admiral Hyman Rickover's complaint that it was precisely such local control that led to undue emphasis on life adjustment instead of the teaching of fundamentals in the country's schools. He joined Bestor in supporting Rickover's solution, a national board that would set forth curriculum standards for all forty-eight states. The real challenge, Ascoli argued, was to convince thousands of school boards that subjects like math and English were more important than "vocational training and service activities." "The future looks bleak," he wrote, "unless in some way Federal assistance can be made acceptable and some sort of national standard can be established to which diploma and degree-granting institutions must conform."[38]

A more serious criticism of the administration's education program was that it failed to meet the central issue highlighted by *Sputnik*. At the October 15, 1957, meeting between prominent scientists and the president, Edwin Land had told Eisenhower that the nation needed to change its priorities and give greater rewards and recognition to scientific and intellectual achievement. Milton Eisenhower made the same point in an interview with *U.S. News & World Report* in February 1958, pointing out that it was not considered "fashionable" for the schools to give the emphasis and recognition to scholarship that they gave to sports and extracurricular activities. The *New Republic* argued that the reason for the shortage of math and science teachers was the low pay and status of the teaching profession. *Time* concurred, citing statistics that showed that much higher salaries had led two thousand of the five thousand college science and engineering graduates in 1957 to go into industry instead of the classroom. Until teaching offered the same rewards as the private sector, there was no way to fill the shortage of eight thousand high school science teachers.[39]

Nor did the administration's modest program take account of the enrollment trends facing the nation's educational system. The number of college students had doubled by the late 1950s from the pre–World War II level; enrollment had increased by 40 percent in the 1950s alone. Despite the fact that nearly half of those in the top 30 percent of their high school classes did not go on to college, each year the number of students entering universities increased by more than the normal population growth. The baby boom generation, still in the elementary and high schools, would soon advance like a tidal wave into the colleges and universities. There was nothing in the administration's program to help higher education meet this coming challenge. Milton Eisenhower took solace in his perception that *Sputnik*, "more than any other circumstance in my lifetime, has caused the American people to look critically and—I hope—thoughtfully at our entire educational enterprise." Unfortunately, Dwight Eisenhower chose not to take full advantage of this rare opportunity but decided instead only to do what was politically necessary to quiet the clamor.[40]

V

The president's efforts to defuse the *Sputnik* crisis depended ultimately on the success of the nation's satellite program. Increases in military spending, reorganization of the defense department, and even federal aid to education would do little to reassure the American people until the United States finally joined the Soviet Union in space.

Throughout January Eisenhower waited, knowing that the single most important thing his administration could do to restore national confidence would be to announce the successful launch of an American earth satellite.

The president was aware that two test launches were scheduled for Cape Canaveral: one for Vanguard on January 18 and another for the army's Jupiter-C, with a satellite dubbed *Explorer,* on January 29. Technical problems delayed the Vanguard shot for several days. On January 22 an aide asked Ike if he wanted to issue a lengthy statement the next day if Vanguard went off as expected. Eisenhower replied that he would prefer a brief White House release stating simply that the first in a series of scientific experiments had been conducted successfully. Republican congressmen, however, were ready to take full political advantage of a successful launch; several had already taped speeches to be released when the Vanguard satellite went into orbit.[41]

Once again Vanguard proved to be disappointing. On January 28, after a ten-day delay, the test shot at Cape Canaveral had to be aborted when a fuel leak was found just fourteen seconds before ignition. The next day Wernher Von Braun's army team took over the launch site and began preparations to send *Explorer* into space. The Jupiter-C launch vehicle was actually a tried-and-true Redstone rocket to which Von Braun had added three clusters of solid-fuel rockets to provide the necessary propulsion for the thirty-pound *Explorer.* A shift of the jet stream southward forced a postponement, first to January 30 and then to January 31, the last day the army was scheduled to use the Cape Canaveral facility.[42]

The President had gone to Augusta, Georgia, to play golf and relax, but he stayed in close touch with developments in Florida. Press Secretary James Hagerty had a line kept open to the White House, where Andrew Goodpaster was in direct contact with Cape Canaveral. On January 30, fearing that the Soviets would launch a third satellite before the United States sent up its first, Eisenhower approved a press release prepared by Hagerty and Killian covering this contingency. As it turned out, there would be no further Soviet satellites for several more months. The original *Sputnik* had finally broken into eight pieces, all of which had dropped out of orbit by January 10, but the massive, 1,120-pound *Sputnik II* continued to revolve around the earth as a reminder that the Soviets were still alone in space.

The news Eisenhower received in Augusta on January 31 fluctuated throughout the day. At first it was feared that continued high winds would force the launch to be scrubbed, but by late afternoon the jet stream had moved northward, making an *Explorer* shot possible that evening. While Ike played bridge in his cottage next to the Augusta National Golf Course, Hagerty kept checking on the progress at Cape Canaveral. At 10:48 p.m. the Jupiter-C blasted off without incident. Aware that it would be another hour before an orbit could be achieved. Ike reacted cautiously, telling an aide, "Let's not make too great a hullabaloo on this." But shortly after midnight on February 1, Goodpaster confirmed that *Explorer* was in orbit. "That's wonderful," Eisenhower exclaimed. "I sure feel a lot better now." He then authorized Hagerty to release a brief statement to the waiting press corps.[43]

The American people hailed *Explorer* with joy but, even more, with a sense of profound relief. Beneath a headline reading "NEW MOON MADE IN U.S.," *Life* claimed that the American satellite made up, "to some extent, for the U.S. humiliation due to the Russian Sputniks." Noting that nearly four months had gone by since the Soviets began the space age, *Time* said that "the 119 days between Sputnik I and Explorer were as important to the U.S. as any similar span in its history." But the editors still rejoiced in what they described as a "Promethean gift." Most Americans responded with smiles on their faces and the unspoken thought, "It's about time." Even Wernher Von Braun was subdued, admitting that "we are competing only in spirit with Sputnik so far, not in hardware yet."[44]

The most enthusiastic response came from abroad. American allies rejoiced at the knowledge that the United States had now ended the Soviet monopoly in space. "U.S. honor had been saved, its dignity and prestige recovered," claimed a Tokyo newspaper. A Buenos Aires headline was more dramatic: "AT LAST, AN UNCLE SAMNIK." Only the Soviets were disdainful, stressing the size differential between *Explorer* and the two *Sputniks*.[45]

The long-awaited orbit of an American satellite finally ended the months of anxiety in the White House. "With the January 31 launching," Ike wrote in his memoirs, "a long and difficult period had ended." But at the same time the success of Jupiter-C strengthened the army's claim that it could have launched a satellite a year before *Sputnik*. Eisenhower's decision to keep the satellite project separate from the military missile program had proved profoundly mistaken. The Russians had used the fact that they were first in space to score a major political victory over the United States. By failing to recognize the importance of the prestige in being the first nation into outer space, the president had weakened America's international reputation and underminded national self-confidence.[46]

The problems with Vanguard continued to haunt the White House even after the successful launch of *Explorer*. On February 5 the Vanguard test postponed for January finally took place. The first stage had flown for only fifty-seven seconds when a malfunction in its guidance system forced officials to destroy the rocket before the satellite could be put into orbit. Once again Eisenhower had to explain that such "failures" were to be expected "as long as we pursue a vigorous search for more advanced vehicles." Wernher Von Braun agreed, admitting that the Vanguard was a much more sophisticated rocket than the army's Jupiter-C. "Ours is based on older and more proven components," he explained, then added wryly, "Ours is a little more obsolete."

However primitive the rocket that thrust *Explorer* into space may have been, the result was more significant than many realized. Although under seven feet long and just six inches wide, the cylindrical *Explorer* carried a much more important set of scientific instruments than either of the *Sputniks*. The "Van Allen package," named after its designer, physicist James Van Allen of the University of Iowa, had the capability of measuring cosmic rays in the area beyond the earth's atmosphere. Two tiny radio transmitters sent this cosmic ray data back to earth, eventually leading to the discovery of the Van Allen radiation belts. This knowledge was vital to the design of spacecraft, which would require shielding to guard against the cosmic rays discovered by *Explorer*'s instruments.[47]

Thus the *Explorer* flight not only ended the national agony resulting from *Sputnik* but marked the beginning of the American effort to conquer space. For the first time since the Soviet feat, Americans began looking forward to the exploration of space and the possibility of manned flight to the moon. The United States, claimed *U.S. News & World Report*, was in "a vital contest with the Sovet Union . . . to be the first to control space itself." It was time now to take up the challenge that Lyndon Johnson had laid down on in his January 7 speech—for the administration to design a space program that would enable the United States to reach for the stars.[48]

CHAPTER SIX

The successful launch of the first American satellite led to a spirited debate about the nation's role in space. Within a week after *Explorer I* went into orbit, the Eisenhower administration, Congress, and the general public began to discuss proposals for creating a new space agency and for an ambitious program of space exploration. The public discussion had been developing ever since *Sputnik,* but it took on a new sense of urgency with the long-awaited arrival of the United States as the second nation in space.

For several months space enthusiasts had been calling on the Eisenhower administration to develop a comprehensive and long-range program of space exploration. On November 6, 1957, Robert Truax, president of the American Rocket Society, had written to I. I. Rabi urging the creation of a new civilian space agency to direct a $50 million a year program. The American Rocket Society, he argued, opposed "stop-gap measures" or "stunts" designed to match the Soviet *Sputnik;* he called instead for a well-designed, long-term effort to probe the mysteries of the universe. He enclosed a report by the society's Space Flight Technical Committee, headed by Krafft Ehricke of Convair, which laid out a twenty-five-year program that included orbiting the earth, sending instrumented flights to the planets, and launching manned missions to the moon. Such activities, Ehricke asserted, would further American prestige by putting the United States "in the forefront of those who will explore the new environment about to be entered by man." "For the individual," he concluded, "the largest direct benefit will be a sense of participation in a great adventure . . . and a better understanding of the universe around him."[1]

Wernher Von Braun became the most eloquent advocate of an ambitious space program. In an interview with *Life* magazine and in testimony before LBJ's preparedness subcommittee, Von Braun spoke of man going to the moon as the natural result of a desire to satisfy human curiosity about the nature of the universe. Space travel, he claimed, would "free man from his remaining chains, the chains of gravity which still tie him to this planet," and "open to him the gates of heaven." Claiming that flights to the moon and back would be possible within twenty-five years, Von Braun saw in space flight a way to "raise the status of scientists in the public eye in this country."[2]

Other scientists had greater difficulty in justifying space exploration, but they were sure it would benefit society. "If the United States doesn't do it," explained Homer Stewart of the Jet Propulsion Laboratory, "why, someone else will, and if you don't stay up with the new things, why, you gradually fall behind." He then added that if we fell too far behind we would be like the Australian Bushmen—"they fell behind 40,000 years."[3]

Air force spokesmen were even more enthusiastic about the military possibilities in outer space. Lieutenant General Donald Putt, air force deputy chief of staff for development, startled a congressional committee when he advocated placing a military base on the moon and using it to rain missiles down on the earth. But he did not see even this bold move as the "ultimate means of ensuring peace." "It is only a first step toward stations on planets far more distant from which control over the moon might then be exercised." Putt's deputy, Brigadier General Homer A. Boushey, was even more outspoken in a speech to the Aero Club of Washington. Asked what he expected to find on the moon, he replied, "Russians." Portraying the moon as the ultimate "high ground," General Boushey said by controlling the lunar surface we could observe Soviet behavior on the earth and establish missile bases that would offer a secure second-strike force for American nuclear weapons in case of a Soviet attack. "Whoever gains the ultimate supremacy of space," Boushey concluded, "gains control—total control—over the earth for purposes of tyranny or for the service of freedom."[4]

Lee DuBridge, the president of Cal Tech, offered a sharp rebuttal to the talk of militarizing space. In a speech to the Western Space Age Conference in Los Angeles, DuBridge called the idea of launching missiles from the moon "utter nonsense." "Why transport a hydrogen warhead together with all men and equipment 240,000 miles to the moon, just to shoot it 240,000 miles back to earth, when the target is only 5,000 miles away in the first place?" The moon was simply too far away to have any influence on hostilities on the earth; it would take five days for a missile to arrive, and by then "the war might be over."

In additon to warning against "wild programs of Buck Rogers stunts and insane pseudomilitary expeditions," DuBridge doubted even the usefulness of manned space flight. "For most scientific explorations in space," he argued, "the presence of man involves quite unwarranted complications and expenditures." It would be far simpler and cheaper, he explained, to concentrate on unmanned flights that relied on instruments alone to probe the mysteries of space.[5]

Some scientists questioned whether there was any real value in entering into a space race with the Soviet Union. Paul Sears, chairman of the conservation program at Yale University, denounced the "present hysteria" over space in his presidential address to the American Association for the Advancement of Science in December 1957. "Outer space is one more item that diverts attention and energy from the prosaic business of setting our terrestial space in order." Citing problems of overpopulation, urban sprawl, and environmental pollution, Sears viewed the fascination with space as an "incredible type of escapism." "Our future security," he warned, "may depend less upon priority in exploring outer space than upon our wisdom in managing the space in which we live."[6]

Sears may have represented an extreme position, but other scientists felt it was imperative that the exploration of space be under civilian rather than military control. In early 1958 twelve scientists at the Los Alamos National Laboratory proposed the creation of a civilian agency dominated by scientists to oversee the nation's space efforts. The editors of the *New Republic* agreed on the need for civilian direction, claiming that nothing that "can be called 'control' of space is going to turn up for many, many years to come." More surprising, *Life* championed civilian control, asserting, "The conquest of space, however militarily important its co-products may prove, is first of all an adventure of the human will and brain, Promethean in spirit."[7]

This lively debate raised two key issues the Eisenhower administration could no longer avoid. The first was the issue of military versus civilian control. The early American satellite program, while divorced from the IRBM and ICBM efforts, had been conducted by the armed forces. Yet many scientists whose services would be indispensable to a successful space program were uneasy about working under military control. Equally important, the president and his advisers would need to decide on how extensive a probe of outer space they wished the nation to undertake. Would the orbiting of satellites and the sending of instruments in unmanned vehicles satisfy the public desire to know more about the universe, or would it be necessary to engage in manned flight in order to fulfill the American desire to recapture the lead in space from the Soviet Union? How well Eisenhower could resolve these issues might well determine his success in defusing the crisis in public confidence arising from *Sputnik*.

I

Growing pressure from Democrats in Congress forced the administration to begin active consideration of space policy during the first week in February. Senators Albert Gore of Tennessee and Clinton Anderson of New Mexico introduced bills to put all space programs under the Atomic Energy Commission. At the same time, Senators Hubert Humphrey and Estes Kefauver sponsored legislation to create a new Department of Science and Technology, which would take charge of all space efforts. And on February 6 the Senate passed a measure sponsored by Lyndon Johnson creating a new Senate Committee on Outer Space, which the majority leader would chair.

The administration replied by making public plans that Secretary of Defense Neil McElroy had been working on since December to put all military space programs under the control of the newly formed Advanced Research Projects Agency (ARPA). McElroy named industrialist Roy Johnson of General Electric to head the new Pentagon board and Herbert York, a member of the PSAC, to serve as its chief scientist. ARPA would supervise the development of rockets, satellites, and other space-related projects by the three services as well as plan and carry out all future American ventures into space. At the same time, however, the administration made it clear that it was still considering a separate civilian agency for the nonmilitary aspects of space exploration.[8]

White House Chief of Staff Sherman Adams presided over a key meeting on February 3 called to decide how the administration should respond to the spate of congressional proposals for space organization. Herbert York, representing PSAC in Killian's absence, played down the military significance of space, commenting that "missiles simply pass through outer space" and urging a separate civilian agency to conduct scientific experiments beyond the earth's atmosphere. A spokesman for the National Science Foundation urged creation of a "blue ribbon organization" to decide this question, pointing out that the scientific implications of space exploration were too important to give the Defense Department exclusive control.

Others stressed the urgency of the situation. Budget Director Maurice Stans spoke of the need to establish priorities and to expedite any project "if its psychological importance is great in relation to the Russians." Adams concurred, pointing to the "intense public interest" in space ventures and the need to make a "convincing response" to the pressure from Congress. Expressing his dislike for "blue ribbon" study groups after his experience with the Gaither committee, Adams finally asked York to have Killian prepare a presidential announcement that PSAC would conduct a study and make its recommendations on space-program organization as quickly as possible.[9]

While York and Killian prepared a public statement, the president expressed some surprising views in a meeting with the GOP congressional leaders on February 4. When the issue of where a space agency should be located arose, the president spoke out sharply for leaving it entirely within the Defense Department. "Our major interest in this for some years will be a defense one," he pointed out; when challenged, he argued that the only "practical" space venture for the foreseeable future would be a reconnaissance satellite. "That's military—that's the big thing," Ike added. Killian immediately objected, claiming that a "truly scientific space aspect does exist." Vice-President Nixon backed him strongly. It would be much better for world opinion, Nixon argued, "if non-military research in outer space were carried forward by an agency entirely separate from the military." The president finally agreed to let Killian and PSAC design a civilian agency to complement the military space effort under ARPA. But he continud to worry about the "tremendous big operational cost duplication" that would result from setting up a civilian space agency alongside ARPA. "Defense *has* to be involved," he exclaimed. "Why duplicate?"

Eisenhower was equally dubious about the benefits that would flow from space exploration. When Killian, in response to a senator's question, said a lunar probe might be possible by 1959 with a crash effort, the president said a "rule of reason" must apply to space ventures. He spoke out against pouring "unlimited funds into these costly ventures where there was nothing of value to the Nation's security." Senator William Knowland of California objected, pointing to the great "psychological" impact of *Sputnik* on world opinion to argue for an American lunar probe. Eisenhower replied, "I'd rather have a good Redstone than hit the moon. I don't think we have an enemy on the moon!"[10]

Later that day, the White House released a statement saying that the president had asked Killian's PSAC to conduct a study and report back with a recommendation for the organization of the American space program. At his press conference on February 5, Eisenhower confirmed the decision to proceed with a dual space effort, with ARPA to be in charge of military applications and Killian's scientists to design a complementary civilian agency. Although he did not make public his own reservations about the value of space exploration, it was clear that he would insist on holding down expenditures in space, just as he had with defense spending after *Sputnik*.[11]

Killian certainly was aware of Eisenhower's determination, as the president had expressed it to the Republican leaders, not to "rush into an all-out effort on each one of these possible glamor performances without a full appreciation of their great cost." In a meeting on February 4 with Killian, York, and George Kistiakowsky, a Harvard chemist and member of PSAC, Eisenhower restated his conviction that military space objectives had to have the highest priority "because they bear on our immediate safety." He appreciated that the "psychological factor" also was important, especially in regard to our allies abroad, but above all he wanted to avoid unnecessary duplication between military and scientific space programs. Ike emphasized that he wanted "to get the broad principles of organization right, not bowing to pressures."

Three days later, in another small meeting, Eisenhower told Killian that he wanted the space program focused on general capabilities rather than specific goals. "His thought," an aide summarized, "seemed to be that we should aim at having the capability of doing certain types of things at certain times, rather than committing ourselves to specific actions." Above all, the president wanted to avoid getting involved in a space race with the Russians—an expensive contest to see who could perform the most spectacular feat to impress world opinion.[12]

II

The future of American space policy was now in the hands of James Killian and the President's Science Advisory Committee. Killian quickly appointed a PSAC panel headed by Nobel laureate Edward Purcell, which included Herbert York, James Doolittle, and Edwin Land as members. Their task was twofold: to decide how the space program was to be organized and then to set up the broad policy objectives, which the president asked be presented to the National Security Council in early March. Pushing this panel hard, Killian gave Purcell just two weeks in which to write its report.

The first task was to reach agreement on who would administer the nation's space effort. Members of PSAC had been wrestling with this problem for several months and had already arrived at tentative conclusions. In a meeting on December 10, 1957, PSAC reached agreement on the need for "a separate agency largely centered about non-military activity." Several members spoke out vigorously against letting the military dominate space. While admitting that the services would provide the rockets, I. I. Rabi felt that space exploration "would thrive best under civilian organization." Detlev Bronk agreed, stressing the need for "separating space technology from [the] means of getting there."[13]

In a memorandum written on December 30, Killian set forth what he felt was the consensus emerging within PSAC. While he realized it would be necessary for military space programs to continue within the Defense Department, he warned against limiting American space efforts "to narrowly concerned military objectives." Such an approach would discourage civilian scientists and would "place the U.S. in the unfortunate position before the world of apparently tailoring all space research to military ends." Instead he argued for a separate civilian agency in addition to the military program. "We must have far more than a program which appeals to 'space cadets,'" he argued. "It must invoke, in the deepest sense, the attention of our best scientific minds if we as a nation are to become a leader in this field."[14]

The organization that Killian and the other PSAC members thought would be best suited to direct the civilian space program was the National Advisory Committee for Aeronautics (NACA). Founded in 1915, this body oversaw three major aeronautical laboratories and worked closely with both the armed services and private industry in seeking to improve America's traditional position as the world's leader in aviation. The director, Hugh Dryden, reported to an independent board made up of both military representatives and distinguished scientists. Although NACA had taken little interest in space flight after World War II, its new chairman, James Doolittle, had begun to direct its activities into this new arena in the mid-fifties.[15]

The scientists, who had always appreciated the role they had played on NACA's board and the independent status of the agency, saw it as the logical choice for overseeing a civilian space program. Killian had noted the "enthusiasm" that PSAC members had shown for NACA when they first discussed the space program in December. He especially liked the good record of NACA in working closely with the military and thought it would lend itself to "a cooperative arrangement" with the Department of Defense in managing the nation's space efforts. NACA would provide, he believed, "the means and incentives for pure scientists to move effectively into space research without regard to practical applications."[16]

PSAC diligently explored other alternatives but found problems with all except NACA. The armed services made strong claims. The army boasted of the achievements of Wernher Von Braun's Army Ballistic Missile Agency, which had sent *Explorer I* into orbit, and the work of the Jet Propulsion Laboratory at Cal Tech. The air force countered by pointing to its experience with the Bell X-15 experimental flights at the very limit of the earth's atmosphere and by citing its role in developing the Atlas and Titan boosters, which would provide the rocket thrust for any serious space exploration in the near future. Even the navy had claims, given its interest in satellites for navigation and its oversight of the Vanguard program. Herbert York made the case for relying primarily on ARPA, but the other members of PSAC strongly opposed an exclusively military space program. They wanted an agency "devoted to scientific advance in general," one that could be presented to the world "on a peaceful and international basis for the benefit of all mankind."

In a sense, NACA won out through a process of elimination. The members of PSAC felt that space was too far removed from the main concerns of the Atomic Energy Commission and too large an undertaking for the National Science Foundation. There was little enthusiasm for the idea of creating a new Department of Science and Technology. Indeed, one of the most attractive features of NACA was that it was already in existence and could simply be expanded to include space within its purview. James Doolittle stressed the strength of

NACA in organizing and coordinating the efforts of many different groups toward a common end. Serving both as chairman of NACA and a member of the Purcell space panel, he played a key role in gaining approval for making NACA the vehicle for the new civilian space agency.[17]

James Killian presented the recommendation to the president on March 5. Joining with Budget Director Percival Brundage and Nelson Rockefeller, chairman of the committee on government reorganization, he submitted a memorandum for putting all civilian space activities under NACA, provided that it was "substantially reconstituted and made responsive to Presidential direction." In making the case for the new National Aeronautics and Space Administration (NASA), as NACA would now be known, Killian contended that "an aggressive space program will produce important civilian gains in the form of advances in general scientific knowledge and protection of the international prestige of the United States." He stressed NACA's long history of "close and cordial cooperation with the military departments," claiming that it would be "a great asset in minimizing friction between the civilian space agency and the Department of Defense." To ensure executive control of space policy, the memorandum recommended making the director of NASA a presidential appointee who would report directly to the White House and not to the agency's board, which would be purely advisory in nature. Finally, Killian and his cosigners urged an "all-out attempt" to draft legislation in the next few weeks so that "the full civil space program . . . can be launched this year."

Eisenhower, who had apparently had second thoughts about an exclusively military space program, responded enthusiastically. He expressed his belief that "discovery and research should be scientific, rather than military," and added that he felt that there was "no problem of space activity (except ballistic weapons) that is not basically civilian." He still worried, however, about the problem of duplication and the ability of NASA to coordinate its efforts with the Pentagon. Killian replied that both ARPA and NASA would have to bring all proposals to the president for final approval, thus giving him the decisive vote. Moreover, Killian explained, "NASA will be in the dominating position with respect to space activities."

Eisenhower closed the meeting by seconding the call for prompt action in creating the new space agency. He asked Killian to work with the Bureau of the Budget in preparing the legislation, which he wanted presented to Congress before the Easter recess in April. Now that he had a strong proposal to put forward as the administration's program, he wished to act quickly to forestall any attempt by Congress to impose its own solution. And whatever early attraction he had had to a purely military agency now had given way to strong support for

NASA as a body that would appeal not only to American scientists but to world opinion in general.[18]

III

Eisenhower's second charge to Killian, the design of an overall space policy, led to long discussions in the President's Science Advisory Committee. At the outset the scientists stressed the need to avoid "space cadet stuff" and setting objectives in terms of "stunts." PSAC should give the president "bona fide scientific objectives," argued Edwin Land, and not turn space into an "athletic contest." Killian felt it would be wise to play down the military aspects and instead emphasize the romance of space flight in order to capitalize on the strong public interest. Members of Congress wanted to see a space program based on "vision" and "bold thinking," one that strove to enhance national prestige, Killian asserted.

There was some dissent within PSAC. Herbert York continued to argue the case for military projects in space, pointing out that there were still "some important future military applications." George Kistiakowsky had a different objection to giving in to the public's craving for space exploration. Saying that we "are in the middle of a great tragedy," he bemoaned the willingness to spend huge sums on space voyages at the expense of a whole range of more serious and more deserving scientific endeavors. I. I. Rabi agreed, talking about "shoestring" support for many scientific projects and the "distortion of moral values" involved in spending more to beat the Russians to the moon than in trying to cure cancer. But Killian countered that the new public interest in space would "work to benefit the rest of science." Hans Bethe thought it would be "a real mistake" to resist popular enthusiasm, even if it was "misguided," while Land urged joining in what he termed "one of [the] best human crusades."[19]

The PSAC panel completed its work in less than a month. On March 6, with Eisenhower vigorously nodding his approval, Edward Purcell and Herbert York outlined to the National Security Council a space program that stressed scientific values and goals. They played down the military significance of space, debunking the notion of seizing the "high ground" by arguing that space was not "up" but "out" and then contending that it made far better sense to put nuclear warheads aboard ICBMs than to launch them from satellites. The main purpose of space exploration, they argued, would be to find out more about the universe and the origins of the solar system. They spoke of using telescopes in space and sending instruments to distant planets as the prime scientific experiments, but they also said it would be feasible to launch a lunar probe within eighteen months and even send a manned flight to the moon before the end of the next decade.[20]

Eisenhower was so pleased with this report that he asked Purcell and York to give the same briefing to other groups within the administration. In a presentation to the cabinet on March 14, they again stressed the scientific value of space travel and played down its military benefit, calling notions of space warfare "clumsy and ineffective." Purcell spoke of sending instruments near the moon in the next year or so, placing a man in orbit within five years, and conducting a manned flight to the moon by the late 1960s. York was more specific, pointing out the need to develop rockets with over a million pounds of thrust—compared to the 250,000 pounds of the current Atlas and Titan boosters—to take men to the moon and back. To achieve such ambitious objectives, he forecast an annual space budget that would rise from $300 million to a peak of $600 million a year, estimating that the total cost of landing a man on the moon would be $3 billion.[21]

In their final briefing, given to the Republican congressional leaders on April 1, the PSAC members were more cautious. Killian stressed the importance of not letting fascination with space blind them to the "great importance of scientific inquiry on earth." Purcell played down the idea of manned flight, pointing to the value of relying on instrumented satellites to assist in communications, observe the earth's weather, and obtain critical measurements and observations of the solar system. "All a man can do is read a meter and turn a dial—and an instrument can do that much better," he claimed. When York explained the timetable for various space projects, the Republican leaders expressed a strong preference for a lunar shot within the next year. The ARPA scientist quickly cautioned that the agency did not plan to hit the moon, but rather simply send a package of instruments close to the lunar surface. Even so, he gave the chances of a successful mission as only one in four.[22]

The great interest shown in these briefings finally led the president to ask PSAC to prepare a public version of its report. On March 25 Eisenhower announced the release of a brochure written largely by Purcell and York entitled "Introduction to Outer Space," which the president called "the most interesting and fascinating thing in this field that I have seen." This document reflected PSAC's decision to deemphasize the military aspect of space and stress instead the scientific benefits. As Killian pointed out, the brochure "took a dim view of space as a theater of war." Instead the author spoke of the "compelling urge of man to explore and to discover" as they argued that "space technology affords new opportunities for scientific observation and experiment which will add to our knowledge and understanding of the earth, the solar system, and the universe."

Purcell and York presented an agenda of space flight in very general terms, dividing the projects into categories of "early," "later," and "still later," without setting any goals in terms of years. The early phase included satellites to help forecast the earth's weather and speed communications, as well as "minimal moon contact." Instrumented flights to Venus and Mars and manned orbit of the earth would come later, while the brochure postponed possible manned flight to the moon to the "still later" period. The main stress was on instrumented probes to the moon and nearby planets, activities that "could absorb the energies of scientists for many decades." Citing the high cost of manned flights, the brochure pointed out that "the cost and difficulty of sending *information* through space will be comparatively low."

The document ended with two cautions. First, the public would have to expect "failure of equipment and uncertainties of schedule" as the nation embarked on this ambitious program. And equally important, the members of PSAC called for a "balanced national effort" that would not harm other important but less glamorous undertakings. "It would not be in the national interest," the authors asserted, "to exploit space science at the cost of weakening our efforts in other scientific endeavours."[23]

This four-thousand-word document summed up the cautious and moderate approach to the space age that Eisenhower had hoped that his scientists would formulate. The president's reluctance to engage in a race with the Russians to see who could achieve the greater space spectaculars and his insistence on fiscal restraint were embodied in this carefully phrased brochure. The stress on instrumented rather than manned space flights and the refusal to set any early goals for either a lunar probe or a manned expedition to the moon indicated that the scientists shared Eisenhower's belief in the need to curb the public's enthusiasm. By setting forth a sober and realistic agenda, the members of PSAC enabled the Eisenhower administration to assert control over the space issue without giving in to the post-*Sputnik* hysteria.

IV

The growing success of the American space program strengthened the president's position. After a fourth-stage failure sent a second *Explorer* satellite tumbling out of control on March 5, Wernher Von Braun's team succeeded in placing *Explorer III* into orbit on March 26. This satellite weighed thirty-one pounds and carried a package of instruments designed to measure cosmic rays.[24]

The most heralded American feat, however, came a week earlier with the first successful Vanguard launch. Just after 7:30 on the morning of March 17, Alan Waterman, the director of the National Science Foundation, informed Ike that the navy had sent the long-awaited *Vanguard* into the highest orbit of any satellite yet, reaching nearly twenty-five-hundred miles out into space at its furthest point. Although the *Vanguard* was tiny, just six inches in diameter and weighing three and a half pounds, it contained sensitive scientific instruments powered by solar batteries that could measure temperature and cosmic radiation in the areas beyond the earth's atmosphere. Scientists expected the sophisticated *Vanguard* to stay in orbit for as long as two hundred years, with its radio transmitters sending back vital data throughout its long life. In contrast, the first *Sputnik*, which lacked serious instrumentation, had burned up while descending into the atmosphere in January, and *Explorer I* was not expected to stay in orbit for more than a few months.[25]

Eisenhower's attempt to play down the significance of the *Vanguard* launch backfired. Despite a brief White House statement stating simply that "a small test vehicle" had been placed in orbit as part of the American participation in the International Geophysical Year, the press greeted the news with unrestrained enthusiasm. *Life* hailed the launch as the beginning of an ambitious American space program. A feature story suggested that this small satellite would soon be joined by a stream of American space vehicles, ranging from lunar probes to manned satellites, and that eventually the United States would send men to the moon and instrumented space ships to Mars, Jupiter, and beyond. *U.S. News & World Report* predicted a new race with the Russians to be the first to hit the moon. Claiming that the Soviets were hard at work on their own lunar probe, the editors asserted that "the U.S. armed services are vying to launch rockets to, near or around the moon—to send up moon markers, cameras, instruments, flags, animals, even human beings."

Government officials appeared to confirm the sense of urgency. General Thomas D. White, the air force chief of staff, told a congressional committee, "We ought to hit the moon as fast as we can. . . . I think we could do it in a year." The army was equally optimistic. Secretary Wilber M. Brucker said his service planned to fire a moon rocket in "not too many months," and the Russians would now "have to hustle" to beat the United States to the moon. An army scientist, while admitting the race would be close, predicted that the United States would fire a rocket to the moon within months, put a man on the moon by the early 1960s, and establish a permanent lunar base by 1975. Dr. John Hagan, the director of Project Vanguard, gave the most authoritative comment. It would be possible, he claimed, to fly a camera past the moon within the next year or two and return with pictures of the mysterious far side of the lunar surface.[26]

The president was furious at what he considered irresponsible statements. He told Republican congressional leaders on March 18 that none of his scientific advisers believed that we could reach the moon so quickly. He was particularly upset at Hagan's remarks, pointing out that Project Vanguard had experienced repeated failures and had yet to put up "a full-sized satellite." "I keep sending down word—will you please keep your mouths shut," Ike told the GOP leaders. But he explained, "Some scientists get a little too enthusiastic when suddenly in the limelight." The president went on to argue against getting involved in a race to the moon with the Soviets, citing the huge expenditures entailed and the cost to other worthwhile scientific programs. When Senator Knowland of California still wanted to know if we could get to the moon first, Ike carefully explained that a lunar probe could come only after "a long series of painstaking steps."[27]

The pressure for a moon shot, however, was too great for the president to resist. The next day, March 19, Secretary of Defense McElroy sent him a recommendation from ARPA Director Roy Johnson asking for approval for three new space projects costing nearly $8 million. The first was for $5 million for the army to launch four more *Explorer* satellites between August 1958 and January 1959, with the last two to be in the hundred-pound range. The air force wanted more than $2 million for three lunar probes to be conducted as soon as possible, "consistent with the requirement that a minimal amount of useful data about the moon be obtained." Finally, the navy made a modest request for $200,000 to set up a ground tracking station in California to follow the lunar probes.

These proposals grew out of discussions between the PSAC space panel and ARPA. In reporting to Killian, Herbert York placed the highest priority on the need to reach the moon ahead of the Soviets. He argued that "the USSR can make a lunar shot at any time now, and will probably do so before the US can, and that the US must do all it can to mitigate the Sputnik-like reaction which would follow the USSR announcement." When the president referred the ARPA proposals to Killian, he quickly approved, pointing out that they all fell within what PSAC had discussed as "a minimum program" of space exploration. The science adviser suggested, however, that the president reserve the right to transfer these projects from the armed services to the new civilian space agency when it came into existence.[28]

Eisenhower gave his reluctant approval to the ARPA space proposals on March 24. As Killian had requested, the president said that they were subject to review and possible transfer to the future civilian space agency. In addition, he insisted on using funds already in the Pentagon budget and on making it clear that these projects were under the control of ARPA rather than the individual services.

A March 26 Pentagon statement on the ARPA space program was deliberately low-key. It said that the president had approved of "several projects . . . for launching a number of small unmanned space vehicles," without giving any details or timetable. The statement avoided any hint of a race with the Russians to hit the moon, referring instead to "efforts to determine our capability of exploring space in the vicinity of the moon." It concluded by calling this effort part of "an orderly program for space exploration."[29]

Despite this cautious wording, Eisenhower had in effect given in to the public's demand to try to beat the Soviets to the moon. Fearful of another blow to national prestige, the president had agreed to try to launch a lunar probe that had little scientific justification. Neither the elegant references to man's need to explore the unknown in the PSAC space brochure nor the specific proposals of research scientists had led to the hasty decision to try to reach the moon before the United States had perfected its satellite program. Instead, political realism had dictated an effort to satisfy the public's desire to capture the lead in space exploration now that America had finally closed the *Sputnik* gap.

The race for the moon also served to hide a far more realistic objective of Eisenhower's space program. Ever since the first satellite went into orbit, the president's primary concern had been to achieve a reconnaissance satellite that would replace the vulnerable U-2. Although the American people were unaware of this spy plane, Eisenhower knew that the Russians bitterly resented the overflights and were searching for a way to bring them to an end. The fact that no nation had objected to *Sputnik* passing high over its territory had encouraged Ike to redouble American efforts to develop a satellite equipped with high-resolution cameras that would enable the United States to continue monitoring Soviet military progress without risking an international incident.

The WS-117L reconnaissance satellite was the single most important project that ARPA supervised. Authorized in 1955 and administered by the air force under contract to Lockheed, the military satellite program involved three components: SAMOS, the camera in the sky, MIDAS, an infrared sensor to detect missile launches, and Discoverer, an experimental system to recover satellite data and film high in the atmosphere. By 1958 these programs cost $152 million, nearly one-third of ARPA's total budget and far more than the $8 million authorized for scientific satellites and the highly publicized moon shot.[30]

For Eisenhower and the PSAC scientists, the military reconnaissance program had top priority. Edwin Land, who had helped develop the U-2's cameras, called WS-117L "fantastic," pointing out how vital it was to cover all parts of the world and detect any missile launch instantaneously. For the president, whose knowledge of outer space continued to amaze aide Andrew Goodpaster, there was no doubt about the importance of a reconnaissance satellite. When Alan Waterman informed him that *Vanguard* had gone into orbit on March 17, his first question was whether or not the satellite faced the earth most of the time so that it could be used for reconnaissance. The president was pleased when Waterman replied that "it would look steadily at the earth." A successful lunar probe would satisfy Congress and the American public, but Eisenhower knew that, in regard to national security, the real payoff in space still lay in another ARPA project that remained totally hidden from view.[31]

V

Throughout March 1958 James Killian worked hard to meet Eisenhower's April 1 deadline for framing legislation setting up the new civilian space agency. Working with representatives of the Bureau of the Budget, he and his aides spent several weeks drafting a satisfactory measure. The main difficulty came over the board for NASA. The NACA governing board had broad authority; the director reported to this body and it made the basic policy decisions. The Bureau of the Budget insisted that the NASA director report directly to the president and that the board serve purely in an advisory capacity. Killian feared that prominent scientists would not serve on a weak board, but he finally gave way, realizing that space policy, unlike the more technical issues of aviation research that NACA had supervised, involved vital national interests that demanded presidential approval. On March 27, with just a few days to spare, Killian circulated a final draft to other government agencies, giving them virtually no time to make significant additions. As Lyndon Johnson later noted, the legislation had "whizzed through the Pentagon on a motorcycle."[32]

On April 2 President Eisenhower sent Congress the legislative proposal to transform "the tried and tested" NACA into the new National Aeronautics and Space Administration. The message called for a director appointed by the president and confirmed by the Senate, with an advisory board to consist of government scientists, academic and industrial experts, and at least one military representative. The president stressed his commitment to a civilian space program focused on exploration of outer space and "devoted to peaceful and scientific purposes." ARPA would contine to supervise space activities until NASA came into existence, but then all except strictly military projects would be shifted to the civilian agency.[33]

At the same time, the president sent a memorandum to both the secretary of defense and the chairman of NACA making clear his determination to move all space programs "except those peculiar to or primarily associated with military weapons systems or military operations" to NASA. He asked the two agencies to conduct a joint review of all programs. ARPA would continue to supervise the military efforts in space, while NASA would consult with the National Science Foundation in an effort to enlist the services of the nation's entire scientific community.

It soon became apparent that the president's decision to divide space projects between the Pentagon and NASA would be the source of controversy. In responding to the president's memo, the Defense Department proposed retaining most of the $520 million assigned to ARPA for space projects in the 1959 budget. In addition to clearly military programs such as the WS-117L reconnaissance project, the Pentagon planned to retain the lunar probe and share in any future man-in-space effort. As a result NASA would receive less than $100 million of ARPA's budget, thus requiring an additional appropriation of nearly $200 million for the new agency. Killian soon realized that, instead of resolving the space issues, the creation of NASA would mark only the beginning of the fight to ensure full civilian control over the nation's space program.[34]

The press, unaware of the looming bureaucratic struggle, hailed the NASA proposal as a statesmanlike step by the Eisenhower administration. Some editors were concerned about a continued military role in space but admitted that it was difficult to draw a precise line between civilian and military activities. "The difference," commented the *Nation*, "would seem to lie at the business end of the missile: is it a dog and a beep-beep, or is it a nuclear warhead?" *Time* called the plan for a new space agency "bold but durable." The editors of the *New Republic* were more enthusiastic. "President Eisenhower has overtaken Lyndon Johnson in the race to outer space," they proclaimed, arguing that Ike had regained the initiative from LBJ with a "well thought-out program."

By early April the national mood on space had changed radically. The gloom brought on by *Sputnik* and the early Vanguard failures had disappeared overnight with the successful satellite launches in March. "For the first time, three instrument-laden American satellites were in the sky," boasted *Life*, "while only one of Russia's two Sputniks was still aloft." The release of PSAC's persuasive brochure on the future of space exploration and Eisenhower's prompt action in proposing a civilian space agency had relieved the sense of national anxiety and had enabled the president to assert control over space policy.[35]

Yet despite his efforts to play down space spectaculars and the sense of competition with the Soviets, Eisenhower had been forced to make crucial concessions. The quick approval of the lunar probe and the vague promises of eventual manned space flight to the moon went far beyond what the president felt was prudent. In committing the nation to long-term exploration of space by men as well as instruments, Eisenhower gained valuable breathing space in the wake of *Sputnik* at the cost of championing goals that would prove both expensive to achieve and difficult to change. And he continued to keep from the American people the one space program he considered most vital to national security—WS-117L, the quest for a satellite that could spy on the Soviet Union.

CHAPTER SEVEN

Of all the issues raised by *Sputnik,* missiles remained the most criti-cal. On February 4, 1958, James Killian and George Kistiakowsky, who was heading up a PSAC panel on the missile program, gave the president an interim report. In their view the United States was mak-ing "real progress" in developing both a first generation of liquid-fuel missiles and a second generation relying on solid propellants. Kis-tiakowsky believed that there were no further scientific challenges in regard to the first generation; it was now simply a matter of overcom-ing engineering problems.

The scientists felt it was time to begin making decisions designed to narrow down the American missile arsenal. Kistiakowsky pointed out that the Jupiter and Thor IRBMs were "almost identical" and favored concentrating on the air force Thor because it was closer to produc-tion. He also claimed that the Titan ICBM was superior to the Atlas, even though it would not be ready for deployment as soon. Accord-ingly, he favored terminating Atlas after eighty missiles and replacing it with Titan ICBMs in the early 1960s.

The future of missiles, both men made clear, lay with the second generation of solid-fuel weapons that could be placed in hardened silos or on board submarines and fired almost immediaely, in contrast to the liquid-fuel rockets that required hours to be loaded with highly explosive fuel and oxygen before they could be launched. The diffi-culty, however, lay in timing. The navy's Polaris was not scheduled for deployment before 1963, while the earliest date for a solid-fuel ICBM was 1965, leaving a gap of five years between the two generations of long-range missiles.[1]

Eisenhower grasped the essence of the dilemma he faced in regard to missiles. Fearful that the Soviets would open up a substantial lead, he had authorized a wide range of first-generation missiles in all three services. Now he had to decide whether to continue this expensive effort on weapons that would soon be obsolete or to concentrate American efforts on the second generation of solid-fuel missiles. And if he chose the second alternative, he still faced the further question of whether to make a crash effort to close the five-year gap between generations, with the attendant duplication and heavy expenditures, or instead to insist on a slower, more careful approach, limiting the number of solid-fuel missiles and insisting on thorough research and development before going into production.

As he began to confront these decisions, Eisenhower made it clear to his scientific advisers that he favored a cautious and prudent response. Kistiakowsky estimated that the Soviets were about a year ahead of the United States on rocket propulsion for an ICBM, a year behind on warhead design, and just a little behind on guidance. Given the thrust of the rockets they had used to launch the two *Sputniks,* he felt they could speed up their ICBM by relying on a relatively simple warhead. The president was aware that American intelligence had estimated in January that the Soviets might be able to deploy their first ICBM as early as mid-1958 and could have as many as one hundred by mid-1959. Eisenhower, however, discounted the Russian ICBM threat. He told Killian and Kistiakowsky that it was vital to consider "relative probabilities." Ike thought it unlikely that the enemy would develop enough missiles "to destroy all our bases simultaneously and thus prevent retaliation by us." "Our deterrent remains effective," he concluded, despite the Soviet lead in the ICBM race. "We would make a mistake to credit [the USSR] with total capabilities."[2]

On another occasion Eisenhower telephoned Killian to challenge the prevailing view that we were falling dangerously behind the Russians in missiles. The president explained that he believed we would not be in hostilities with the Russians in the next five years. He admitted this estimate was based on an "intuitive feeling," but he felt confident that the Pentagon and Congress were exaggerating the Soviet strategic threat.[3]

Killian informed Secretary of Defense McElroy of Eisenhower's preferences. The president wanted to limit the deployment of first-generation missiles, especially the Atlas and Thor, rely on an improved Titan as an interim ICBM, and postpone any production of solid-fuel missiles while the Defense Department supervised a centralized effort to perfect a more advanced solid propellant for all second-generation missiles. Finally, the president wanted the Pentagon to prepare a comprehensive study of all future missile programs, which would include cost estimates as well as show the relationship of missiles to other deterrent forces.[4]

It is thus clear that Eisenhower had decided by early February not to engage in a crash program for second-generation missiles, such as the navy Polaris and the air force Minuteman. Disturbed by the waste and duplication that had characterized the development of the first generation of missiles, the president was intent on moving more deliberately on the next stage. He would do all he could to curb interservice rivalry and the inevitable proliferation of weapons system it entailed. Convinced in his own mind that the national security was not in peril, he still faced the task of persuading Congress and the American people of the wisdom of proceeding slowly and prudently in face of the Soviet threat.

I

American missile policy became a subject of intense public scrutiny in February 1958. The administration, in an effort to reassure the nation, announced that agreement had been reached with Great Britain to station sixty Thor IRBMs at bases in England, with the first units due to arrive before the end of 1958. General Lauris Norstad, the Allied Supreme Commander in Europe, felt this was not enough. He requested that an additional ten IRBM squadrons, 150 more missiles, be assigned to defend the NATO countries. The air force also pressed for an increase in the planned total of IRBMs from the original 120 (60 Thor and 60 Jupiter) to 180 (135 Thor and 45 Jupiter).[5]

Critics were quick to point out that the IRBMs were at best stopgap weapons that had grave weaknesses. The *New Republic* described the Thor as "a typically unstable, liquid-fueled rocket of low reliability, unknown accuracy and high launching time." Robert Albrook, writing in the *Reporter,* warned that the IRBMs in Europe were vulnerable to a Soviet first strike. "Like the American fleet tied up at Pearl Harbor," he claimed, "these 'ultimate weapons' could well be knocked out in a massive surprise attack." Instead of relying on the vulnerable and very expensive Thors, he argued, it would be better to "skip the liquid-fuel missile era altogether" and concentrate instead on developing the Polaris and other solid-fuel weapons.[6]

The Polaris soon became the most popular of all the proposed American missiles. *Time* ran a story in early March congratulating Rear Admiral William Raborn for taking the initiative in developing this remarkable weapon. Praising Raborn and the scientists for devising more reliable solid-fuel propellants and an underwater navigational system, the editors claimed that ten such subs on patrol could fire missiles that would reach 95 percent of the Soviet population. While admitting that the Polaris would not be tested until later in 1958, *Time* claimed it was far ahead of schedule, with three submarines likely to be operational by 1960. Admiral Hyman Rickover was equally enthusiastic, telling the American people how Polaris submarines could hide beneath the polar ice cap and thus deter a Soviet first strike.[7]

The navy pushed very hard for its sole strategic weapon. Admiral Raborn found a shortcut by taking a nuclear sub under construction in New London, cutting it in two, and inserting a new midsection with Polaris missile launchers. The Eisenhower administration included a request for $350 million for this and two other Polaris submarines in the supplement to the 1958 defense budget sent to Congress in January. By reducing the range of the Polaris missile from fifteen hundred to twelve hundred miles, the navy was able to move up the operational date for these three vessels, each carrying sixteen missiles, from 1962 to 1960.

Pressure quickly built up for a major expansion of the Polaris program. In hearings before a House appropriations subcommittee, Secretary of the Navy Thomas Gates revealed that the navy would prefer to have nine Polaris submarines, six more than authorized. Admiral Arleigh Burke, the chief of naval operations, estimated that such an expansion would cost an additional $1 billion. When Secretary of Defense McElroy testified before Lyndon Johnson's Defense Preparedness Subcommittee in late February, he was asked why the administration planned only three Polaris submarines, instead of the nine the navy wanted. McElroy explained that the Polaris was still untested but added that the Pentagon was planning to ask Congress for additions to the 1959 budget to build two more. This answer did not satisfy Senator Henry Jackson of Washington. Going the navy one better, he asked for a greatly stepped-up Polaris program, telling McElroy, "I hope that you will give consideration to laying down a minimum of 15 keels of Polaris submarines this year."[8]

The popularity of the Polaris led the air force to move more quickly with its own solid-fuel missile, the Minuteman. An outgrowth of a project known as Weapon System Q, the Minuteman had evolved into a three-stage solid-fuel rocket with a range of fifty-five hundred miles. Despite the fact that this missile was still in the early research and development phase, the air force incorporated the Minuteman into its missile program in February 1958. The plans called for a hundred Minutemen to be deployed in hardened silos by 1964, with four hundred more in 1965.

The air force fought hard to convince the American people that the Minuteman was a better investment than the Polaris. Unofficial spokesmen told *Time* that the air force could have sixty Minutemen operational by 1962 and that eventually they planned on as many as four thousand at a cost of $3.5 billion. Noting the high cost of the Polaris, which required three submarines be built for every one on patrol, the air force pointed out that the $350 million budgeted in 1958 for the Polaris paid for only forty-eight missiles; for the same sum, the nation could have sixteen hundred Minutemen. When McElroy asked the Joint Chiefs which weapon to favor, a deadlock ensued, with Admiral Burke making the case for Polaris, General

Thomas White, the air force chief of staff, championing the Minuteman, and the army chief, General Maxwell Taylor, contending that the United States already had an "overkill" capability and needed more ground troops rather than more missiles.[9]

When Secretary of Defense McElroy testified before Johnson's subcommittee in late February on missile progress, he tried to cool some of the popular enthusiasm for second-generation missiles. He claimed that since *Sputnik* the Eisenhower administration had speeded up the Atlas ICBM by a year and IRBM deployment by two years. This achievement, he asserted, gave the United States the time it needed to proceed more deliberately with the second generation of solid-fuel missiles. While claiming "great progress" in this area, he repeated Eisenhower's concern that we avoid the duplication and wasteful overlap that had marked the crash programs for the first generation of missiles. It would be much better, he asserted, to engage in extensive research and testing of solid-fuel missiles before deciding on which ones to put into production.

Lyndon Johnson was not impressed with McElroy's description of the American missile effort. He asked the defense secretary point blank, "Are we ahead or are we behind or are we losing to the Soviet Union?" When McElroy evaded this question by saying simply that the administration had speeded up the missile program since *Sputnik,* Johnson asked specifically what had been done since his subcommittee concluded its hearings in January. McElroy cited the $1.3 billion in additional funds for the 1958 budget requested in January and, to Eisenhower's displeasure, revealed that the administration was preparing to ask Congress for an even larger supplement to the 1959 defense budget. Even that answer did not satisfy LBJ, who said he wanted to get down to "brass tacks" by asking, "Do you feel that everything is being done that can prudently be done to contribute to the survival of this country?" McElroy replied by stressing the need to spend such large sums prudently, but he finally said, "I do think that everything is being done that I would recommend be done."[10]

On February 27, 1958, a day after he testified before Johnson's subcommittee, McElroy reported to the National Security Council on the status of the American missile program. He outlined the current plans for 130 ICBMs by 1963, 90 Atlas and 40 Titan. The air force, he pointed out, wanted a far larger force. It was proposing to have all 90 Atlas missiles deployed by 1962, to increase the number of Titan operational by 1963 from 40 to 110, and to plan for the Minuteman to go into production by 1963, with a goal of nine squadrons of fifty each. If these plans were approved, the goal would be to increase the American ICBM force from a projected 130 to more than 600 by 1964.

Secretary McElroy also informed the NSC that the navy was seeking funding for additional Polaris submarines. He had referred this request to the Joint Chiefs, who had yet to make a decision, but it was clear that it would be in competition with the air force requests for additional funding.

President Eisenhower was not yet prepared to approve such large additions to the projected American missile force. He preferred instead to limit funding to research and development for the second generation of missiles and defer any decision over how many Polaris and Minutemen to approve until they were ready for production. As a result, at the end of February the authorized American missile program remained at 130 ICBMs (90 Atlas and 40 Titan) and 120 IRBMs (60 Thor and 60 Jupiter), with tentative plans for 48 IRBMs aboard the three Polaris submarines that had been approved. It remained to be seen, however, how long the president could resist the pressure building up for a crash program in second-generation missiles.[11]

II

In the early months of 1958, Dwight Eisenhower went through his winter of discontent. He could not seem to shake off a nagging cold. His throat was sore and his voice husky, and the result, noted his secretary, Ann Whitman, was "a correspondingly bad temper." In January Sherman Adams called the White House staff together, asking everyone to work as hard as possible to relieve the president of unnecessary burdens. "This man is not what he was," Adams confessed. James Killian recalled that in a meeting in early February, stung by the constant chorus of criticism, Ike put his head down on his desk and "remarked that he didn't know whether his poor brain was going to be able to take it or not."[12]

The press quickly picked up hints of the president's malaise. John Fischer, the editor of *Harper's,* issued a call for his resignation. Citing Eisenhower's heart attack, ileitis, and recent stroke, Fischer felt that it would be best for both Ike and the nation for him to step down. At a time when the country desperately needed someone in charge, we had "a leaky ship, with a committee on the bridge and a crippled captain sending occasional whispers up the speaking tube from his sick bay." Periodicals on the left, ranging from the *Progressive* to the *New Republic,* also wanted Ike to resign, but others, such as the *Reporter,* feared that Nixon would offer little improvement.

The most serious sign of public disenchantment came in late February when *Time,* usually the president's strongest booster, expressed deep concern over Eisenhower's stamina and ability to lead the nation. Reporting that he had spent most of the month on George Humphrey's Georgia plantation recuperating from his cold, the story portrayed Ike as playing bridge, napping, and doing very little work each day. White House aides claimed that the president still worked hard when he was in Washington but admitted that he tended to run out of steam as the day progressed. *Time*'s most damaging disclosure was the staff estimate that the president had cut back about 25 percent on his workload since his November stroke.[13]

On February 25 Eisenhower returned to the White House to face his critics. Ann Whitman noted that he had shaken off the cold completely and seemed to be "in better spirits than any time in the last three months." An old army friend, General Alfred Gruenther, thought Ike had never "looked better, either mentally or physically." When a thorough medical exam showed him fully recovered from the stroke, Ann Whitman commented, "Certainly he seems to be—he looks wonderfully well, and most importantly, has regained his sense of humor and desire to get into things." The president himself, asked at a press conference about *Time*'s claim that he had cut back 25 percent on his work schedule, flashed his famous grin and replied, "I wish it were reduced, but—no, I don't think it has at all."[14]

Public opinion polls taken in the winter of 1958 reflected an ambivalent attitude toward Eisenhower's leadership. A special Gallup survey taken in February on the *Sputnik* crisis gave the administration high marks. 72 percent of those questioned thought that the administration was doing a good job on national defense, with only 19 percent expressing disappointment. Most Americans tended to blame themselves rather than their leaders for the apparent Soviet lead in technology and scientific education. One Cleveland woman summed up the prevailing feeling by saying, "Instead of making more beautiful cars, we should have been working on space travel." But a more general Gallup survey showed a steep decline in Eisenhower's popularity. His rating fell from 79 percent at the start of his second term to 52 percent by March 1958, the lowest point yet in his presidency. In just the last month, his rating had fallen six points.[15]

The sharp drop in Eisenhower's public standing stemmed more from the deepening recession than from his handling of the *Sputnik* crisis. Unemployment rose to over five million by February, the highest level since World War II. The president confessed to his brother in mid-March that the economy had "touched rock bottom." Democrats in Congress began to shift their attention from attacks on the administration's national security policies to new demands for increased spending on highway and public works to stimulate the sagging economy. Some even began to talk of a possible tax cut to increase consumer purchasing power. And as the president's popularity fell with the continuing slump, Democrats looked forward to picking up as many as fifty seats in Congress in the fall elections.[16]

The administration's best hope for an early recovery rested on the impact of higher defense spending. Monthly expenditures for national security had hit a peak in August 1957 at $3.5 billion, then had dropped to $3 billion a month as a result of Charles Wilson's economy moves. Despite the acceleration of the missile program and the heavier defense spending authorized after *Sputnik,* the monthly outgo for national security did not rise in the first three months of 1958 but instead stayed relatively stable at about $3.1 billion (see Table 2). When Senator Symington asked for an explanation, Pentagon officials said it was due to the long lead time involved in missile development; most were still in the research phase and would not go into full-scale production until later in 1958 at the earliest.[17]

While the lack of an immediate stimulus from defense spending worried Democrats, Eisenhower and his advisers continued to show greater concern over the long-range effect of high spending on the American economy. In a speech he was planning to give to newspaper editors, Eisenhower planned to "try to show what the enormous expenditures for defense are doing to our economy." As he explained to his brother Milton, his main concern was not the present decline but the long-term outlook. He wanted to show how important it was to hold down defense spending, "to keep this thing in the size a free economy can carry indefinitely."

Eisenhower was especially upset by the waste and duplication involved in the nation's response to *Sputnik.* He warned his aides to be on guard against the danger of "hysteria" and to be vigilant to cut out the "useless things" that were being proposed in the name of national security. He asked Killian to find out how the Pentagon had been able to spend $25 billion for research and development over the past five years. The president found it "difficult" to understand how the nation "got $25 billion worth out of it."[18]

Other cabinet members shared the president's concern. John Foster Dulles told Treasury Secretary Robert Anderson that in his opinion "we are going crazy on military stuff." The United States, Dulles argued, already had sufficient nuclear striking power to deter the Soviet Union. "We don't need any more." Anderson agreed on the need to put a ceiling on defense spending but warned that the Democrats "are playing up the expenditures as a means to counteract the depression."[19]

Eisenhower had a clearer understanding of the relationship between increased defense spending and the economy than did his critics. The vast sums Congress voted for the overlapping missile programs had little immediate impact on the recession of 1958, but they were bound to lead to sharp rises in future budgets. Two economists reported in mid-1958 that defense spending would jump from $43.5 billion in 1958 to $45.6 billion in 1959 and then to nearly $47 billion in 1960. Although these levels were far below those recommended in both the Rockefeller and Gaither reports, the result would be to lift the costs of national security to more than 10 percent of the GNP. The question the nation faced, they concluded, was "What is the U.S. willing to forego in other lines of spending for the sake of security?"[20]

The president was intent on making sure the nation was aware of

TABLE 2: Monthly Rate of
Defense Spending in Fiscal 1958

Month	Amount (*in millions*)
July	$3,200
August	3,532
September	3,036
October	3,216
November	3,063
December	3,313
January	3,143
February	3,168
March	3,068

Source: Senate Armed Services Committee, "Inquiry into Satellite and Missile
Programs," 2384.

the long-term cost of increased defense spending. In the midst of the
recession, he could no longer hope to balance the budget, but he was
determined to hold down spending for missiles to as reasonable a sum
as he could consistent with the nation's security. It was this sense of
purpose that helped him regain his strength after his February slump.
Like the economy, he had hit "rock bottom" but now was on his way
back up once again.

III

The Eisenhower administration made the key decisions on the second
generation of missiles in the first half of March 1958. The PSAC panel
headed by George Kistiakowsky delivered its formal report, entitled
"Whither Ballistic Missile Systems," to Killian on March 4. Four days
later the science adviser prepared his own recommendations and submitted them, along with the panel report, to the president on March
10. Eisenhower accepted nearly all these recommendations, which
then shaped American missile policy for the next decade.

Kistiakowsky's panel began with the assumption that ballistic missiles would be an "indispensable part" of the retaliatory forces of both
the United States and the Soviet Union for the foreseeable future.
The group focused its attention on what it termed the "greatly improved weapons systems" made possible by the use of solid fuels. The
only value of the first generation of liquid-fuel missiles lay in their
early deployment and their relatively high degree of thrust. At the
same time, however, the Thor, Jupiter, Atlas, and Titan missiles were
not very reliable, unsuited to quick response, and very vulnerable to
an enemy first strike. The second generation, in contrast, had the
"great advantages" of "instant readiness and high reliability."

Accordingly, the missiles panel recommended a centralized research and development program within the Defense Department

designed to perfect a more sophisticated solid propellant for all second-generation missiles. While such a program might delay the development of the Minuteman for as much as two years, it would result in a much more efficient and dependable fuel and thus a more advanced ICBM for the future.

Beyond its recommendation for concentrating on the perfection of a solid propellant, Kistiakowsky's group made specific recommendations for individual missile programs. It favored phasing out the Atlas ICBM and replacing it with an improved Titan that used storable liquid fuel and thus could be deployed in hardened silos. The panel called the Titan II "distinctly superior" to the Atlas and pointed out that its greater thrust also made it more suitable for America's space program. The panel agreed that the air force Minuteman was very attractive and was likely to "provide us for many years with an effective retaliatory capability." But the PSAC members opposed a "crash program," recommending instead that the air force wait for the development of better solid propellants before building any Minutemen. Instead of rushing a low-performing Minuteman into operation in 1963, the panel recommended relying on the Titan in the early 1960s and then gradually replacing it with an improved Minuteman in 1965.

The missiles panel was equally candid in its appraisal of the IRBMs. It believed that the Thor was superior to the Jupiter, largely because it was closer to going into production, and therefore recommended that the Jupiter program be canceled. Kistiakowsky's group held the Polaris in high regard, observing that it "offers us a retaliatory weapons system of superior reliability, which has a high probability of surviving a surprise attack." Its only drawback, the panel pointed out, was its high cost. Since three submarines had to be built to keep one on patrol at all times, each Polaris missile cost the taxpayer between $20 and $30 million. Nevertheless, the panel concluded, "as a long term deterrent force, submarine based Polaris has probably no equals if costs are disregarded."[21]

In his own recommendations, Killian followed the panel closely. In particular he reiterated the need to avoid the waste and duplication that marked the first generation of missiles. "It is dangerous," Killian told Eisenhower, "to plunge into rigidly fixed hardware and development programs without due allowance for advance development." Therefore he strongly seconded the panel's recommendations to delay design of the Minuteman and concentrate instead on a "well-conceived basic research effort on solid propellants." Killian thought it was especially important to insist on "a strong central mechanism for the management and planning of our strategic missile program."

Killian favored replacing the Atlas with an improved version of the Titan based in hardened silos, and he wanted to terminate Jupiter so that the Thor became the only land-based IRBM to go into production. He also supported the idea of delaying the Minuteman while developing better solid propellants, then gradually deploying it in the mid-1960s. His view of the future composition of the American strategic arsenal consisted of a "mixed force of missiles, as for example, a combination in the future of Titans, Polaris, and possibly Minuteman missiles." Such a mixture, he concluded, "reduces the vulnerability of our retaliatory capability and greatly increases the problem of the enemy in countering such missiles."[22]

The president was very pleased with the recommendations of the scientists. He approved all the major suggestions except the idea of canceling the Jupiter, since he thought it important to keep Wernher Von Braun's unit in operation at Huntsville. Ike agreed to replace the Atlas with the improved Titan II "as soon as consistent with an adequate rate of buildup of the total missile forces." Eisenhower was most enthusiastic over the recommendation for "central direction" of the research effort for improved solid fuels. He suggested giving ARPA this task. He expressed his belief that "all research on fuels should be kept centralized, avoiding the wastes of duplicating effort." In fact, he wanted to go one step further and remove all missiles from the individual services, except possibly the navy's Polaris, and give them to "a single missile command."[23]

Eisenhower made clear his misgivings about the Pentagon's management of the missile program in a meeting with Secretary of Defense McElroy and his deputy, Donald Quarles, on March 20. When he repeated his suggestion that ARPA take charge of the solid-fuel effort for all second-generation missiles, Quarles said that this Pentagon agency "is not intended . . . to be the manager of the missile development aspects." McElroy objected when Ike went on to voice his belief that Minuteman should be developed by the Defense Department itself "and should not be assigned to any of the services." The secretary said he had given the air force exclusive control over "the development and operational use of all ICBMs and IRBMs." Citing the duplication of effort between the solid-fuel Polaris and Minuteman, Ike told the Defense Department officials that "he had reservations as to the wisdom of this way of going about future missile development."

The Pentagon's determination to follow custom and let the individual services oversee the design of the second generation of missiles confirmed Eisenhower's belief in the urgent need for a thorough reorganization of the Defense Department. The president lectured McElroy and Quarles on the need to free "our minds from existing systems and organizations." "We continually find ourselves," he said passionately, "prisoners of free-wheeling activities that have been going on for a number of years in each of the Services." McElroy's only response was a promise to place all missile programs under the supervision of the future undersecretary for research and engineering once Congress approved the proposed reorganization plan.[24]

Despite the Pentagon's continued footdragging, Eisenhower was determined to cut out much of the waste and duplication of the original missile program as the nation moved toward the second generation of these weapons. Once again, the assistance of scientists like Kistiakowsky and Killian had proved invaluable. Free of the bureaucratic claims of the armed forces, the members of PSAC gave the president the broad overview of the missile program that he so clearly wanted. The result was a sensible plan to move as quickly as possible beyond the obsolete first generation toward reliance on solid-fuel missiles like Polaris and Minuteman. Deployment of Titan II as an interim weapon provided the administration with a way to ward off the air force pressure for too early a commitment to Minuteman. By insisting on the prior development of improved solid fuels, Eisenhower and his scientists laid the foundation for a well-designed and invulnerable strategic arsenal for the 1960s.

IV

The question of how much these missiles programs would cost continued to plague the Eisenhower administration. In an effort to keep the 1959 defense budget as close as possible to his original ceiling of $38 billion a year, the president had asked Congress for $1.3 billion in supplemental 1958 funds for the Pentagon in January. But the heavy development costs for the second generation of missiles forced McElroy to consider asking for an even larger supplement to the 1959 budget. When the three services submitted requests totaling nearly $10 billion, the defense secretary worked hard to reduce them to $1.8 billion.

Eisenhower was furious at what he considered irresponsible behavior. He told Killian that "he found it hard to retain confidence in the heads of the Services when they produce such proposals." The 1959 defense budget had already risen to nearly $41 billion; these additional sums would put it over $42 billion, much higher than the $40 billion level that Ike felt would be desirable. Most of the money would go for research and development of second-generation missiles, thereby building in future increases in spending when these weapons reached the production phase in the early 1960s. He was especially troubled by the fact that simply adding two Polaris submarines would cost nearly $400 million. Speaking to congressional leaders, he talked of the need to avoid "hysteria and demagogery" and instead "exert some reasonable control" over defense spending. "I'm trying to be a Horatius at the bridge to keep from going out of bounds," he told the legislators.[25]

On April 1 McElroy and Quarles submitted a formal request for an additional $1.8 billion in defense spending for the 1959 budget. When the president and his budget director, Maurice Stans, continued to object, McElroy made one final effort to pare down the request. Later that day the defense secretary informed the president that he had cut some other Pentagon programs to reduce the amount to $1.6 billion. A grateful Eisenhower thanked McElroy for his efforts, saying that "the extra 2 hundred million meant a lot to him." It was, the president felt, "a moral victory."[26]

The administration announced on April 2 that it was asking Congress to approve an additional $1.6 billion in defense spending for 1959. The next day, Secretary McElroy went before LBJ's Defense Preparedness Subcommittee to give another interim report on the administration's response to the *Sputnik* crisis. He gave a breakdown on the additional $1.6 billion. Over $400 million would be spent for B-52 bombers, keeping the Boeing assembly lines open through 1960; over $300 million more would pay for two more Polaris submarines; nearly $100 million was for solid-fuel research; and another $50 million was needed for the improved Titan II ICBM. In addition, the administration was asking for $140 milllion more for ARPA for a variety of projects, including the highly classified reconnaissance satellite.

In contrast to the president, the senators expressed disappointment at what they considered the limited nature of the administration's request. Senator Prescott Bush, a Connecticut Republican, wanted to know why the Pentagon was asking for funds for only two more Polaris submarines when the navy wanted an additional six. McElroy patiently explained that the Defense Department was waiting for successful tests of the Polaris missile; he wanted to be sure it was "a proven system" before expanding the program.

Once again it was Democrat Stuart Symington who was most critical. He claimed that *Sputnik* undercut the traditional American claim of qualitative superiority in the face of Soviet advantages in the sheer number of weapons. The Missouri senator pointed out that the two administration requests for additional defense spending came to just under $3 billion; the Gaither committee had recommended an $8 billion annual increase, and the Rockefeller report called for $5 billion more a year. McElroy said that cuts in domestic spending had brought the increase in defense funding up to $4 billion, a level he felt was "about right." When Symington then asked point-blank if we were still behind the Russians in the ICBM race, McElroy said the administration was acting on that assumption. "But we have no positive evidence," he added, "that they are ahead of us in long-range missiles."[27]

This exchange reflected the uncomfortable position in which Neil McElroy found himself. On the one hand, he needed to placate an angry Congress, which felt the administration was too complacent in view of the Soviet missile threat. Democrats in particular were intent on portraying the Eisenhower administration as risking national security for the sake of budgetary restraint. At the same time, however, he needed to assure a worried president that the Pentagon would not repeat the waste and duplication that had marked the development of the first generation of missiles. Eisenhower had been forced to abandon his $38 billion ceiling on defense spending, but he would continue to do everything possible to keep the military budget in check.

The administration tried to resolve this dilemma at a National Security Council meeting on April 24, 1958. The president stood firm on his decision to limit the first generation of ICBMs to the 130 previously approved, 90 Atlas and 40 Titans in squadrons of ten each. In order to make these liquid-fuel missiles more secure from attack, the NSC authorized that the last five Atlas squadrons be deployed in hardened sites that could withstand blasts up to 25 psi (pounds per square inch) and that the four Titan squadrons be placed in underground silos hardened to 100 psi. At the same time, Eisenhower agreed to expand the Polaris program to five submarines, two more than previously authorized, but far fewer than the navy and Congress advocated.

The real fight came over the Defense Department's proposal to increase the number of IRBMs to be deployed in Europe from 120 to 180—nine Thor squadrons and three Jupiter, of fifteen missiles each. The president, expressing his fear of the way "our defense programs pyramid," suggested holding the IRBMs at eight squadrons until a second generation of Jupiters and Thors could be developed. Donald Quarles argued that 180 missiles was a "minimal figure"—only half the number the Gaither committee called for and barely enough to meet the need for European deployment. Eisenhower, to the surprise of several White House aides, finally accepted the Defense Department recommendation of 180 IRBMs, despite his continuing doubts. He would have preferred more of an "austerity program," he commented, adding that he continued to worry that excessive defense spending "could reduce the United States to being a garrison state." And despite the enthusiasm of the Pentagon for the new weapons, the president said he "still had more faith in the delivery capabilities of the aircraft than he had in all these missiles at the present time."[28] (See Table 3.)

Eisenhower's reluctant decision to increase the number of IRBMs reflected his need to hedge his bets while moving ahead cautiously with the second generation of solid-fuel missiles. In order to protect the nation from the possibility that the Soviets would have enough ICBMs to launch a first strike against the continental United States in the early 1960s, the president was willing to expand the IRBM deployment in Europe and follow the Gaither panel's recommendation for hardening American ICBM bases. These stopgap measures would be expensive, but Eisenhower felt that they would be far cheaper than a crash program for second-generation solid-fuel missiles. Accordingly, he insisted on going slowly with the Polaris, despite intense congres-

TABLE 3: Authorization for Liquid-fuel Missiles

October 1957

ICBM	IRBM
40 Atlas (4 squadrons of 10)	60 Thor (4 squadrons of 15)
40 Titan (4 squadrons of 10)	0 Jupiter
80	60

Total missiles: 140

December 1957

ICBM	IRBM
90 Atlas (9 squadrons of 10)	60 Thor (4 squadrons of 15)
40 Titan (4 squadrons of 10)	60 Jupiter (4 squadrons of 15)
130	120

Total missiles: 250

April 1958

90 Atlas (9 squadrons of 10)	135 Thor (9 squadrons of 15)
40 Titan (4 squadrons of 10)	45 Jupiter (3 squadrons of 15)
130	180

Total missiles: 310

sional pressure, and waiting for the development of improved solid propellants before authorizing the air force to proceed with the Minuteman.

The president did not, as his Democratic critics charged, open up a missile gap that endangered national security. Nor did he, as some have claimed, take a calculated gamble by bypassing a large force of first-generation missiles that would soon be obsolete in order to concentrate on the second generation of solid-fuel weapons. Instead he compromised by holding down the number of expensive Atlas and Titan ICBMs while expanding the interim force of cheaper Thor and Jupiter IRBMs. The result was that the United States developed more first-generation IRBMs than it needed but used the time this maneuver bought to proceed more deliberately with the far more significant second generation of solid-fuel missiles. Although Eisenhower ended up spending more on the first generation of missiles than he thought necessary, at least he avoided the huge expenditures that both the Gaither panel and the Democrats in Congress recommended. And by insisting on a cautious approach to the second generation of missiles, the president could claim, as he had told McElroy, that he had won "a moral victory."[29]

CHAPTER EIGHT

President Eisenhower's determination to resist the congressional pressure for greater defense spending in the wake of *Sputnik* spurred him to give high priority to reforming the Pentagon. After outlining his plans for defense reorganization in his January State of the Union address, he had delegated this subject to a Pentagon committee headed by Boston lawyer Charles Coolidge. Meeting with Coolidge and McElroy in late February, Eisenhower made it clear that he expected a drastic overhaul to end the waste and duplication so evident in the missile program. He favored centralized control over all research and development in the Defense Department, criticizing what he termed "decentralized authority" stemming from "having money voted directly to the services." Above all, he wanted to enhance the position of the secretary of defense. As Andrew Goodpaster noted, "The President said the essence of the matter is to establish the power of the Secretary of Defense to get things done."[1]

In March, working with the Coolidge committee, the president emphasized three primary changes he wanted to see in the Defense Department. First, he favored unified commands in place of the traditional role of the three services in conducting operations. He wanted the secretary of defense, acting through the Joint Chiefs, to issue orders to theater commanders who would have full control over all army, navy, and air force units in their area. Second, he insisted on giving the secretary of defense what he termed "fiscal flexibility," that is, the power to allocate the defense budget to the three services, rather than have Congress appropriate money directly to the army, navy, and air force. "Particularly it is important," he told Ann Whitman, "that all Research money be appropriated directly to the Secretary of Defense." Finally, he wanted to create a new position in the

Defense Department to oversee all weapons development and thus cut out the waste and inefficiency that stemmed from interservice rivalry. Only the appointment of a "real boss over research and engineering," the president believed, would enable the nation to achieve "maximum results from the tremendous resources that are being put into our military establishment."[2]

Eisenhower realized that such far-reaching changes would meet with intense congressional opposition. Powerful members of both houses, especially the chairmen of the armed services committees, preferred the existing decentralized system with three distinct and separate services. By appropriating money to each service, Congress retained a degree of control over the army, navy, and air force that would be lost under Eisenhower's plan to weaken the services and centralize control under the secretary of defense. Two Democrats from Georgia, Senator Richard Russell and Representative Carl Vinson, would lead the opposition to defense reorganization. Of the two, Vinson played the more active role. Chairman of the House Armed Services Committee, Vinson had served in Congress since 1914 and had used his position to enhance both his own power and congressional control over the Pentagon. Not wanting to see a strong secretary of defense undermine the influence he and the Congress had enjoyed, Vinson proposed legislation that would bolster the three services by making the secretaries of the army, navy, and air force members of the National Security Council. Eisenhower found this idea absurd, telling Republican congressional leaders that he needed the Joint Chiefs, "not civilian secretaries, advising on *strategic* matters."

The president knew, however, that he would have to find some way to neutralize Vinson and the predictable opposition from Congress. On March 28 he arranged a breakfast meeting with Vinson, Texas Democratic Congressman Paul Kilday, and Representative Les Arends, the GOP whip and ranking minority member of the Armed Services Committee. "All we're trying to do," he told them, "is to set up an establishment that will function in peacetime, as it must in wartime, under the Secretary of Defense." Vinson was not persuaded, putting forth arguments that convinced the president that he wanted Congress to "control in detail every defense activity." When the meeting ended, Ike remarked to an aide, "We're going to have trouble."[3]

Any doubt on that score ended at a meeting with Republican congressional leaders on April 1. Coolidge presented the Defense Department recommendations; removing the secretaries of the army, navy, and air force from the chain of command, enlarging the role and personnel of the Joint Chiefs of Staff, and creating the new post of director of research and development in the Defense Department on a par with the three service secretaries. The most startling suggestion, however, was a change in the appropriation process to achieve "flexibility on money." The Coolidge committee proposed that, instead of dividing the 1960 defense budget among the three services, Congress simply designate eight broad categories (personnel, weapons, construction, etc.) and let the secretary of defense allocate funds to the services as he deemed best.

Senator Styles Bridges of New Hampshire immediately challenged this startling proposal. Giving McElroy power to shift funds between the services, he warned, "involved getting into a field that had traditionally belonged to the Congress, which had always made specific appropriations to the services." Eisenhower responded that change was necessary to streamline the Pentagon "to meet modern requirements" and to prevent the secretary of defense "from being hamstrung in his efforts to get the best defense for the nation." William Knowland of California, the Republican leader in the Senate, continued to object, pointing out that "people in Congress" would be concerned about "maintaining their traditional power of appropriating funds." "Congress," he added, "would not surrender this lightly." Although the president gave a passionate appeal on the need to avoid waste and duplication in a defense budget that had risen to $41 billion since *Sputnik,* Senators Bridges and Knowland made it clear that any effort to change the appropriation process was doomed. The power of the purse stood between the president and his desire for sweeping defense reorganization.[4]

The president refused to be discouraged. On April 1 he told UN Ambassador Henry Cabot Lodge that he was "going to town" on a message to Congress on defense reorganization. "Over the weekend," he confided to Lodge, "I spent a great deal of time on the final draft of the document; I am determined to make it, in all respects, 'mine.'" He devoted most of the next day to working on the message, leaving the Oval Office only for a press conference. Press Secretary Jim Hagerty, who had urged Ike to hold this session, arranged for the first question to deal with defense reorganization. Eisenhower responded by stressing the themes of unification and flexibility. "In modern times," he declared, "there is no such thing as a separate ground, air, or sea war." The secretary of defense, he maintained, must be able to command all operations and, to do so, must have the ability to allocate spending among the services "to meet unforeseen contingencies."[5]

Despite his deeply held convictions, however, the president realized that there was no chance of getting Congress to grant the secretary of defense such discretionary power over the budget. Regretfully Ike dropped the proposed change in the appropriations process from his message to Congress, asking only that the secretary of defense be given limited authority to shift funds between the services in special cases. The rest of the message, sent to Congress on April 3, 1958, reflected the other recommendations of the Coolidge committee. The administration asked that the secretary of defense, acting on the advice of the Joint Chiefs, issue commands for combined operations without going through the service secretaries and that the staff of the Joint Chiefs be expanded to allow the chief of each service to devote more time to advising the secretary of defense rather than administering his own branch.

Aside from the more centralized chain of command, the main emphasis of he message was on a more efficient system of weapons development. "The Secretary must have full authority to prevent unwise service competition in this area," the president advised Congress. He proposed creating the new post of director of defense research and engineering in the Pentagon, with the same salary and rank as the service secretaries. The individual who held this position would be "a nationally recognized leader in science and technology" who would be able to "minimize duplication and rivalry among the three services."[6]

The president's proposals received a generally favorable response. Commentators praised the concept of unified commands and the effort to centralize research and development in the Pentagon. Ike's claim that the scaled-down authority of the secretary of defense to shift funds between services would "go far toward stopping the services from vying with each other for Congressional and public favor" also met with approval. But many observers felt that the president faced opposition from the armed forces. The air force was expected to give in gracefully, the army reluctantly, but the navy was seen as likely to resist most strongly, fearing that it would lose its separate identity in the new Pentagon alignment.

Congress remained the real stumbling block. The navy had influential allies on Capitol Hill who would be sure to charge that Eisenhower wanted to transform the secretary of defense into a "czar" and to impose a Prussian general staff on the services. But most of all, legislators like Vinson and Russell would do everything they could to protect the control that Congress exercised by keeping each of the services dependent on that body for its appropriations. The president already had been forced to give up his quest for a centralized defense budget. In the continuing struggle to streamline the Pentagon, he would be forced on the defensive as Congress did everything possible to protect the power of the purse. Yet even more than in the case of space policy and missile deployment, Eisenhower had a personal commitment to defense reorganization that gave promise of a classic showdown between the executive and legislative branches of government.[7]

I

In the first two weeks of April, the president focused his attention on his two main opponents, the navy and the Democratic leadership in Congress. On the evening of April 8, he invited Scretary of the Navy Thomas Gates and Admiral Arleigh Burke, the chief of naval operations, to an informal session at the White House. Gates and Burke said they supported the general plan for reorganization but admitted they feared it might have a negative impact on the navy's morale. It was possible that a future president might let a secretary of defense abuse his powers to the detriment of the navy and the marine corps. When they expressed concern about advocating the administration's program in congressional testimony, Ike finally got them to agree to stress the advantages of "unified strategic planning and command direction." The evening ended on a friendly note as the president assured the worried navy leaders that he had no intention of downgrading the services but only wanted to end wasteful duplication of effort in the armed forces.[8]

Dealing with Congress proved more difficult. On the one hand, Eisenhower used his press conferences and public addresses to defend his reorganization plan and especially to rebut the charges of wanting to make the secretary of defense a Pentagon "czar." He denied that he wanted to usurp congressional authority or merge the three armed services into one unified force. His only goal, he claimed, was to convince the American people of his desire to provide for both "their pocketbook" and "their safety." He planned to take his case to the nation by television, saying he was willing to "get onto the air as often as the television companies would let me get on." And he was even willing to pull rank. "I don't care who is against this thing," he told reporters. "It just happens I have got a little bit more experience in military organization and the directing of unified forces than anyone else on the active list."[9]

At the same time, the president saw the need to compromise. In a meeting with Republican congressional leaders on April 15, he explained that he no longer was seeking a lump sum appropriation to the secretary of defense. Instead he would be satisfied if Congress would simply delegate to the secretary of defense the authority to shift 10 percent of each fiscal year's budget between the services as circumstances required. In that way, he explained, flexibility could be preserved while "90% of the budget could be nailed down tight." In submitting the draft defense reorganization bill to Congress on April 16, the president pointed out that there was no provision for a lump sum appropriation, but instead he would ask for the 10 percent discretionary feature during the budget deliberations for 1960.

In a press conference that same day, he was less than honest with reporters, saying that he had never advocated a single, lump sum defense budget. All he wanted to do, he explained, was let the secretary of defense control money allocated for research and development of new weapons. Bothered by follow-up questions, Ike finally cut off further discussion by observing, "Let's try to use some common sense and not just get a Sputnik attitude about everything."[10]

Ike made his most eloquent statement on defense reorganization in a speech to the American Society of Newspaper Editors and the International Press Institute on April 17. He worked on the text for nearly a week, taking it back to his private quarters at night and improving it "tremendously," he told Ann Whitman. His text was simple. In the missile age, the nation could no longer afford interservice rivalry and costly duplication of weapons systems. "I am quite sure," he commented, "that the American people feel it is far more important to be able to hit the target than it is to haggle over who makes a weapon or who pulls a trigger." He had no intention of infringing on congressional prerogatives, he explained. All he wanted to do was work with Congress to make the annual defense budget "adaptable to rapidly changing strategic conditions in the world."[11]

This carefully orchestrated campaign had little impact on its primary target, Carl Vinson. The chairman of the House Armed Services Committee, known variously as "Uncle Carl" and the "Swamp Fox," branded the administration's bill as an invitation to some future "man on horseback" and a clear attempt to create a "Prussian-type supreme command." Responding to Ike's reference to the needs of the missile age, Vinson claimed that "space ships, satellites and guided missiles cannot abrogate the Constitution of the United States." He was especially incensed at the idea of giving the secretary of defense discretionary power over the defense budget. "I know of no concept more dangerous to the security of the United States," he declared on the floor of the House. "I am convinced that the collective wisdom of the Congress of the United States supersedes the collective wisdom of the Secretary of Defense."[12]

Eisenhower and McElroy were most concerned about the possibility of individual members of the Joint Chiefs speaking out against the administration's plan in testimony before Vinson's committee. Vinson had raised this issue with McElroy in advance of the hearings, and on April 21 the defense secretary asked Eisenhower how he should respond. "The President said that if any man gratuitously goes out and opposes the President's proposal publicly, he should be out," Andrew Goodpaster recorded Ike as telling McElroy. If asked, an officer could express his own views to Congress, but "the test is whether he can and will support the program within the Department." With his usual tact, McElroy promised to try to avoid any such direct conflict between Vinson's committee and members of the Joint Chiefs of Staff.

The subsequent hearings went about as well as Eisenhower could expect. The chairman of the Joint Chiefs, air force General Nathan Twining, supported the president's legislative proposal "solidly," in the words of Army Secretary Wilber Brucker. The only negative testimony came from the navy. Arleigh Burke backed the proposal in general terms but voiced his "misgivings" and "apprehensions" about the impact on the navy. Marine Commandant Randolph Pate was more openly critical, claiming that the administration's plan threatened the survival of the marines as a separate unit.[13]

Speculation over far-fetched consequences of defense reorganization finally caused Eisenhower to lose his temper, something he often did in private but rarely in public. During a press conference on April 23, Sarah McClendon, a Texas journalist who had made a career out of being a presidential gadfly, asked Ike if his legislation might enable a dictatorial president or secretary of defense to "transfer all the troop units from the Army, Navy, Air Force, and even Marines, and leave none under the present Secretaries or Chiefs of Staff?" The president, his face flushed with anger, fired back, asking if she had "read the law." When Sarah McClendon said she had, Ike doubted her word and then burst out that it would make just as much sense for her to claim that maybe Congress "is suddenly going nuts and completely abolishing the Defense Department."[14]

When reports that the president was beginning to crack under pressure appeared in the press, Neil McElroy stepped in to cool everyone down. In his testimony before Vinson's committee, he backed Eisenhower's proposal strongly but suggested that some of the phrasing could be softened to reassure Congress. In particular he was ready to guarantee that the service secretaries would retain their right to plead the case for their branches before the congressional committees. Bolstered by a telephone call from Henry Cabot Lodge, who told Ike that he "should not give an inch" until the legislation got into conference committee, the president was still in an angry mood when he met with McElroy on April 28. Referring to Burke and Pate obliquely, he said "their future retention would depend on their loyalty to the success of the plan." But McElroy gradually defused his anger by stressing the need to avoid "excessive rigidity" in regard to the wording of the legislation. Though Ike warned the defense secretary of the "Congressional technique of undercutting objectives by inducing witnesses to accept seemingly innocuous word changes in pending legislation," the president finally agreed to let him soften some of the key phrases.[15]

Eisenhower set out to mend fences when he met with the press again on April 30. Although he offered no apology to Sarah McClendon, he laughed off a reference to his "irritation" at the last press conference and impressed reporters by appearing to be "buoyant, relaxed, cheerful." He signaled a new mood of moderation by speaking out against any thought of merging the three services, saying that the nature of modern warfare simply required much greater cooperation among the army, navy, and air force than in the past. He still thought there was little room for compromise on such a well-thought-out plan, but he allowed that some "slight changes in wording" might be possible.[16]

Despite his new image of sweet reasonableness, Eisenhower was more determined than ever to win this contest with the Congress. He soon embarked on a dual strategy to achieve victory. First, he devoted nearly every public speech to the issue of defense reorganization in an effort to build up public support. Addresses to such disparate groups as the United States Chamber of Commerce, the Advertising Council, and the Republican National Committee dinner honoring GOP members of Congress all dealt at length with the effort to reform the Pentagon. He stressed one theme above all others: the desire for a more efficient defense structure that would guard against wasting the huge sums voted by Congress for the nation's security. The sole aim, he explained, was "to get responsible executive authority clearly established in the Secretary of Defense." He even departed from a speech on civil rights to a group of black newspaper publishers to get in a plug for his reorganization plan. Pointing out that blacks paid taxes like everyone else, he argued that "defense must be kept at the absolute minimum in cost but with the maximum efficiency."[17]

The president's other major lobbying effort came through the written rather than the spoken word. Adopting a suggestion from the president of General Electric, in late April he wrote to more than one hundred of the nation's leading business executives to ask them to bring pressure on Congress on behalf of his defense reorganization plan. The response was overwhelming. Many of the recipients of the president's letter were executives of companies who thrived on defense contracts. They bombarded members of Congress, and especially of the armed services committees, with letters and telegrams endorsing Eisenhower's program. One writer, who sent the White House a copy of his letter to Congress, said Pentagon reform was necessary "to meet the threat of the lightening-like atomic missile potential developed by Communist Russia today." Another executive reported that he sent out twenty thousand letters to fellow businessmen to enlist them in Ike's crusade against Congress.

Judging from the mail received by Senator Stuart Symington, the letter-writing campaign was very effective. In spring 1958 Symington received scores of letters from bankers, lawyers, and businessmen urging him to vote for the president's reform measure. Given the enormous influence of men who were key components of what Eisenhower would later label the military-industrial complex, it is not surprising that Congress began to squirm under the pressure. When several Congressmen accused the White House of using unfair tactics in going over their heads to appeal to their constituents, Ike was delighted at this clear proof of the campaign's success.[18]

This mobilization of the nation's industrial elite, so uncharacteristic of Eisenhower's usual fondness for more indirect methods of persuasion, proved to be a tonic for Ike's sagging popularity. His standing in the Gallup poll, which had fallen to an all-time low of 49 percent in early April, quickly bounced back to 54 percent by mid-May. The American people, noted *Time*, liked to see their leaders fighting for causes in which they believed so passionately. The contest with Uncle

Carl and the Democrats in Congress seems also to have invigorated the president. The encouraging response from the nation's leading businessmen and the joyous feeling of fighting for a cause so close to his heart filled him with a sense of zest that had been lacking since the ominous beep-beep-beep of *Sputnik* had led Congress and the American people to question his leadership.[19]

II

Despite the president's vigorous counterattack, the Democrats still had the power to deny him the victory he sought. Vinson was willing to go along with the main provisions of the administration proposal, but he made three changes in the draft bill that infuriated Eisenhower. One gave Congress the power to veto any attempt by the secretary of defense to shift combat functions within the Defense Department. A second stipulated that the service secretaries and the individual members of the Joint Chiefs had the right to present their own views to Congress, even if they were in conflict with the administration's position. The final change, and the one Ike felt was most crucial, stated that the secretary of defense could exercise his authority only "through the respective Secretaries of each department." It was this language that threatened to block the president's efforts to subordinate the three services and allow the secretary of defense to give orders directly to theater commanders.[20]

When McElroy and Bryce Harlow, the White House aide in charge of congressional relations, first informed Eisenhower of Vinson's proposed changes, the president was adamant. He felt the measure was "much too restrictive to be acceptable" and instructed Harlow to inform Vinson that he could not agree to these new provisions. Harlow and McElroy tried to soften the president's opposition, pointing out that he had gotten 95 percent of what he had sought from Congress. Ike finally agreed to write a letter thanking Vinson for his efforts and simply asking reconsideration of two features: the clause on the transfer of combat functions and the language appearing to keep the service secretaries in the chain of command.

The original draft of the letter to Vinson even included a sentence in which the president said, "I congratulate you and your Committee for the progress made toward developing a sound defense structure." After thinking it over, Ike ordered this passage removed, but he left in words that expressed his belief that the proposed legislation "seems to deal positively with every major problem I presented to Congress." Then the president raised his two objections and politely expressed the hope that "this language will be suitably adjusted on the House floor."[21]

When the House Armed Services Committee reported out the defense reorganization bill on May 16 with Vinson's changes intact,

Eisenhower was faced with a difficult parliamentary decision. He could either try to have the bill amended on the floor of the House, a dubious prospect in view of the Democratic majority, or wait for the Senate to act and then ask a conference committee to remove the offending sections. The GOP congressional leaders were divided. In a conference with Ike on May 19, several advised that it would be better to work out changes in the Senate than risk a public defeat in the House. But Representative Charles Halleck warned that Vinson could be very tough in a conference committee, a position backed by House Minority Leader Joseph Martin, who felt that with Ike's strong backing they could win on the House floor. Vinson would give way to avoid taking a "licking," Martin predicted. The president finally said he would defer to the House leaders and then added, "I've liked old Uncle Carl for 20 years. But I know how tough and dictatorial he can be."[22]

The longer Ike thought about it, the angrier he became. He expressed great disappointment that the vote in the House committee had been unanimous, with the Republican members refusing to stand up to Vinson. He especially blamed Les Arends, the ranking GOP member of the committee, who claimed that the language Ike did not like was aimed not at him but at a future president who might abuse his authority. The president asked Bryce Harlow to work on Arends, who he claimed had been "ducking out" on his responsibilities. Eisenhower finally confronted Arends personally, telling him, "Les, remember that you're my boy—not Uncle Carl's."[23]

Nearly two weeks after the House committee vote, the president went public with his objections to the bill. In a statement that James Hagerty released to the press on May 28, Eisenhower argued that the legislation "directly conflicted with the reorganization that I proposed to the Congress." Singling out the three changes made by Vinson, Ike charged that they "imply Congressional approval of wasteful duplications, administrative delays and interservice rivalries." While admitting that the bill achieved most of what he wanted, Eisenhower argued that when it came to national defense "going part way is not going far enough." "America, having started on this reorganization," he concluded, "wants the job done right."[24]

Ike bridled when the press claimed he had changed his stand on the Vinson bill. In a letter to *New York Times* columnist Arthur Krock on May 30, the president denied Krock's assertion that Eisenhower had endorsed the House bill in his May 16 letter to Vinson and then had reversed himself with the May 28 statement. Ike explained that the letter had been an attempt to win over Vinson by gentle persuasion, but when it had not worked he felt he had to make his true feelings known. Never again, he told Krock, would he make "the mistake of assuming that a polite indication of disagreement . . . can be interpreted as weakness in will."[25]

Now that the issue was out in the open, the president used all the weapons at his command. On May 27 he told the GOP leaders that he had "everyone working" on Congress. He had written letters to members of the Business Advisory Council and the U.S. Chamber of Commerce, asking prominent industrialists and corporate executives to pressure Congress. Expounding on the need to purge the bill of Vinson's changes, he vowed to "fight it every step of the way," in an effort to overcome "one man's arrogance and pride & egotism." In a Memorial Day speech to Medal of Honor winners in the White House rose garden, Ike explained his objections to the House bill and asked these heroes to join in his crusade against Congress. "We need a clean-cut bill that makes it possible to have a security that is not only sound and strong," the president declared, "but also leaves the country solvent."

Convinced he was locked in a personal struggle with Uncle Carl, Eisenhower decided to send a letter to every GOP member of the House stating why he objected to Vinson's changes and asking for what he called "solidarity of vote on this bipartisan issue." He even appealed to the House Democratic leader, John McCormack of Massachusetts. After Ike made his case for removing the three offending features from the pending bill, McCormack politely commented that he thought the president had a good chance of succeeding, but he refused to make any formal commitment. Bryce Harlow, who was present, recorded Eisenhower as saying that "he intended to do everything he properly could to garner support for his amendments." McCormack still refused to commit himself, commenting that "the President, in his opinion, ought to hold to his position."[26]

Despite his appeal to McCormack and his attempt to describe the issue as bipartisan in nature, the president was facing defeat in the heavily Democratic House. On the day before the vote was to be taken, he told GOP leaders that it came down to a matter of principle. Pledging never to compromise, he added, "If we have to abandon one single item of principle, as far as I'm concerned I'd rather veto and make it an election issue." But he seemed to realize that he faced failure, adding ruefully that there was "no use of me making another speech."

Ike was right. On June 11 the House voted along straight party lines to reject three amendments by Les Arends designed to strike Vinson's changes from the bill. By making it a partisan issue, Eisenhower had solidified Democratic support behind Vinson. The defeat was not only humiliating for the president but unnecessary. As McElroy and Harlow had pointed out, he had gained nearly all his major objectives. Vinson had simply insisted on a few face-saving changes that could have easily been altered in a conference committee after the Senate acted. But now even Senate action was in doubt as the Democrats vowed not to allow the president to win a political victory.[27]

III

The key figure in the Senate was an old adversary, Democratic Senator Stuart Symington of Missouri. Although he had been one of the most vocal critics of the administration in the wake of *Sputnik*, Symington was in fact sympathetic to the president's plans for defense reorganization. He had long felt that the secretary of defense should have greater authority over the individual services, and he had spoken in favor of the administration's proposal before the Coolidge committee. He thought Ike went "a little far" in proposing to give the secretary of defense "the complete power of the purse," but once the administration dropped that feature Symington agreed to support the effort to achieve "true unification of the services."[28]

Two liberal Democrats, Paul Douglas of Illinois and Mike Mansfield of Montana, tried to get Symington to lead the Democratic fight against the administration's plan in the Senate. Calling the House bill "a dangerous surrender of Congressional responsibilities established by the Constitution," they warned that Ike wanted to amend it to give even greater power to the secretary of defense. The result, they claimed, "would almost completely take away our Congressional authority to provide for the common defense."

Symington immediately rejected this advance and made it clear that he "strongly favored" the administration's effort to achieve a "long overdue reorganization of the Department of Defense." "I believe that prompt action to modernize our defense structure is vital to the security of the United States," he replied. Not content with this move, Symington then sent copies of his letter to Douglas and Mansfield to every member of the Senate. "I believe," Symington told his colleagues, that the president's "defense reorganization legislation is at least as important as any legislation which will come before the Congress during the present session." When the Senate Armed Services Committee began its hearings on this measure, Symington urged Chairman Richard Russell to include more witnesses favorable to the measure, notably Robert Lovett, Omar Bradley, and Nelson Rockefeller. He also consulted with Vinson and Lyndon Johnson, the Senate majority leader, to ensure that there would be room for compromise when the bill finally reached conference committee.[29]

Compromise was a word that now had a new appeal to Dwight Eisenhower. After a conference with the president on July 24, Bryce Harlow told Ann Whitman that "he now seems willing to accept the provisions that were branded as totally objectionable." In a meeting with GOP congressional leaders that same day, Ike agreed with Minority Leader William Knowland's assessment that it was "obvious we can't get all we want." In order to persuade the Senate to remove the service secretaries from the chain of command and to allow the secretary of defense to shift combat functions without a congressional veto,

Ike was now willing to give in on Vinson's third change, permitting members of the Joint Chiefs to give their independent views to Congress. "In this room," Ike finally admitted, "if we can get [the] first two straightened out, I'll take it." Although the president had earlier referred to the idea of the chiefs testifying against administration policy as "legalized insubordination," he was confident that he could control his own appointees. If not, he could always fire them!

The president confirmed the bargain that he had first outlined to the congressional leaders in a telephone conversation with Neil McElroy on June 30. Aware that the defense secretary had been sounding out Chairman Russell and other members of the Armed Services Committee, Ike told him to give in on the issue of the Joint Chiefs testifying independently to Congress in return for rejecting Vinson's changes on the other two matters in dispute. Moreover, in conducting these delicate negotiations with the Democratic senators, Eisenhower agreed that McElroy "could say that he has talked to the President about it." At the end of the call, Ike also asked McElroy to convey his personal thanks to Stuart Symington for his help.[30]

Meanwhile Eisenhower continued with his own lobbying efforts on behalf of the administration proposal. Acting on the advice of Bryce Harlow, he held private breakfast meetings with Styles Bridges, the ranking Republican member of the Armed Services Committee, something the president had never done before. Harlow informed Ike that "Bridges is susceptible to flattery, and that he is a walking 25 votes in the Senate, the most skilled maneuverer on the Republican side." Richard Russell and Lyndon Johnson regularly relied on him to deliver GOP votes on key measures; it was only fitting for Eisenhower to do the same thing.

The president succeeded in winning Bridges's support, but he had no luck when he tried to woo Russell. When he called the Georgia senator to ask for his help on the defense reorganization bill, Russell replied, "No soap." Saying that the bill was as good as it was going to get, Russell claimed he faced a tough fight, presumably with Vinson in the conference committee, over removing the service secretaries from the chain of command.[31]

Despite this setback, the Senate hearings went well as McElroy, Army Chief Maxwell Taylor, and Nathan Twining, chairman of the Joint Chiefs, all backed the bill strongly. Arleigh Burke, the chief of naval operations, created a problem, however, when he told the committee that he opposed removing the civilian secretaries from the chain of command and supported the congressional veto on the secretary of defense's power to transfer combat functions between the branches. Since these were the two points that Vinson had added and McElroy was trying to persuade Russell to drop, the secretary of defense chewed out Burke in public, calling his testimony "regrettable." Russell then came to Burke's defense, blasting McElroy as a "totalitarian" who wanted to muzzle his service chiefs. The defense secretary finally apologized to Russell, admitting that the administration had agreed to let the chiefs speak their minds to Congress. But he did reserve the right to voice his disappointment over the views they expressed.[32]

Although the senators and reporters focused on the question of the independence of the Joint Chiefs, the real issue at the hearings was control of the defense budget. McElroy stated clearly his conviction that the primary purpose of defense reorganization was to stop the waste involved in duplicate weapons programs, like the Thor and Jupiter IRBMs. What the administration wanted above all else was for Congress to "give the President's office more power to choose among the missiles." Ike felt even more strongly than McElroy that Congress should let the president decide issues of national security. Appalled when congressmen and senators voted funds for nine Polaris submarines, four more than the administration had requested, Ike burst out to McElroy that the Democrats were "apparently planning to 'kill every Russian three times' in the development of our forces for massive retaliation." Reiterating his distaste for the "duplication of weapons through the development stage," Ike made it clear that his greatest concern in fighting for Pentagon reform was "national solvency."[33]

Despite the fireworks at the Senate hearings, the committee quickly agreed to report the bill with one key amendment. The language relating to the role of the army, navy, and air force that Vinson had added was changed from "separately administered" to "separately organized," which had the effect of removing the three services from the chain of command. The secretary of defense, acting through the Joint Chiefs, could issue orders to combined commands throughout the world without consulting or working through the army, navy, and air force. In return, McElroy had to accept the congressional veto over the transfer of combat functions, such as the marines or naval aviation, as well as preserve the right of individual service chiefs to give their dissenting views to Congress. Eisenhower had already agreed to the latter point. He regarded the other concession, curbing the power of the secretary of defense to shift combat functions among the services, as of little consequence. In his memoirs he dismissed it as "a small hole in the doughnut."

Peace and harmony now reigned in place of discord. The Senate passed the revised bill unanimously. It took the feared conference committee only twenty-seven minutes to reconcile the differences between the House and Senate versions; Vinson went along gracefully with the compromise Russell and McElroy had worked out. The president was more than willing to bury the hatchet. When both houses passed the conference report, he expressed his satisfaction with the result, noting that "except in relatively minor respects, the bill adequately meets every recommendation I submitted to the Congress on this subject." He even had some kind words for Vinson and Russell, congratulating them for their contributions and lauding their committees for doing "a praiseworthy job on this important legislation."[34]

IV

When the president signed the bill into law on August 6, 1958, he called it "a major advance in our organization of defense." He was particularly pleased with the reform of the Joint Chiefs of Staff. Not only would this body now have direct command over American forces through the secretary of defense, but the legislation provided for the vice-chief of staff to take over responsibility for day-to-day oversight of each service, freeing the chief of each branch to devote himself to advising the secretary of defense and the president on national strategy. This was a step Eisenhower claimed he had been seeking for eleven years, ever since he had served as army chief of staff just after World War II. But as Lawrence Korb, the foremost historian of the Joint Chiefs, points out, it takes more than changes in organizational charts to alter bureaucratic behavior. "The problem of the service chief is not that he cannot divest himself of his service duties," Korb writes. "The real problem is that he does not want to." Men like Arleigh Burke and Maxwell Taylor would continue to place the interests of the navy and the army first; their primary loyalty was to the branch of service they represented, not to the president or the secretary of defense.[35]

In the long run, the most significant change achieved by the legislation was the one that had never been in dispute, creating the new post of director of defense research and engineering. What men as different in their approach to national security problems as Dwight Eisenhower and Stuart Symington agreed on was the need to stop the wasteful duplication in the development of new weapons. Interservice rivalry had transformed the missile race with the Russians into an expensive nightmare as each service sought to develop its own rockets without any consideration of an integrated national effort. Thus the navy advocated the Polaris, the army the Jupiter, and the air force the Thor, with each branch appealing to congressional allies for support.

Eisenhower had taken a vital first step to gain control over this process with his appointment of James Killian and the President's Science Advisory Committee. But Killian had too many responsibilities to play the role of missile czar. The selection of a distinguished scientist as director of defense research and engineering, with the same status as the service secretaries, gave promise of ending the interservice squabbling and allowing the Pentagon to control the evolution of new weapons in an orderly and coherent manner. As the editors of the nation's major scientific periodical noted, the new post "reflects the formal recognition of science's critical role in the military." They looked forward to the appointment of a director who would have "the position, the prestige and the explicit authority" to provide centralized management over the vital task of channeling the nation's scientific and technological resources to serve the goal of national security.[36]

In September Secretary McElroy began a three-month search for the right man to fill this critical position. Turned down by several leading candidates, McElroy finally settled on Herbert York, the chief scientist of the Pentagon's Advanced Research Projects Agency (ARPA). Well-qualified by experience as Edward Teller's right-hand man at the University of California's Livermore Laboratory and as a key member of Killian's Science Advisory Committee, York agreed to discuss the post with President Eisenhower just before Christmas 1958. When York commented on how long the post had been open, Ike said, "You were my choice from the beginning, but they [in the Pentagon] had wanted someone older and more distinguished." York was ready to accept the job, but he warned the president that GOP leaders might oppose his nomination since he was not a Republican. "I wish you were a young Republican," Ike confessed; "it would be easier." When York explained that both his wife and father were Republicans, Ike laughed and commented, "That's a new political concept, absolution by association."[37]

York proved to be an excellent choice, providing the central management needed in weapons development in the Pentagon. Indeed, Eisenhower was pleased with the overall outcome of his fight for defense reorganization, telling some of the business leaders whose help he had enlisted that the legislation adopted by Congress "assures a strong, more effective and more economical defense for our country."[38] But he also must have known that he had mismanaged what could have been a much smoother legislative process. His refusal to compromise with Carl Vinson at the outset had led to a humiliating defeat on the floor of the House and had allowed partisan wrangling to endanger a measure that commanded broad bipartisn support, as Symington proved in the Senate. The problem, uncharacteristically, was that Ike had become too personally involved, too passionate, and too emotional over an issue that required the patience, tact, and flexibility that usually marked Eisenhower's relations with Congress. The problem, one suspects, is that the president's own reputation as the nation's most distinguished military leader led him astray. Convinced that he knew far more than members of Congress about the requirements of national security, he became rigid and unbending when the situation called for moderation and conciliation. Fortunately, he finally realized the error of his ways and let Bryce Harlow and Neil McElroy work out a compromise with Congress that achieved his major goals with only minimal concessions to partisan pride.

CHAPTER NINE

On May 15, 1958, the Soviet Union launched *Sputnik III* into orbit around the earth. The third Soviet satellite was a huge, cone-shaped vehicle weighing one and a half tons that had been sent into space by a rocket with a thrust of over half a million pounds, a far more powerful booster than any under development in the United States. Unlike the earlier versions, *Sputnik III* carried a full array of scientific instruments designed to detect cosmic rays and measure the earth's atmosphere. Although the United States now had three satellites in orbit (two *Explorers* and one *Vanguard*), the sheer size of the *Sputnik III* enabled Nikita Khrushchev to remind the entire world of the continuing Soviet lead in space technology. The United States would need "very many satellites the size of oranges," he told Arab diplomats visiting Moscow, "in order to catch up with the Soviet Union."

The American people reacted calmly to the latest Russian feat. *Time* viewed it as "a stern warning that the U.S. must push harder on its own missile program," but the editors of *U.S. News & World Report* pointed out that the navy would launch a fourth American satellite soon, with eight more to follow before the end of 1958. Privately James Killian expressed surprise that the Russians had undertaken "a solid scientific effort instead of something spectacular like shooting the moon." He told the cabinet that the latest *Sputnik* proved the Soviets "were substantially ahead of us with delivery capability that we will not have until mid-1959." Under questioning by Eisenhower, Killian admitted that *Sputnik III* confirmed that the Russians had succeeded in miniaturizing their instruments and thus would be able to develop reconnaissance satellites.[1]

Critics continued to charge the Eisenhower administration with complacency in the face of the Soviet achievement. Pointing out that the Russians were launching satellites a hundred times heavier than American ones and that they were two to five years ahead of us, the *New Republic* claimed that the president appeared to "lack the interest to meet this crucial challenge." "What other nation in history," asked one of its columnists, "ever let its arms superiority lapse to an enemy so quietly and calmly?" Eisenhower tried to correct this impression, telling reporters that, even though we had started later than the Russians and were thus behind, we would soon have "all the engines of all the strength we shall need." The contrast between Soviet satellites two-thirds the size of an automobile sharing the heavens with American probes no larger than softballs gave these brave words a hollow ring.[2]

I

Consciousness of the continuing race with the Soviets served as a dramatic backdrop to the administration's efforts to persuade Congress to enact the space legislation submitted earlier in the spring. By May committees in both branches of Congress were busy revising the proposal to transform the obscure but respected National Advisory Committee for Aeronautics (NACA) into the National Aeronautics and Space Administration (NASA). Two related issues soon came to the fore in the legislative process. The first was the degree to which military programs in space would come under NASA control; the second focused on the size and power of the governing board of the new space agency.

The Senate committee, dominated by Lyndon Johnson, insisted on revising the administration's proposal to make clear that the Pentagon would be free to develop and control all military uses of space independently of the civilian agency. Roy Johnson, the director of the Advanced Research Projects Agency (ARPA), stated the Pentagon's concerns most forcefully in his testimony. He told the legislators that it would be "disastrous" if the military uses of space were limited by NASA. If, for example, the Defense Department felt it was desirable to put a man into space, "it should not have to justify this activity to a civilian agency." He was even more blunt in responding to a question by Senator Johnson on the rationale for all space activity. National policy could not be based on "space for peace or space for fun," Roy Johnson answered, but rather had to be "set up with a military connotation."[3]

Eisenhower was furious with Johnson for his testimony to Congress. He reminded General Nathan Twining, chairman of the Joint Chiefs, that "Secretary McElroy and the scientists had agreed with him" on the wisdom of assigning all space activities except military applications to a civilian agency. When Ike complained to the secretary of defense that the ARPA director was "publicly opposing the President on this issue," McElroy said he had talked to Johnson and gotten him to agree to the administration's position. Johnson's insubordination, however, proved effective. The Senate Republican leaders told the president that the legislation would have to be amended to give the Pentagon the freedom to pursue its own space activities independently of NASA.[4]

The division of authority between ARPA and NASA made the question of who would determine space policy crucial. The House committee favored the administration's plan, which called for a seventeen-member advisory panel to guide the director of NASA; the Senate preferred a smaller board, which would be charged with framing an overall national space policy. Beyond the question of the size and authority of the governing committee for NASA lay the question of who would actually decide which projects were military and which ones were civilian in nature—NASA, the Pentagon, or the president himself.

In mid-May Eisenhower sought to resolve these issues by making a few key changes in the proposed legislation. While still affirming that American activity in "outer space be devoted to peaceful and scientific purposes," the president approved changes in wording to make it clear that the activities "peculiar to or primarily associated with weapons or military operations will be the responsibility of the Department of Defense." He still clung to the original concept of a seventeen-member advisory board but now specified that at least three of the seats be filled with Pentagon officials. Finally, in case of conflict over whether a space project was essentially civilian or military in nature, the president himself would make that decision.[5]

Despite the president's efforts at compromise, the House and the Senate proceeded to pass bills creating two very different versions of NASA. The House measure, adopted unanimously after only a two-hour debate on June 2, continued to emphasize civilian control over the nation's space program and limited the military's role sharply. It also followed the original administration position in calling for a strong director who would report directly to the president, using the seventeen-member board purely as an advisory body. Finally, to avoid intergovernmental conflict, the House bill provided for two liaison committees to coordinate space policy with the Pentagon and the Atomic Energy Commission.

In contrast, the Senate measure, which also was adopted unanimously, exempted all space activities related to weapons and military applications from NASA's authority and insisted on a smaller, seven-member policy board charged with overseeing all aspects of the nation's ventures into outer space. In an accompanying report, the Senate committee warned that giving NASA power over military projects could lead to "great mischief." The justification for the policy board stressed the need to provide for coordination between the two separate aspects of space activity provided in the Senate version, civilian and military. The Senate report argued that "any differences arising among the agencies concerned in the course of the execution of their functions must be established at a governmental level higher than that occupied by any of those operational agencies."[6]

It was precisely this effort to impose a high-level body between the head of NASA and the president that disturbed Killian and other advocates of civilian control within the Eisenhower administration. Killian felt that such an arrangement would leave the NASA administrator in a weak position and encourage "interdepartmental logrolling." Few first-rate scientists would want to work under such conditions, and thus he felt "it would be better to have no agency at all and no board rather than to have this combination." The president was equally concerned at what he saw as a congressional attempt to undercut his authority. He told his aides that it would be a "tragedy" if the president did not have the power "to decide who handles what subject." Eisenhower also opposed the liaison committees proposed in the House measure and wanted to remove clauses in both bills that denied him the authority to transfer space activities between the Pentagon and NASA without prior approval by Congress.[7]

The fate of NASA now resided with a conference committee steered by the two Democratic legislative leaders, Senator Lyndon Johnson and Representative John McCormack. The administration sought to bolster the House position, despite its objection to the liaison committees. Eisenhower met with Majority Leader McCormack to affirm his support for the House version, and both men agreed that "civilian control over outer space is essential." Senator Johnson was equally determined that the upper chamber's insistence on a separate military role in space and a high-level policy board should prevail. LBJ lobbied other Democrats on the need to preserve a "clear distinction" between civilian and military space activities, asking Stuart Symington to try to persuade James Doolittle of the need to limit NASA's control over the military. The conference committee became deadlocked as members of both branches refused to give way.[8]

The president finally broke the stalemate by inviting Senator Johnson to meet with him privately at the White House. LBJ slipped into the Oval Office on Monday evening, July 7, and in a few minutes he and the president reached agreement. The president would accept the Senate's policy board, rechristened the Space Council, but only if it were modeled after the National Security Council, with the president as chairman. LBJ agreed to this arrangement, provided that the Space Council was expanded to nine members, with three to be from outside the government. The conference bill would embody the Senate measure's language on exempting military space ventures from NASA control and would give the president the power to transfer space projects between government agencies without congressional approval prior to December 31, 1958. Despite the fact that he had to surrender on the seventeen-man advisory board, Eisenhower was pleased with the bargain he struck with LBJ, telling an aide that "his conversation with Senator Johnson was very satisfactory."9

Once the principals had reached consensus, the conference committee acted quickly. Meeting briefly on July 15, the members approved a measure that gave NASA control over "aeronautics and space activities sponsored by the U.S. except that activities peculiar to or primarily associated with the development of weapons systems, military operations or the defense of the U.S." should be the responsibility of the Department of Defense. The bill provided for a nine-member National Aeronautics and Space Council composed of the president as chairman, the secretaries of State and Defense, the chairman of the AEC, the NASA administrator, one other government official, and three private citizens. As finally written, the measure dropped the House proposal to coordinate with the AEC but provided for a civilian-military liaison committee to try to work out any conflicts between NASA and the Pentagon at a low level. It was clear, however, that in cases of continuing disagreement, only the president could decide which body would have jurisdiction.10

Eisenhower was content with the outcome, expressing agreement when Killian called the congressional action "acceptable." The president indicated that he planned to give NASA control over all nonmilitary space ventures as well as anything "not yet proved as to technical feasibility." He instructed Killian to work out the actual transfer of space projects from ARPA to NASA, specifically telling him to deal only with the Pentagon and not with the individual armed services. As for the Space Council, Eisenhower made it clear that he had no intention of convening this body regularly, nor of acting as its presiding officer. He refused to use his discretionary power to appoint an executive secretary or create a separate staff for the Space Council, and he asked Killian to preside at its infrequent meetings. Lyndon Johnson may have forced Eisenhower to accept the Space Council as his price for creating NASA, but the president would make sure it would remain a minor body that would never threaten his full control over the nation's space policy.11

President Eisenhower had every right to take satisfaction in the final shape of the space legislation. He had proved far more skillful at parliamentary maneuvering than on defense reorganization, playing off the House against the Senate to get a measure that delegated surprisingly broad powers to the president in this new field.

What is even more surprising, however, is how little attention the American people seemed to pay to the creation of NASA. Both *Time* and *U.S. News & World Report* commented on the lack of fanfare for the final passage of the legislation, a striking contrast to the public uproar over *Sputnik* just a few months earlier. Eisenhower contented himself with a brief statement at the signing ceremony, calling the measure "an historic step, further equipping the United States for leadership in the space age." It was Lyndon Johnson, even though outmaneuvered on NASA, who put its creation in the broadest perspective. "In the long view of history," he told the Senate, "possibly the most important step we took during this session was to establish an agency to guide America's effort in the exploration of space."[12]

II

Congressional approval of NASA did not end the bureaucratic struggle for control of the nation's space efforts. Jim Killian now had to carry out Eisenhower's difficult mandate to divide the existing programs between the Pentagon and NASA. As in all intergovernmental quarrels, it finally came down to a question of money.

A three-cornered fight over space funding began in early July, while Congress was still debating the legislation creating NASA. On July 2 Killian convened an informal space panel consisting of representatives of NACA, including its director, Hugh Dryden, ARPA, notably Roy Johnson and Herbert York, and of the Bureau of the Budget (BOB), led by Maurice Stans. Although the administration originally had planned to allocate only $200 million for space ventures in 1959, it soon became clear that the interested parties wanted at least twice that amount. The result was a fierce round of bureaucratic infighting.

Hugh Dryden presented NACA's estimate of what NASA would need in its first year. The total, $259 million, included large sums for administering NACA's existing aeronautical laboratories as well as for such new responsibilities as "space science" and "man-in-space." NACA hoped that much of this money could be transferred from space funds previously assigned to ARPA.

Herbert York quickly dashed these hopes. In presenting the ARPA request, he asked for $169 million in space spending for the Pentagon agency, including $48 million for "man-in-space." Of this sum, York proposed transferring only $16 million to NASA. When Killian's aide suggested shifting the entire $169 million to NASA, York claimed that this would still necessitate asking Congress for an additional $130 million to fund a total space budget of $300 million.

Maurice Stans quickly brought the space enthusiasts back to earth. Pointing out that the administration faced a $10 billion deficit in 1959 as a result of the recession, Stans advocated that 1959 space spending be held to no more than $250 million ($50 million more than originally projected) and that as much of this sum as possible be transferred from money already appropriated to the Department of Defense. In addition to ARPA funds, Stans pointed to another $70 million allocated to the air force for space programs as fair game for NASA funding. He felt the greatest problem lay with the false expectations that members of the administration were raising in the public mind. "In particular," he argued, "it will be necessary to assure that future public statements avoid claiming more than can be accomplished."[13]

The budget director's blunt words forced the other members of the space panel to begin taking a more realistic look at the components of the space program. Three issues came to dominate their deliberations as they sought to bring their preliminary figures into line with budgetary reality.

The question of who would be in charge of manned space flight was the most hotly debated issue. ARPA, led by the aggressive Roy Johnson, staked its claim strongly. The agency asserted that its man-in-space program was closely linked to the development of reconnaissance satellites and that it had to guard against the possibility that the Russians would perfect an orbiting bombardment system. But its strongest argument was tactical: Deputy Secretary of Defense Donald Quarles claimed that Congress was much more likely to appropriate money for manned space flight to the military than to a civilian agency.

NACA fought back by pointing out that manned space flight would be the touchstone of the nation's space program. The president had already declared that U.S. ventures beyond the atmosphere "should be devoted to peaceful purposes for the benefit of all mankind." In its early stages, manned flight would be primarily a research program to determine "man's basic capability in a space environment as a prelude to the human exploration of space and to possible military applications of manned satellites." Dryden pointed to the success of NACA's direction of the X-15 program and its proven record of close cooperation with the military.[14]

Dryden gained support from two key sources. Robert Piland, Killian's deputy, quickly backed NACA's position, claiming that it would be far better for public relations to have a civilian agency exploring outer space. Arguing far more eloquently than Dryden, Piland said it would set a bad precedent to have the military in charge of space exploration when the ultimate goal was to impress mankind with a flight to the moon. Equally important, Maurice Stans weighed in on the side of NASA, claiming that any attempt to impress Congress by stressing the security aspect of space exploration would be "stretching the facts."

In desperation Quarles finally suggested that any final decision on who would be in charge of manned space programs be deferred. In the short run, each agency could pursue those aspects best suited to its resources. Despite strong objections from both ARPA and NACA spokesmen, Piland accepted this solution. He advised Killian to let NASA design the capsule for manned flight and ARPA the rocket boosters. As the program developed, it would then be easier to decide which agency would have the final responsibility for putting astronauts into space. Killian quickly accepted this shrewd compromise.[15]

The possible transfer of two key Pentagon agencies involved in space research proved less difficult to resolve. Although the navy was willing to give up supervision of the Vanguard scientific satellite program to NASA, the army wanted to retain Wernher Von Braun's Army Ballistic Missile Agency (ABMA), which had launched *Explorer I*, America's first satellite, in Huntsville. NASA was more interested in acquiring another army asset, the Jet Propulsion Laboratory at Cal Tech. Since its director expressed a desire for a transfer to NASA so that his institution could become known as "the national space laboratory," it was agreed that the army would retain control over ABMA for the time being, while NASA would take over the Jet Propulsion Laboratory before the end of 1958.[16]

The final issue that came up during the budget negotiations was the size and nature of WS-117L, the secret reconnaissance satellite program directed by ARPA. Killian made it clear from the outset that this project, which Eisenhower had given the highest priority throughout the *Sputnik* crisis, was not a candidate for either transfer to NASA or budgetary cuts. During the discussions, however, a number of scientists objected to the huge budget for WS-117L, $186 million in 1959, more than the rest of the ARPA space budget and nearly as much as NASA was requesting. In particular, civilian specialists questioned the fact that twenty-seven of the sixty space vehicles included in the 1959 budget were for the reconnaisance satellite program. Herbert York promised to review these figures, but Killian refused to make any changes in the WS-117L budget, simply adding its $186 billion to the sums finally agreed upon for NASA and ARPA for 1959.[17]

By mid-July representatives of NASA and ARPA had reached rough agreement on a budget and now joined together to persuade Maurice Stans to grant new money for space in 1959. They worked out three possible combined space budgets, ranging from as low as $240 million, BOB's target, to as high as $400 million, close to what the two agencies had originally requested. Piland reported to Killian that $240 million "is considered completely inadequate by the agencies concerned." When Stans raised the figure to $290 million, Killian argued that $325 would be a "rock bottom" budget. As ARPA and NASA struggled to cut their joint requests down from $400 million to $325 million, Killian finally reached agreement with Stans on July 28 on the sum of $350 million for the combined space effort.[18]

The space budget was a genuine compromise. ARPA retained $108 million for space activities other than WS-117L, with NASA gaining $117 million from ARPA and the air force, along with $125 million in new funds. The total space budget, including the sacrosanct reconnaissance satellite project, came to $536 million (see Table 4). Maurice Stans described this figure to President Eisenhower as "a very

TABLE 4: Space Budget for Fiscal 1959

Original Request		Final Allocation
$259 million	NASA	$240 million
169 "	ARPA	110 "
186 "	WS-117L	186 "
614 "	Total	536 "

large sum for outer space activities" and added that "it will have substantial implications as to the future level of authorizations." His only hope was that the ARPA portion would decline as the years went by and that NASA's share would not "grow too rapidly."

For Dwight Eisenhower the outcome was quite satisfactory. At his insistence, WS-117L escaped intact. The president still believed that satellite reconnaissance was by far the most important military consequence of the space age, and he was determined to try to have American spy satellites replace the vulnerable and political sensitive U-2 as soon as possible. While he was sympathetic to the BOB's efforts to hold the line on space funding, he recognized the political importance of giving NASA enough resources to satisfy the national desire to beat the Russians in space. But at the same time, he insisted on avoiding what he termed "hysterically devised crash programs and propaganda stunts" and was especially pleased with the conservative division of the man-in-space program between ARPA and NASA.[19]

The individual most effective in the entire process proved to be James Killian. Working quietly behind the scenes, Killian showed himself adept in both scientific administration and bureaucratic maneuvering. From the outset he had used PSAC to frame a carefully crafted and scientifically oriented space policy. Relying on the advice of the nation's foremost scientists, he had protected the administration from congressional pressure for a space race with the Soviets and had skillfully led the effort to have NASA, a civilian agency, take control from the Pentagon's ARPA. And in the final budgetary bargaining he had proved masterful, making sure that NASA was funded well enough to design an intelligent space effort but not so lavishly as to encourage wasteful spending on space spectaculars.

The quiet man from MIT had thus emerged in only six months' time as Eisenhower's key post-*Sputnik* adviser. He had established close ties between the administration and many of the prominent scientists who had been alienated earlier in the decade by the Oppenheimer affair. Yet at the same time, he made sure that the PSAC panels were strictly apolitical, choosing scientists for the quality of their advice, not for their ideological positions. His standing instruction to the scientists he consulted was "never, never to let political viewpoints influence scientific judgments." Most impressive of all, he had won the complete confidence of the man who mattered most, the president. "Let's see what Jim thinks about this" became a familiar refrain in the Oval Office whenever an issue involving scientific or technical matters was involved. In his service as the midwife to NASA, Jim Killian proved once again that Eisenhower had picked the right man for the job of scientific adviser to the president.[20]

II

The creation of NASA was the highlight of a summer that witnessed a number of significant developments in American space policy. By the end of August, the administration had chosen a new director for NASA, decided on which agency would supervise manned space flight, adopted a broad statement of space policy, and achieved a mixed record in its continuing efforts to match the Soviet feats in space.

Eisenhower once again relied on Killian to help him select the right person to head NASA. Their first choice was James Doolittle, the chairman of NACA's advisory board. The World War II hero at first politely rebuffed Killian's overtures. When Killian continued to press, Doolittle finally agreed to take on the job for a year or two, but only if the president made it a personal request, something Ike declined to do. Hugh Dryden, the NACA administrator, seemed like a good second choice, but the president was unenthusiastic, and congressional leaders thought Dryden was too cautious and conservative in his approach to space issues.

Killian finally settled on T. Keith Glennan, the president of Case Institute of Technology in Cleveland. Glennan had many advantages: He was a distinguished engineer, an experienced administrator who had served on the Atomic Energy Commission, and a lifelong Republican. After meeting with the president, who expressed little concern over Soviet space advances and said he wanted NASA to pursue a program that was "sensibly paced and prosecuted vigorously," Glennan accepted the position on the condition that Dryden serve as his deputy. The two men formed a good team for the new agency, with Glennan concentrating on policy issues and Dryden on the technical aspects of the space program.[21]

Eisenhower made their task easier by taking an important political decision before NASA formally came into being. The issue of who would supervise the manned space program still remained unresolved, though both Killian and Dryden were pressing the case for NASA hard. Despite several ambitious man-in-space projects pushed by the separate services, the Pentagon gave way gracefully when Eisenhower decided in mid-August to give NASA overall control of manned space flight. ARPA would still be responsible for providing the boosters, which had to come from the Atlas and Titan ICBM efforts. The Pentagon designated the funds allocated for manned space flight as the lion's share of the $117 million it transferred to NASA. Project Mercury, an outgrowth of NACA research, would thus become the focus of national attention as NASA's effort to send a man into space ahead of the Soviet Union.[22]

At the same time, the National Security Council adopted a broad statement of national space policy, NSC 5814. At the request of the Joint Chiefs of Staff, this document omitted any reference to military missiles and placed the emphasis on the scientific rather than the military aspects of space. Thus the introduction spoke of the need to deny the Soviet's superiority in space, which could be used "as a means of undermining the prestige and leadership of the United States," NSC 5814 expressed a contradictory desire: American leadership in space exploration for peaceful purposes to enhance the nation's world prestige, and reconnaissance capabilities free from international control or oversight. "Space for peace" had to coexist with "space for security," and, despite all the rhetoric about openness and international cooperation in exploring the heavens, the Eisenhower administration gave the quest for a spy satellite to replace the U-2 highest priority.[23]

NSC 5814 was secret, as was WS-117L, the reconnaissance satellite that received more funds than any other space program. Public attention continued to focus instead on the scientific satellites, *Vanguard* and *Explorer*. The navy had more bad luck. In June two rockets failed to put *Vanguard* satellites into orbit; after four attempts only one sophisticated *Vanguard* was sending signals back to earth. Wernher Von Braun's army team had greater success, however. On July 6 they launched the heaviest American satellite yet, *Explorer III*, weighing 38.43 pounds and carrying a battery of instruments designed to measure cosmic radiation. Using a new solid-fuel rocket perfected by the Jet Propulsion Laboratory, *Explorer III* followed an elliptical orbit that took it over the Soviet Union. By August Killian could report to President Eisenhower that the four American satellites circling the globe were sending back vital information about radiation extending more than six hundred miles out into space, thereby confirming the existence of the Van Allen belts.[24]

For the American people, however, these scientific achievements paled beside the question of who would get to the moon first, the United States or the Soviet Union. Although ARPA had made a guarded announcement in March about future moon shots by the army and the air force, the administration tried its best to avoid raising false expectations. When General Samuel E. Anderson announced in June that the air force would launch the first of its three lunar probes in August, ARPA director Roy Johnson immediately silenced him.

The editors of the *Nation* approved of this action, asking rhetorically, "What, if anything, can be done to make general officers realize that in the technological contest between the Great Powers, one does the thing first and talks about it afterwards?"[25]

Eisenhower was in full agreement. After Army Secretary Wilber Brucker made a public reference in early July to forthcoming army "moon shots," the president called in Andrew Goodpaster to say he took "strong exception" to Brucker's remarks. He made it clear that he wanted the Pentagon to play down the lunar probes in advance, and he insisted that only ARPA was authorized to release information about such projects. Goodpaster conveyed Ike's wishes to Brucker and also spoke to Secretary of Defense McElroy, who assured him that "he would take steps to see that the matter was made crystal clear to the top officials of the services."

The press, however, continued to run stories about the forthcoming moon shots, citing one general as saying the plans were so secret that they never even used the word *moon* in the Pentagon. In early August, *U.S. News & World Report* reported that the air force was planning to fire a rocket in an attempt to put a radio transmitter into orbit around the moon. Although admitting the Russians were also preparing a lunar probe, the story claimed that "U.S. experts were confident last week that the U.S. would be the first to 'shoot the moon.'"[26]

By mid-August, despite administration efforts at secrecy, more than three hundred reporters had converged on Cape Canaveral to witness the launch of the first moon probe. Dreading what might happen, the president told the cabinet that he hoped it would be "nothing like [the] first Vanguard." Unfortunately, it proved to be little better. The first lunar rocket blew up in the sky just seventy-seven seconds after take-off. The administration had tried hard to play down the significance of this first moon shot; as Roy Johnson informed Killian, it was following a "deliberate program to create the feeling in America that space programs are experimental and that many failures will accompany each success." Nevertheless, the American people, who had been subjected to headlines like "U.S. FORGING AHEAD IN SATELLITES" and "WOULD AMERICA BEAT RUSSIA TO THE MOON?" were very disappointed.[27]

Some responded by questioning the whole concept of a space race with the Soviet Union. Former Secretary of Defense Charles Wilson commented, "Maybe I'm old and not as curious as I was, but I think the other side of the moon is much like this one." After all, he went on, it was just a case of competition "between two bunches of German scientists, those with the Russians and those with us." But for most Americans the race to reach the moon before the Soviets was a vital concern. In creating NASA and planning a manned space program, the Eisenhower administration was trying to meet the public's wishes without going to extremes. Killian and the president realized how much the American people wanted to be first in space. An advertisement for North American Aviation perhaps best captured the national feeling that they could not ignore: "The day an American returns from outer space will be another V-Day for the free world—greater perhaps than any it has yet known."[28]

CHAPTER TEN

The creation of NASA left education as the last remaining legislative issue stemming from the *Sputnik* crisis. In his special message to Congress on January 28, 1958, President Eisenhower had outlined a very limited program of federal aid to education. The chief features were ten thousand scholarships a year over a four-year period to encourage gifted high school graduates to attend college, graduate fellowships in science, engineering, and foreign language to develop more teachers in those fields, and matching grants to the states to improve the quality of math and science teaching. When critics pointed out how modest these recommendations were in view of the crisis in education, the president made clear his belief that the primary reponsibility lay with local and state officials, not the federal government. If Washington took over the schools, he responded, then the nation would "have lost a very great and vital feature of our whole free system."[1]

The Democrats, who controlled both the House and Senate, responded with bills calling for much larger numbers and heavier federal expenditures than Ike thought prudent. Sponsored by Senator Lister Hill and Representative Carl Elliott, both of Alabama, the opposition measure called for forty thousand college scholarships annually for six years, along with an additional fund to provide loans up to $1,000 a year to college students. At $1,000 a year, the 240,000 scholarships alone would cost more than the $1 billion ceiling the president had placed on the HEW proposal. Moreover, the Democratic plan went beyond the simple appeal to national defense to state the goal of assuring "the intellectual preeminence of the United States, especially in science and technology." Accordingly, it based scholarships on merit rather than need, in the belief that the nation had to do all it could to advance the education of its most talented youth.[2]

Eisenhower was in no mood to compromise on either the number of scholarships or the nature of the program. As he saw it, the only reason for the federal government to pay college costs was "to help the good student who otherwise wouldn't get an education." He wanted a program based solely on need and clearly temporary. The Democratic plan appeared to him to be the beginning of a permanent federal commitment to financing education, rather than a measure designed to meet a crisis situation. HEW Secretary Marion Folsom argued that Hill and Elliott were simply engaging in legislative bargaining, asking for a lot more in the beginning than they expected to get. The president stressed to Folsom, who would soon leave the cabinet due to ill health, that "you ought not indicate any readiness to compromise."

Eisenhower was equally adamant on the loan issue. When Folsom said this approach had considerable support in Congress, Ike expressed his own doubts, citing the bad experience he had had with loans to medical students at Columbia University. When James Killian offered contrary evidence from his MIT presidency, Eisenhower agreed to withhold judgment on this issue. He made it clear, however, that whatever the final shape of the program, he would insist that students receiving federal help "would have to maintain high quality work" or lose their funding.[3]

By June the president was determined to stand firm behind his education proposals. After a conference with Folsom, Killian, and key White House aides, he insisted that administration spokesmen oppose the loan proposal in the Democratic bill, block any effort to increase the number of scholarships beyond ten thousand a year, and reject any provision that would remove the means test for a scholarship. Eisenhower felt most strongly about the last point, telling the group that "the real purpose behind legislation such as this is preventing the loss of a student with real ability, one who would not get an education without this help."

The president was skeptical about the whole idea of federal aid to education. Under the pressure from Congress and public opinion in the wake of *Sputnik,* he was willing to accept a modest program of federal support, but only if it were temporary and limited in both size and cost. He really believed that education was primarily a local responsibility. When he met with a group from Huron, Ohio, who had developed a community program relying on their own resources, he was ecstatic. The Huron experience, he told former Harvard President James Conant, was "an excellent example of what a community *can* do itself, on its own initiative." "And the crowning achievement," he continued, "was when the salary of the science teacher was raised to equal that of the football coach."[4]

I

The legislative impasse between Congress and the president coincided with a drop in public interest in the education crisis. The launching of *Explorer II* on January 31 reassured those who had been worried about the United States falling behind the Soviet Union in science and technology. *Life* magazine punctured this mood of complacency and reawakened concern over the state of American education with a five-part series in March and April of 1958.[5]

The most influential weekly magazine in the country, *Life* entitled its picture essays and accompanying editorials "The Crisis in Education." The editors made no effort to hide their concern. "The schools are in terrible shape," they claimed. "What has long been an ignored national problem, Sputnik has made a recognized crisis." The pictures and the accompanying text hit at specifics—overcrowded schools, underpaid teachers, easy courses. Pointing to the lack of agreement on a national curriculum, *Life* commented, "Most appalling, the standards of education are shockingly low."

Three themes ran through the installments: a comparison with Soviet education, the neglect of the gifted, and the need for greater stress on science and technology. Soviet high school students received far better training in math and science than did American youth and thus were two years further along in their studies by the time they entered college. At the same time, American schools neglected the academically gifted, thus allowing "the geniuses of the next decades" to "slip back into mediocrity." Worst of all was the failure to prepare American students for "the technicalities of the Space Age." "Space ships and intercontinental missiles were not invented by self-educated men in home workshops," wrote novelist Sloan Wilson in one of the editorials. "They are developed by teams of highly trained scientists, most of whom begin (and get much of) their education in the public schools."

The editors of *Life* made it clear who was to blame—the "educationalists" who placed life adjustment ahead of learning. The followers of John Dewey had created schools with too many electives and too many extracurricular activities. Instead of "coddling and entertaining the mediocre," it was time to "recapture an honest respect for learning and for learned people." They even found a few bright spots in this generally dim picture, praising innovations in the teaching of math and science that stressed basic principles rather than rote memorization. The editors spoke highly of James Conant's study of American high schools and the new physics course pioneered at MIT with the help of the National Science Foundation. But truly effective educational reform could only come, they concluded, at the grass roots, when concerned citizens became involved in the revitalization of the nation's schools.[6]

The president was in full agreement with *Life*'s approach. In a letter to Time-Life executive and sometime White House speechwriter Emmet Hughes, Eisenhower expressed his thanks by saying, "Educators, parents and students alike must be continuously stirred up by the defects in our educational system." Convinced that federal funding alone was not the answer, Ike emphasized the need for "a return to fundamentals in both high schools and indeed in the higher grades of the elementary schools." "We should stress English, history, mathematics, the simple rudiments of one or more of the sciences, and at least one language," he concluded. In what she described in her diary as this "wonderful letter," Ann Whitman noted Ike's belief that *Life* had captured the essence of the educational crisis by its insistence that the nation "get away from the John Dewey frills."[7]

The *Life* series touched off a lively debate over American education in the spring of 1958. Critics of the educational system such as Arthur Bestor and Hyman Rickover repeated their pleas for more emphasis on the basics before national audiences. Attacking progressive education, Rickover urged that schools "concentrate on what is properly their function—the education of young minds." Writer John Keats echoed the same themes in calling for the creation of "citizens' grand juries" to insist on curriculum reform at the local level. Even professional educators joined in the chorus. A Gallup poll showed that 90 percent of the nation's principals, compared with only 51 percent of the parents, felt that their schools were not demanding enough from students, and more than half were already taking steps to strengthen the curriculum.[8]

The comparison of Russian and American schools continued to attract great attention. Educators who returned from tours of the Soviet Union gave glowing accounts of the Russian schools. Alvin C. Eurich called Soviet education "exceedingly impressive" and noted that the system turned out more than twice as many scientists and engineers as did American schools. The U.S. Commissioner of Education, Lawrence G. Derthwick, after a government tour of Soviet schools, lectured a national radio audience about the amazing degree of Russian commitment to education "as a means of national advancement." Such statements alarmed humanists like Pulitzer Prize–winning poet Karl Shapiro, who warned against "the Russian Revolution in American education." Pleading the case for resisting a misplaced emphasis on science and mathematics, Shapiro feared that *Sputnik* would lead to "the brutalization of our people by science hysteria, by politics, and by promises of technological rewards."[9]

A special report on education by the Rockefeller Brothers Fund tried to strike a more balanced note. It was issued in late June by a panel on which James Gardner of the Carnegie Corporation had replaced James Killian as Chairman. The fundamental theme was the pursuit of excellence in all fields of knowledge and human endeavor.

While calling for the training of more scientists and engineers and for special programs for the gifted, the Rockefeller report stressed the need for diversity in both the curriculum and in society as a whole. "Our conception of excellence," the report stressed, "must embrace many kinds of achievement at many levels." The panel called for a doubling of spending on public education, with the federal government to play a new but limited role in providing the additional resources. The real challenge, it concluded, was to make "intellectual excellence" the overriding goal of the American educational system.[10]

James Killian agreed with the broad conclusions of the Rockefeller report and tried to have the President's Science Advisory Committee play a constructive role in the debate over the nation's education policy. In March 1958 he created a PSAC education panel headed by Lee DuBridge, president of Cal Tech. Killian charged this body with two tasks: advising PSAC on the current education legislation before Congress, and drafting a report on the future of American education. The focus of this document, Killian suggested, should be on the "need to create higher national standards and greater quality in education."

Killian felt it was vital to use the *Sputnik* crisis to work for broad reform of American schools rather than simply improve education in science and technology. When an engineering dean wrote to request federal aid to produce more engineers as well as scientists, the president's science adviser opposed such a piecemeal approach. "Science and technology will be strengthed if our overall education is strengthened," he replied, "but I also feel that a sustained effort to modernize science and engineering education can serve to lift the level of all education, as indeed it must." He stressed the same point in a speech in March, saying, "If we are to have better science education, we must have better overall education."[11]

The members of the PSAC education panel agreed. In their discussions they spoke of the need to use the current sense of crisis to achieve long-overdue reforms in American education as a whole. They wanted science to "lead the way in strengthening other parts of the curriculum," and they especially saw a need to increase scientific literacy so that the American people would be better able to deal with "the great issues of our time arising out of science." The key problem, they agreed, was how to identify and assist the intellectually gifted without neglecting the needs of all students. The education panel opposed separate schools for those with "high talent" but favored special courses and programs for such individuals. The most important point, they stressed, was that "the government be prepared to assure the education of the most talented students."

One point that troubled Killian was the panel's insistence that it should set national standards to help schools across the country improve the quality of their curricula. While Killian agreed this was an important concern, he soon realized that it would bring PSAC into conflict with local school officials who resented the idea of Washington imposing criteria on their districts. The administration draft of education legislation had included a section on national standards for secondary and primary education, but Killian decided to drop this feature in June when congressional leaders persuaded him that there was "little public expression of interest in the question of standards."[12]

Realizing the need for legislative compromise, Killian decided to have the education panel concentrate on developing a "white paper" that would deal with such topics as identifying and supporting "intellectual giftedness" and setting forth national standards for the schools to adopt. The white paper would take months to complete (the report did not finally appear until the spring of 1959) and thus would keep the PSAC panel occupied while the administration made the best possible bargain with Congress on school legislation. This approach avoided the dilemma noted by one member of the education panel—how to write a report "which is critical, but which enlists the support of the public school people."[13]

II

The logjam in Congress over education legislation began to break up in early July. Chairman Carl Elliott of the House Education and Labor Committee abandoned the original Hill-Elliott measure and worked closely with HEW in fashioning a bill designed to meet Eisenhower's limited objectives. On July 2 the House committee reported out the amended bill. In addition to relatively noncontroversial features including graduate fellowships and aid to local schools for the teaching of science and math, the measure proposed up to twenty-three thousand college scholarships a year for four years, along with an additional loan fund.

At his press conference that day, Eisenhower avoided any direct comment on the terms of the legislation. He made it clear, however, that he had "very definite ideas" about school reform and that the administration's proposals were the result of long consultations "with every educational authority we could think of." He admitted that years of neglect had created a need for governmental action, but he did not favor "any more federal interference or control or participation than is necessary," reiterating his fundamental belief that "the educational process should be carried on in the locality."[14]

At a meeting later on July 2 with a group of congressmen from the House committee, the president spelled out his reservations. He was willing to accept the loan fund he had opposed earlier, but only if the number of scholarships were reduced and the loans required "high scholastic competence and good standing." He was still adamant that the scholarship program be based on the need of the applicants, not on the principle of identifying and rewarding the most promising high school graduates. "The President," the notes of this meeting recorded, "felt Federal money should not be paid to a student who did not actually need it."

Representative Stuyvesant Wainwright, a New York Republican who had opposed federal aid to education in the past, wrote to Eisenhower asking him to endorse the House bill. He pointed out that the measure reflected the president's preference for "state and local participation and administration of the proposed programs" and said the loan provision "conforms to your philosophy of 'God helps those who help themselves.'" Eisenhower replied in a public letter giving qualified support for limited federal action "to help meet emergency needs in American education" but also stressing his belief that the number of scholarships should be reduced from twenty-three thousand to ten thousand a year and be restricted to qualified students who "need financial help in order to get a college education."[15]

In meetings with Republican congressional leaders later in July, Eisenhower revealed his willingness to challenge more conservative members of his own party who opposed all federal aid to education. When Representatives Charles Halleck of Indiana and Ralph W. Gwinn of New York voiced their objections to using federal money to fund college scholarships, the president countered that there was a genuine national emergency that called for the training of more scientists and engineers. Killian came to his support, citing estimates that as many as one hundred thousand of the top 25 percent of high school graduates did not go on to college. Finances held many back, and thus, he argued, it was vital to offer federal aid to help these bright students fulfill their potential. Eisenhower added that he regretted we had to spend so much on "negative" things like B-52s; here was a chance to support something much more "constructive."

By the end of July, it was clear that the president had full control over the fate of education legislation. Given the strong opposition of many conservatives in both political parties, any chance to enact federal aid depended on his strong support. And Eisenhower made it abundantly clear that he would insist on limiting the number of scholarships to ten thousand annually over a four-year period. In a note to the budget director on July 22, 1958, a White House assistant summed up the administration's position: "The President stressed the emergency nature of the recommendation he made to meet a national need with a program specifically limited as to duration."[16]

With Congress due to adjourn by late August, time became a major factor in the final deliberations over education legislation. The Senate waited for the House, where the outcome was much less certain, to act first. On August 4, 1958, the House committee voted out a bill that called for twenty-three thousand scholarships a year based on merit rather than need. Knowing of the president's firm views, a bipartisan group of congressmen met later that day to inform the White House that, when the bill went to conference committee, they would cut the number of scholarships to ten thousand, all to be awarded on the basis of financial need. Eisenhower replied with a public statement simply reiterating his insistence on a limited number of scholarships and the assurance that "no tax dollars are paid to any scholarship winner who does not need those dollars to finance his college education."

While many observers foresaw a new deadlock in Congress, the legislative struggle turned out differently than anyone would have predicted. In the House, Representative Walter Judd, a Minnesota Republican, succeeded in deleting the provision for twenty-three thousand scholarships a year and transferring the amount allocated, approximately $300 million, to a revolving loan fund. The Senate still held out for scholarships but reduced the amount from the original $1,000 a year to just $250 while accepting Judd's proposal for most of the college assistance to be in the form of loans. When the measure went to the conference committee, a realization that conservatives in the House would block any measure involving federally funded scholarships allowed Judd's amendment to prevail. The conferees removed the scholarship provision and set up a $295 million loan fund for individual loans to be granted primarily on the basis of the student's financial need.[17]

As enacted by Congress later in August, the National Defense Education Act (NDEA) authorized the expenditure of slightly less than $1 billion over a four-year period. There were three main provisions. The first, on which nearly all the debate had centered, established a $295 million loan fund. Students could borrow $1,000 a year for five years, but only if they could show financial need. Repayment was due within eleven years after graduation. The measure called for special consideration for students planning to teach or specialize in science, math, or foreign languages; those who became teachers would be forgiven half of their total loan. A second part of the NDEA provided $280 million in federal matching funds for the purchase of equipment for the teaching of science, math, and foreign languages in both public and private schools. The third major section of the law authorized the spending of $59.4 million for fifty-five hundred graduate fellowships in areas relating to the national defense, including science, engineering, and foreign area study. In addition to fellowships ranging from $2,000 to $2,400 a year, this provision also granted universities $2,500 a year per student to help offset the high cost of expanding graduate programs in these areas. Finally, the NDEA also provided relatively small sums for supporting guidance and counseling programs in the schools, for vocational education, for research in educational radio and television, and for foreign language institutes at selected universities.[18]

In signing this legislation on September 2, 1958, the president was aware that his views had prevailed. Calling NDEA "a sound and constructive piece of legislation," he emphasized that it was "an emergency undertaking to be terminated after four years." He went on to remind the American people that the real challenge in American education was on the local level, and he called on everyone to take up that task.

Eisenhower had succeeded in blocking the attempt to set up a large-scale college scholarship program that could mark the beginning of a permanent federal role in higher education. Although he had been willing to accept ten thousand scholarships for a four-year period, he was happy with the Judd amendment and the resulting loan fund with its relatively short duration and its requirement that all loans be granted on the basis of financial need.[19]

Others regretted the outcome. The editors of *Life,* who had crusaded so fervently for educational reform, called NDEA "a compromise bill, good as far as it went." The *Nation* was more critical, terming the measure "just good enough to be impossible to veto and just penurious and misguided enough to make an angel curse." The editors regretted the miserly expenditures involved and the loss of the scholarship provisions; loans seemed to them an accountant's approach to education. The only solace to the *Nation* was that "the bill does at last crack the ice of resistance to federal aid to education," but it warned that "the crack is so tiny it must be widened very soon if it is not to freeze solid again."

Senator Lister Hill was one of many who felt that the loss of scholarships was tragic. It meant, he argued, "the defeat of the attempt to give national recognition to intellectual achievement." The editors of *Science* felt even more strongly on this point. The final version had dropped the clause in the original Hill-Elliott bill setting forth the goal of assuring "the intellecual preeminence of the United States, especially in science and technology." By basing all loans on need rather than merit, and even dropping a proposal to award congressional citations to the top 5 percent of each high school class, NDEA made no effort to advance "intellectual preeminence" or reward "outstanding scholastic achievement." Instead of mandating the government to seek out actively those who displayed "superior intellectual achievement," the editors lamented, the law simply "makes available the machinery and the funds for those students who are qualified and who do need financial aid."[20]

The passage of NDEA reflects the narrowness of Eisenhower's view of the *Sputnik* crisis. Unlike his critics, he believed that there was no great national emergency requiring fundamental changes. Instead he intended to make only limited responses that would not further add to what he perceived as the true national problem, heavy government spending and the danger of a large deficit. Passage of the education legislation added less than $200 million to the 1959 budget—$66.2 million to the National Science Foundation for graduate fellowships and language institutes and $116.5 to HEW for the loan fund and matching grants to local school districts. Compared to the several billion added to the $40-billion-plus defense budget, the spending on education was very slight. Yet, faced with a growing deficit caused by the recession-induced decline in revenues, Eisenhower insisted on this cost-saving approach.[21]

When the new school year began in the fall of 1958, the modest nature of Eisenhower's educational program became apparent. Enrollments, which had been rising steadily since 1954, went up again sharply at all levels. There were now 42.9 million students in class, an increase of 25 percent over the last five years. Yet college science courses were only up slightly, and engineering enrollment actually declined. The most encouraging news came from the local schools themselves. In Miami high school students had to take an extra year of English and math; in Texas a new requirement added a year of world history to the high school curriculum, along with a second year of laboratory science. From across the country came reports of a new emphasis on science and math in the elementary grades, more homework being assigned, and the adoption of new courses for students "with high intellectual potential."

Sputnik, rather than Eisenhower, had led to a long-overdue shakeup of American education. Those who had been criticizing American schools throughout the 1950s now suddenly were not only being heard but heeded. In a sense, the president's faith in local action in education was being fulfilled as school districts sought to strengthen their courses as part of a response to a national crisis. But Eisenhower's insistence on limiting federal action and balancing the budget had prevented him from playing a leading role in educational reform. The changes took place in spite of, rather than as a result of, White House initiatives. Yet even with his modest approach, Eisenhower was beginning a process of federal involvement that set important precedents for the much more extensive educational programs that Congress would enact in the 1960s.[22]

CHAPTER ELEVEN

Congressional passage of the space and education legislation left the issue of a possible missle gap as the greatest concern stemming from *Sputnik*. Despite many reassuring statements by the Eisenhower administration, the American people still feared that the Soviet success in launching large earth satellites proved that they were far ahead of the United States in the race for the ICBM. President Eisenhower, convinced that the American missile program was progressing well and opposed to heavy increases in the defense budget, continued to try to persuade a dubious Congress and an uncertain public that the apparent Soviet lead in the missile race did not endanger national security.

In the spring and summer of 1958, the president was encouraged by the reports of progress on first-generation liquid-fuel missiles. The two land-based IRBMs, the air force Thor and the army Jupiter, seemed to be moving ahead on schedule, despite some problems with the pumps on their rocket engines, which were overcome by July. PSAC's ballistic missile panel believed that the first Thor squadron would be deployed in England by the December 1958 target date. These IRBMs would probably not become fully operational until mid-1959, since it still took the crews nearly two hours to fuel them for launch and then only one in two could be expected to reach its target.[1]

The two first ICBMs, the Atlas and the Titan, were also making progress. After an initial failure, an Atlas flew successfully at full power in early August. In a flight that lasted twenty-two seconds, the ICBM traveled twenty-seven hundred miles, less than half its full range. What *Time* called "the longest and best flight of the nation's biggest bird" led the air force to proclaim that the United States now had "a 6,000 mile ICBM that we can use in a hurry if war comes."

Although the Atlas was already in production, actual deployment was still more than a year away. And PSAC scientists were recommending that greater emphasis be given to the Titan, which had larger engines and could be placed in hardened silos if its fuel were changed from liquid oxygen to a new form of storable liquid propellant. The president agreed to make this switch, which delayed its IOC (initial operating capability) from mid-1961 to the following April, in the interest of developing "a more reliable weapon."[2]

The best news of all came in a major technical breakthrough on nose cone design. The original Altas and Thor nose cones were blunt in shape and made of copper to shield the warhead from the heat generated during reentry into the earth's atmosphere. Heavy and clumsy in design, they slowed the warhead to the point where some feared it could be hit easily by an anti-missile missile. The army tried out a lighter, more streamlined nose cone that used the principle of ablation; instead of copper, the Jupiter nose cone was made of fiberglass with coatings of polymer plastics that melted during reentry while protecting the warhead within. Tested successfully in the spring of 1958, the new Jupiter nose cone was quickly adopted for all American missiles, permitting them to carry much more substantial payloads. In July a combined Thor-Vanguard missile flew some six thousand miles with the new ablation nose cone working perfectly.[3]

The outlook for second-generation solid-fuel missiles seemed even brighter. PSAC's ballistic missile panel commented favorably on future prospects of both the Polaris and the Minuteman on July 18, 1958, but recommended changes that would delay their deployment. The scientists reported that the Polaris tests were going well. The early version, due to become operational in late 1960, had a range of less than a thousand miles; it would be 1963 before it was likely to reach the goal of fifteen hundred miles. Minuteman was still in the early research and development stage, with an IOC of 1963–64. The panel favored increasing Minuteman's thrust from sixty-five thousand to eighty-five thousand pounds, to ensure a range of fifty-five hundred miles. "Such [a] weapon system," the report concluded, "will truly be a 'second generation' advanced missile with increased reliability, resistance to attack and of reduced installation cost."[4]

The main problem confronting the Eisenhower administration was the growing public enthusiasm for Polaris and Minuteman, untested weapons that would not be fully deployed until well into the next decade. *Life* magazine hailed the Minuteman, which it claimed would be in place by 1962, as "a fabulous arms system which will revolutionize U.S. military defense." The public notices for Polaris were even more glowing. *Life* called it "the most dramatic weapon in the U.S. underseas arsenal," and Senator Henry Jackson advocated a fleet of one hundred Polaris submarines as the backbone of the nation's strategic defense.[5]

The president, who was trying to hold the line at five Polaris subs while the navy pressed for nine, felt that it would not be prudent to invest heavily in these future weapons at the expense of the first generation—Atlas, Titan, Thor, and Jupiter—needed to offset Russian missiles already in production. At the same time, he did not want to waste taxpayer dollars by building up too large an arsenal of soon-to-be-obsolete weapons. Thus the dilemma he faced in 1958 was complex: how much to spend for national defense without risking a dangerous missile gap in the early 1960s or the mammoth expenditures that he feared would undermine the American economy.

I

The first battle came over the final size of the fiscal 1959 defense budget. The president, who had sought to limit defense spending to a ceiling of $38 billion in 1958, tried to keep the annual defense budget near that goal by asking Congress for special supplemental appropriations. Thus in his January 1958 budget message he had called for a defense budget of $39.1 for 1959, along with a supplement of $1.67 billion for the 1958 budget to pay for a post-*Sputnik* missile buildup and requests in the spring of 1958 for nearly $2 billion in supplements to the forthcoming 1959 budget.

There was a certain method to this apparent budget madness. Much of the additional money was for strategic weapons still in the development stage. In approving these requests, Congress was giving the administration "new obligational authority"—the power to commit funds in future defense budgets to pay for weapons that would not go into production for several years. These appropriations did not increase current spending, which Eisenhower was intent on keeping below $40 billion a year after *Sputnik*. They satisfied advocates of a bigger defense buildup, but the president knew he could cut back on these expenditures if the world situation warranted, and he could certainly spend the money more slowly than Congress desired. Polaris was a good example. Congress responded to pressure from the navy and voted funds for six missile-firing submarines, but Eisenhower refused to begin building more than five.[6]

The president made clear his views on defense spending at several press conferences in the spring of 1958. In response to a question, he admitted that a fall in revenue due to the current recession would produce a $10 billion deficit in 1958, the largest ever in peacetime. He still hoped to pare expenditures to achieve a balanced budget again, but he admitted it was unlikely in the next year or two. Defense spending, he said, had become "enormous," and it was time to bring it under control. "Now I do believe this: I do believe that the United States has now caught its breath and is not quite so apt to use the words 'urgent' and 'critical' as it was last fall after the first Sputnik was put into the air." Admitting that the new weapons like Polaris and Minuteman would be "very expensive" once they went into production, he stressed the need to cut back in other areas and to "keep sanity in this whole business of expending."[7]

Congressional leaders were far more concerned about the threat to national security than to the American economy. At a final point hearing by the preparedness subcommittee, Senators Stuart Symington and Lyndon Johnson both criticized the administration for not doing enough to bolster the nation's defenses. Symington expressed disappointment at Eisenhower's response to *Sputnik,* citing the Gaither report as an example of what he thought should have been done. Privately the Missouri Senator vowed to LBJ that he would do all he could to increase defense appropriations because it affects "the future security of the United States and the free world." Johnson also voiced a "sense of disappointment that I have felt for some time over the lack of a feeling of a grim urgency in the Defense Department." "We must work as though there was not going to be a tomorrow," he told Defense Secretary McElroy. "We must be positive that we are doing all that we can as soon as we can."[8]

Congress made clear its feelings by adding substantially to the 1959 defense appropriation bill. The House included an additional $638 million for three more Polaris submarines and $90 million for speeding up Minuteman development, though it balanced some of these additions with cuts in other areas. The Senate, however, led by Symington and Jackson, voted 71 to 9 for a $40-billion-plus defense appropriation for FY 1959, more than $1 billion more than Ike had requested. In addition to the House increases for Polaris and Minuteman, the senators wanted to increase the number of B-52 bombers and KC-135 tankers to refuel these planes in flight.[9]

The president was furious. He wondered where Symington and Jackson got their "claim to expertise" in a field in which Eisenhower had vastly more experience. Reacting to Congress's insistence on more bombers and missiles, Ike commented that the Democratic senators were apparently planning to "kill every Russian three times" in a massive retaliatory attack. Speaking out again at what he considered overkill, Eisenhower said it looked to him "as if Congress was going on the theory that we need all of everything, everywhere, all the time." His greatest concern was national solvency; he told Republican legislators that "the nation's defenses are certainly hurt if the economy is hurt greatly over the long run."

Realizing that he had little room for maneuver, the president finally instructed his aides to compromise by making sure that most of the increases were in the form of "new obligational authority" on a "no year" basis. As long as the appropriations did not have to be used within a given fiscal year, Eisenhower hoped he and his successors could avoid spending some of the vast sums voted for as yet unproven weapons. As he told one Republican congressman, "he wanted to be sure that funds were spent 'as needed,' not before."[10]

The result was that Symington and Jackson were able to win what the *Washington Post* called only a "half-victory." On August 6 a conference committee settled on a figure of $39.6 billion for the 1959 defense appropriation, $815 million more than Ike had requested but over $1 billion less than the Democratic senators had wanted. Although the president expressed regret on signing the bill on August 22 that it was over $1 billion more than "I consider necessary for our security," he knew that the "no year" feature would enable him to keep defense spending within his $40 billion limit for 1959. Nevertheless, this was the largest defense appropriation passed by Congress in peacetime, nearly $5 billion more than the previous high in 1957.[11]

The congressional action was almost certain to raise defense spending for the indefinite future. The appropriation bill increased the number of Polaris submarines from six to nine, despite Ike's unwillingness to begin building more than five. The additional $90 million for Minuteman would lead to an acceleration of the development and production of that costly weapon. These commitments to the weapons of the future built guaranteed increases into defense budgets for years to come. At the same time, Eisenhower still faced the problem of protecting the nation's security for the three or four years before these second-generation missiles became operational. Whatever the risk to economic health, the president could not neglect the possible peril facing the nation if the Soviets were in fact well out in front in the race for the ICBM.

II

The president and his advisers had reliable estimates of the likely deployment dates for American missiles, but they were in great doubt about the Soviet ICBM program. An Intelligence Advisory Committee (IAC) chaired by the director of the CIA and consisting of representatives from the various intelligence agencies of the government—the three services, the State Department, the Atomic Energy Commission, and the FBI—approved National Intelligence Estimates (NIE) prepared by the CIA. The NIE on Soviet missile development at the time of *Sputnik* predicted that the Russians would not have ICBMs operational before 1960. In November 1957 that estimate was revised downward to 1959, when it was thought possible the Soviet might have as many as ten ICBMs ready for use. A special estimate (SNIE) compiled the following month and approved in January 1958 suggested a possible IOC of mid-1958, with mid-1959 listed as more likely, and predicted as many as one hundred ICBMs operational between the middle of 1959 and 1960. Since the first American Atlas squadron was not due to be deployed until late 1959 at the earliest, the likelihood of a missile gap loomed for at least a year, if not longer.[12]

In the spring of 1958, the CIA began to have second thoughts about the January SNIE. Allen Dulles noted that, while the Soviets had conducted hundreds of tests at ranges up to one thousand miles, they had only held four tests of possible ICBM rockets by the end of 1958. The shorter tests enabled them to put IRBMs into production and deployment, but the handful of ICBM tests—just two of the SS-6 missile itself, at ranges far below intercontinental distance, and the two *Sputnik* launches in fall 1957—suggested that the Soviets had run into serious problems with their ICBM. Two further tests in the spring of 1958—an SS-6 ICBM flown at less than full range, and the May *Sputnik* launch, which had apparently been delayed for five months— seemed to heighten the possibility of a serious design flaw in the Soviet ICBM. Dulles believed that six tests were evidence that the Russians were only one-third to one-half the way along toward perfecting their long-range missile.[13]

Members of Killian's PSAC disagreed. In the spring of 1958, they recommended a halt in nuclear testing to President Eisenhower based on their belief that the United States was far ahead of the Soviets in nuclear warhead development. At the same time, they cautioned against a Russian proposal for a similar ban on ICBM tests. The scientists pointed out that, while the United States could detect missile launches with radar and other instruments, it was impossible to differentiate between military shots and peaceful space flights. But a more compelling reason was their conviction that the Soviets, despite the relatively few tests they had conducted, were far ahead in the race for the ICBM. George Kistiakowksy, who chaired the PSAC missile panel, was convinced that, in view of their extensive testing of shorter-range IRBMs, "the Soviets could complete all the necessary missile firing tests within the next few months." With the earliest time for an American ICBM more than a year away, Killian informed Eisenhower in mid-April that "the acceptance of a stoppage of tests would be highly disadvantageous to the United States."[14]

Secretary of State John Foster Dulles apparently shared his brother's doubts about the Soviet ICBM lead. Citing a PSAC report that indicated that a ban on missile testing would prevent the development of ICBMs, he wrote to Killian to ask the scientists to reconsider the question of how much testing would be required before a long-range missile became operational. The key date in Dulles's view was September 1, 1958, when he hoped the nuclear test ban would take effect. If a ban on all missile tests by that date, in the judgment of PSAC, would prevent the Soviets from perfecting an ICBM, then he thought it would be in the best interests of the United States to make such a proposal. Kistiakowsky advised Killian that it would be wiser to consider the possibility of a future cessation of missile tests only after the United States had reached "certain milestones" in its own ICBM program.[15]

In early May Killian and Kistiakowsky ended all further discussion of a missile test ban by presenting a pessimistic comparision of the American and Russian ICBM programs to the National Security Council. Although their report remains classified, the NSC minutes reveal that they viewed the Soviets as being far ahead of the United States in the deployment of ICBMs. Killian attributed this lead to the fact that the Russians had started much sooner, while Kistiakowsky stressed their superior propulsion systems. Secretary of Defense McElroy challenged the scientists, suggesting that, while the Russians might be ahead in the size of their rocket engines, the United States could be close to them in overcoming such critical ICBM problems as guidance and reentry. The scientists rebutted this criticism, denying that they had exaggerated the Soviet advantage and contending that the "propulsion problem" was still the primary challenge the United States had to overcome.

At the end of the NSC meeting, the president and a few key advisers adjourned to his office to discuss the ICBM race in private. Impressed by the intelligence data cited by Killian and Kistiakowsky, Eisenhower apparently ruled out the secretary of state's suggestion of a possible missile test ban. Instead he approved a recommendation by Allen Dulles that he continue to meet with General Nathan Twining, the Joint Chiefs chairman, Robert Cutler, Ike's national security adviser, and James Killian to conduct a comparative analysis of Soviet and American missile programs. At the CIA director's suggestion, these four men had begun meeting earlier in the spring of 1958 to discuss the missile estimates; they would continue to consult in an effort to compare American and Soviet ICBM progress and keep the president and the NSC informed.[16]

From the available evidence, it is not clear whether it was this small group of high-level advisers or the more formal machinery of the CIA's Board of National Estimates that was responsible for a new NIE on Soviet missiles in the spring of 1958. The new estimate, prepared on May 20 and approved in mid-June, presumably reflected the intelligence data on which Killian and Kistiakowsky had based their pessimistic report to the NSC. In contrast to the January 1958 SNIE, the new estimate made a firm prediction of ten Soviet operational ICBMs by early 1959. More startling, it predicted that the Russians would have as many as one hundred SS-6 missiles by the end of 1959, five hundred by 1960, and one thousand by 1961. With the United States only planning to deploy 130 Atlas and Titan missiles by 1962, this estimate led to the frightening prospect of a massive missile gap by the early 1960s.

Once again it was President Eisenhower who seemed least impressed with this dire prediction. Just as he had when the Gaither committee gave its report to the NSC soon after *Sputnik,* he expressed great skepticism over these estimates. Remembering the earlier bomber gap, when the CIA had predicted in 1956 that the Soviets would have as many as 800 long-range bombers by 1958, he had his staff prepare a chart that showed how the CIA had lowered the number to just 135 in June 1958. He had a memo prepared on which the changing estimates of Soviet missile development were placed just below the falling bomber estimates to drive home his lack of faith in the CIA's ability to predict Soviet strategic behavior.[17]

In a crucial meeting on June 17, 1958, with Allen Dulles and Herbert Scoville, the CIA's director of scientific intelligence, the president cited the bomber gap evidence as an indication of the fallibility of such predictions. Dulles replied lamely that the Russians had apparently decided to shift their resources from bombers to missiles between 1956 and 1958. Then he did agree to change the estimate "to retard by six months to one year the dates on which the Soviets are estimated to have an initial operational ICBM capability." Eisenhower was still not satisfied with this small concession. Seizing on a key point, he told Dulles that he found it impossible to reconcile these estimates with the small number of tests the Russians had conducted, which suggested they were experiencing serious difficulties with their SS-6 missile.[18]

The president responded to the possibility of a future missile gap by authorizing more detailed studies of the strategic balance between the United States and the Soviet Union. On June 25 the NSC formalized the high-level consultation among Allen Dulles, Killian, Twining, and Cutler by creating a Comparative Evaluations Group consisting of these men, along with the undersecretary of state and the chairman of the president's board of advisers on foreign intelligence. They were to meet regularly and to report to the president every three months on the relative status of Russian and American weapons systems. In addition, it was agreed that the NSC would receive a report later in the summer from the Pentagon's Weapon System Evaluation Group (WSEG), a body established in 1957 to weigh the merits of different U.S. weapons programs.

On August 8, 1958, WSEG issued a pessimistic report on the relative military advantages of missiles and aircraft. The report argued that for the next five years the United States would have to rely exclusively on bombers for nuclear retaliation. It discounted the Thor and Jupiter IRBMs to be based in Europe as too vulnerable to a Soviet first strike, and pointed out that the United States would not have enough ICBMs operational to act as a deterrent until 1962. Citing intelligence estimates of a possible missile gap between 1960 and 1962, the WSEG report recommended increasing the number of B-52s on alert and keeping a portion of this bomber force in the air at all times to guard against a Soviet first strike.[19]

The president still refused to panic. In the past he had relied on the information gathered by U-2 flights to arrive at a more realistic assessment of Soviet missile capabilities. In 1958, however, he had curtailed these overflights after a Russian protest against an incursion into their air space in the Far East. Fearful of an embarrassing international incident, in March he had Andrew Goodpaster order Allen Dulles to discontinue "special reconnaissance activities . . . effective at once." The U-2 flights resumed later in the spring, but several accidents, including two fatal crashes within twenty-four hours, led to a second suspension on July 10, 1958. For the next few months, U-2s flew along the borders of the Soviet Union, but there were no direct overflights. The pictures that were taken by mid-1958, however, showed no signs of Russian deployment of ICBMs, leading James Killian to conclude that the Soviets were "far behind" American estimates on ICBM development. The huge size of the SS-6 missile meant it could only be moved by rail, which Killian claimed would make it easy for the United States to monitor any future deployment.[20]

The absence of U-2 flights in the latter half of 1958, along with the president's insistence that the overflights be kept a closely guarded secret within his administration, prevented this aerial reconnaissance from resolving the possibility of a missile gap. Eisenhower's position stemmed more from his own basic convictions than from U-2 photographs. He believed strongly in the deterrent power of the American bomber force, doubting that the Soviets would risk the massive destruction that more than five hundred B-52s could deliver. Even more important, his evaluation of the international arena and Soviet behavior convinced him, he told Killian, that "the possibility of all-out war within the next five years is very small."[21] Where the missile experts focused on a possible divergence in the number of weapons the Soviets might be capable of producing compared with the United States, the president relied on a political analysis that suggested that a nuclear attack was extremely unlikely in the near future. The issue of the missile gap came down finally to the difference between technological possibilities and diplomatic probabilities.

III

Public concern over America's strategic vulnerability began to mount by the summer of 1958. Eisenhower had persuaded the nation that, despite *Sputnik* and the Gaither report, the United States retained a decisive lead in nuclear striking power and thus was invulnerable to attack. Many military leaders, however, especially within the air force, disagreed and began to leak their views to the press. By midsummer the president had to combat a new wave of doubt and uncertainty.

Hanson W. Baldwin, the influential military commentator of the *New York Times,* began the debate with his book, *The Great Arms Race.*

The outgrowth of articles he published in the *Times* in March 1958, Baldwin's book offered a balanced but critical view of Eisenhower's response to *Sputnik*. The author agreed with the president that the United States still retained "a definite superiority to the U.S.S.R. in overall military power." However, he felt that Eisenhower had been too intent on balancing the budget and that as a result we no longer retained "the margin of power over other nations that we had at the end of World War II." And, reflecting his close ties to the admirals and generals in the Pentagon, Baldwin was critical of Ike's efforts to give civilians within the Defense Department the power to make key budgetary and strategic decisions.

Obviously drawing on well-placed sources within the military, Baldwin offered an informed judgment on the status of the missile race. He pointed out that the Soviets were at least a year ahead in the development of IRBMs, having conducted extensive tests at ranges up to one thousand miles and having probably already deployed a seven-hundred-mile missile. He was more guarded about the ICBM, claiming that the Russians had only a "slight" but nevertheless "real" lead in developing that weapon. He did acknowledge, however, the small number of ICBM tests and claimed that in December 1957 an SS-6 had blown up on a launch pad. At most, he wrote, the United States was only a few months behind the Soviets on intercontinental missiles. Therefore, he concluded, "a planned and deliberate major attack by the Soviet Union on the United States is, in the foreseeable future, a very unlikely possibility."

Despite this reassuring assessment, Baldwin felt that Eisenhower was not doing enough to protect American security. While he agreed that the solid-fuel Minuteman and Polaris missiles were excellent weapons, they would not be available in large numbers until the mid-1960s, leaving open the possibility of Soviet superiority early in that decade. Baldwin argued that the Polaris, because it offered "the greatest immunity to enemy surprise attack," was the ideal weapon for America's second-strike strategy of deterrence. The administration, however, had approved only five Polaris submarines, far too few in his judgment, and even Congress, in calling for nine, was being "unimaginative" and "far too modest." Overall, Baldwin concluded, *Sputnik* served the nation well by halting a dangerous decline in defense spending. But Eisenhower's modest increases for the Pentagon proved to be neither "very imaginative or a very dramatic answer to the Soviet satellites." Unless the United States began spending at least $1 billion a year more for defense, it faced the possibility of falling behind the Soviet Union in the years ahead.[22]

General James W. Gavin, who had retired as the army's chief of research and development in January 1958, was a much more outspoken critic of Eisenhower's cautious defense policies. In early August *Life* magazine published excerpts from Gavin's forthcoming book, *War and Peace in the Space Age*. Blaming the same culprits as Baldwin—"hundreds of civilians" within the Defense Department and Eisenhower's insistence on balancing the budget—Gavin claimed that the Soviet Union had already perfected an ICBM while its American counterpart was still several years away. This "missile lag," he warned, would "place us in a position of great peril." Gavin discounted both IRBMs in Europe and America's bomber superiority. A Soviet first strike could knock out the Thors and Jupiters, he argued, and Soviet surface-to-air missiles would soon render the B-52 obsolete. "The ICBM is the consequence of the manned bomber obsolescence," he contended, "not the cause." "We *are* in mortal danger," he concluded, "and the 'missile lag' does portend trouble—trouble of a perilous nature."[23]

Alarming as Gavin's warning was, it was too vague to be fully believable. But at almost exactly the same time, journalist Joseph Alsop published a series of three newspaper columns in which he spelled out in frighteningly specific terms the precise nature of the missile gap facing the United States. Citing unnamed Pentagon sources, Alsop warned that America's military leaders were referring privately to "the gap"—the period from 1960 to 1963 when the Soviet Union will have "unchallengeable superiority in the nuclear striking power that was once our specialty."

For the first time, the American people learned of the projections of American and Soviet ICBM deployment. Pointing out that the United States planned to have only 130 Atlas and Titan missiles operational by 1962, Alsop cited the June NIE that predicted as many as fifteen hundred Soviet ICBMs by that date, and two thousand a year later (see Table 5). Placing these figures side-by-side, he wrote: "This is the true, but unadmitted, response to the warning of the *Sputnik*."

Unlike Baldwin and Gavin, Alsop charged the president with full responsibility for this dangerous state of affairs. Asserting that the administration was "guilty of gross untruth," Alsop claimed that Eisenhower was either "consciously misleading the nation" or, more likely, was "misinformed about the facts." He went on to argue that few Polaris submarines would be operational during this "time of deadly danger" and that the Minuteman, "on which the President is gambling the American future," could not be deployed before the end of 1963.

TABLE 5: Alsop's Projected Gap in Missiles

Year	American ICBMs	Soviet ICBMs
1959	0	100
1960	30	500
1961	70	1,000
1962	130	1,500
1963	130	2,000

The result of this missile gap, Alsop concluded, was to give the Soviets "overwhelming superiority in over-all nuclear striking power" in the early 1960s. Massive retaliation would no longer be a credible deterrent. The Soviets would not have to launch a first strike; just the threat of such an attack could bring them diplomatic triumphs over the United States. "Any man who is not intoxicated by official self-delusion," he argued, "must at least expect the Kremlin to threaten to strike the first blow." Given this prospect, Alsop concluded that the American people would have to act quickly to "save ourselves," presumably by demanding a crash program to duplicate the first generation of Soviet ICBMs.[24]

Alsop's columns had both immediate and long-range impact. Published just before Congress acted on the 1959 defense budget, they helped persuade congressmen and senators to vote for nearly $1 billion more than Eisenhower had requested. The legislators could not force the president to increase the number of Atlas and Titan missiles, but they did appropriate funds for additional Polaris submarines and a speedup in Minuteman development. At the same time, Alsop popularized the concept of a missile gap, thereby intensifying public pressure on the president and Congress for more defense spending. Typical was the response of Senator Richard Russell to a constituent who had written to him about Alsop's columns. Expressing agreement with Alsop, Russell promised to do "everything within the power of one member of the Senate to provide the authorization and the appropriations for an adequate defense."[25]

Eisenhower also felt the pressure generated by Baldwin, Gavin, and Alsop. At a press conference on August 27, he denied that the nation was in peril. Claiming that he had inherited only an embryo missile program from the Truman administration, the president pointed out that he had given missiles "highest priority" since 1955. "From that moment on," he claimed, "there has been no place that I can see where there has been any possibility of gaps occurring." At the same time, he cautioned against "wild" procurement policies to purchase untested weapons. Denying that missiles had made bombers obsolete, he argued that "our enormous strength in fine long-range airplanes" would fill any possible gap in the near future.[26]

IV

Democratic Senator Stuart Symington refused to accept this rosy forecast. On July 21, 1958, he met with CIA Director Allen Dulles to voice his doubts. In an effort to allay Symington's concern, Dulles even allowed him to talk with members of the CIA's Board of National Estimates, the first legislator to do so. The Missouri senator was still not satisfied and began to assemble his own contradictory estimates of Soviet ICBM development. His primary source was Thomas Lanphier, who had served as Symington's aide when he was secretary of the air force and currently was a vice-president of Convair, the aerospace company building the Atlas missile. Lanphier had close ties with air force intelligence, which regularly challenged the CIA estimates of Soviet ICBM development. Led by Major General James H. Walsh, air force intelligence claimed that the Soviets were in the process of deploying hundreds of ICBMs. The debate centered on differing interpretations of photographic data; one CIA officer claimed that "to the Air Force every flyspeck on film was a missile."[27]

Symington held a second meeting with Dulles on August 6 to present his conflicting views. The senator was accompanied by Lanphier, who offered contradictory data on the Soviet ICBM test program. Dulles claimed that the Soviets, while they had tested the IRBM hundreds of times, had only conducted six ICBM tests, and none since *Sputnik III* in May. On the basis of these few tests, the CIA estimated that the Russians would have the capability of deploying five hundred ICBMs by 1962, possibly even by 1961. In contrast, Lanphier maintained that the Soviets had conducted between fifty-seven and eighty ICBM tests and thus were capable of having many more operational missiles much earlier than the CIA predicted. Lanphier's figures remain classified, but he claimed that they were "sufficiently different" from the CIA estimate and were "much more alarming."

Dulles dismissed Lanphier's claims as unfounded, saying that they were based on nothing more than gossip within the American intelligence community. He surmised that General Walsh, unable to get the CIA to accept air force intelligence figures, was using Symington as part of a bureaucratic maneuver. President Eisenhower was equally unimpressed, making "a strong statement in criticism" of the claims Symington and Lanphier had made to the CIA director.[28]

Symington refused to accept this rebuff, insisting that he be allowed to present his views to the president himself. Ike reluctantly agreed to meet with the Missouri senator on August 29. Symington presented Eisenhower with a letter spelling out his position in detail. He recited his meetings with Dulles and their disagreement on how many ICBM tests the Soviets had held. Symington's strongest point was his contention that the CIA claim of only six ICBM tests did not square with the agency's projection of five hundred Russian ICBMs by 1962. The United States, in contrast, was planning about one hundred tests for only sixty-four Atlas missiles. It was incredible that the Soviets would put such a complex weapon into production without proving its performance thoroughly. Therefore Symington was convinced that the CIA had "heavily underrated Soviet missile development to date, as well as planned capabilities."

Symington argued that, even if the CIA estimates were valid, they still indicated a serious imbalance in relative missile strength in the early 1960s. The Soviet Union would have five hundred ICBMs by

1962, according to the CIA figures, while the United States planned to deploy only 130 Atlas and Titan missiles by that year. Thus, he warned, "our currently planned defense programs are insufficient to meet the threat which the CIA estimates the Soviets will pose by 1961." This danger would be even greater if the Soviets were, as Symington believed, much further along in their ICBM development. The result would be to expose the United States to "overt political, if not actual military aggression from the Sino-Soviet alliance—with a relatively slight chance of effective retaliation against such aggression between 1960 and 1962." In other words, Symington claimed that the missile gap that Alsop and Gavin warned about was likely to undermine American security.

The president refused to accept this alarming forecast. He suggested that Symington should confer with Secretary of Defense McElroy for a more accurate picture of the strategic balance. Eisenhower dismissed Lanphier's information as raw data from low-level intelligence sources that did not have the benefit of "high-level analysis," citing the bomber gap that Symington had prophesied in 1956 as an example of a similar misjudgment. The president admitted that the Russians had a head start on missiles, with the United States waiting for the smaller H-bomb warheads before undertaking full development. But he asserted that he had "been through this matter, with intelligence chiefs of all the services present, just a day or two before" and was fully satisfied with the status of the American ICBM program.[29]

Privately Eisenhower was impressed with the detailed information Symington had presented. He was furious when the senator referred to a successful Atlas test the day before, which the president did not know about. Deputy Secretary of Defense Donald Quarles explained that Lanphier, due to his position at Convair, had informed Symington. The test, Quarles added, was successful, with the nose cone landing within the target area, thus confirming Ike's confidence in the Atlas program. The president then referred Symington's letter to McElroy and Dulles for analysis and evaluation. An aide informed Symington that the president would give him the results of this review "as promptly as possible."[30]

The consideration of Symington's claims took much longer than this reply suggested. On October 10 Allen Dulles sent the president a memorandum reviewing his meetings with Symington. The CIA director reiterated his belief that the Soviets had only conducted six ICBM tests so far and predicted that they would reach the level of five hundred intercontinental missiles by 1961, or 1962 at the latest. Dulles discounted Symington's claims of up to eighty Soviet ICBM tests but failed to explain how the CIA could estimate five hundred ICBMs by 1961 on the basis of so few trial launches. He denied any effort within the American intelligence community "to suppress evidence" and concluded that "very careful study" of Symington's claims "leads me to believe that they provide no basis for changing our estimate on Soviet guided missiles as presented to you."[31]

Despite this confident tone, Dulles was concerned by the obvious discrepancy between the small number of Soviet tests and the CIA estimate of five hundred ICBMs by 1961. The day before his report to the president, Dulles asked the agency's Guided Missile Intelligence Committee to restudy the Soviet missile program. In particular he asked this group to determine whether the CIA had missed any ICBM tests or if the Russians had deceived the agency with "concealed tests." He also asked the experts to explore the question of how many tests would be needed "to achieve 500 ICBMs by 1961–62." Equally important, he wanted to know if the apparent lack of tests could indicate "serious difficulty or delay in their missile program."

George Kistiakowsky, the missile expert on the PSAC, had even graver doubts. On October 9 he told a Killian aide that he was "not completely happy" with a draft NIE that lowered the projected number of Soviet ICBMs to just ten by 1959. His study of their program led him to believe that the Russians would have close to one hundred ICBMs by that time. He was willing to accept the CIA's estimate of five hundred missiles by 1961–62, but he termed this a "critical period" that confirmed the warnings of the Gaither report.[32]

The CIA eventually resolved the apparent contradiction between the small number of Soviet tests and the prediction of five hundred missiles by 1961 by reducing its projections of Russian ICBM deployment. The December 1958 NIE revised the June figures downward, predicting one hundred Soviet ICBMs by 1960, three hundred by 1961, five hundred for 1962, and between one thousand and fifteen hundred for 1963 (see Table 6). The Guided Missile Intelligence Committee apparently concluded that the CIA had not missed any Soviet tests and that the Russians had experienced unknown difficulties delaying their ICBM deployment.[33]

Allen Dulles presented this unwelcome news to Senator Symington in a meeting on December 16, 1958. Tom Lanphier, who had accompanied Symington, was asked to leave the room while Dulles, along with General Walsh, another air force intelligence officer, and CIA official Herbert Scoville, briefed the senator on the issues he had

TABLE 6: Changing CIA Estimates of Soviet ICBM Deployment

Year	June 1958 NIE	December 1958 NIE
1959	100	10
1960	500	100
1961	1,000	300
1962	1,500	500
1963	2,000	1,000-1,500

raised. Dulles informed him that the Soviets had still only conducted six ICBM tests, experiencing two apparent failures in July. Consequently the CIA was downgrading its estimates of Soviet long-range missile deployment; it did not expect any ICBMs to become operational in 1958 and predicted only ten prototypes in 1959. There was no hard evidence of any Soviet ICBM production or missile site construction. Based on a belief it would take three years from initial deployment to achieve a goal of five hundred operational ICBMs, the CIA was pushing back its estimate of this critical "yardstick" of missile strength by two years, from 1960 to 1962.

Symington remained skeptical. He pointed out that the CIA estimates suggested that the Soviets "had been way ahead of us but were slackening up" in the ICBM race. General Walsh commented that "maybe they had gone back to the drawing board to fix something up." Symington still felt that "the intelligence picture was incredible." He claimed that, even accepting the CIA estimate of five hundred ICBMs by 1962, the Russians would need to conduct many more tests before going into production. He said that his sources within the aerospace industry assured him that "the test data and the estimate were incompatible." "It didn't make sense," Symington contended, "to estimate so much production in a short time with so little testing."

After the intelligence briefing, Lanphier rejoined the meeting. Under questioning he admitted that his figures on Soviet tests "came from information floating around in the intelligence hierarchy" and that he had deliberately exaggerated the numbers to test out the CIA. Despite this admission, Symington remained convinced that the CIA was wrong on both the test data and its estimates of Soviet ICBM deployment. He implied that the CIA was adjusting the figures to please the president, saying that a slowdown in the Russian ICBM program "was a wonderful thing to believe if it was more important for the US to balance the budget than to have national defense." As the meeting broke up, the senator said he felt it would be necessary to inform the American people of his concerns.[34]

V

Senator Symington went public with his disagreement with the Eisenhower administration in the early months of 1959. In congressional hearings he accused McElroy of deliberately "downgrading" the estimates of Soviet ICBM deployment in order to help balance the defense budget. In February he read the text of his August 29, 1958, letter to Eisenhower into the *Congressional Record* and accused the administration of trying to lull the American people into a "state of complacency not justified by the facts." Convinced that there would be a dangerous missile gap by 1962, he predicted that, instead of the five hundred SS-6s the CIA forecast the Soviets deploying in that year, "they will have 3,000 ICBMs."[35]

A partisan debate over a future missile gap raged for the next two years. Gradually, however, it became apparent that the administration's cautious view was justified. Although the Soviets resumed ICBM tests in April 1959, the CIA could find no evidence that the SS-6 missile had gone into large-scale production. Finally, in early 1960, U-2 flights detected the first modest deployment of the Soviet ICBMs in an arc along the trans-Siberian railroad. The missile, with its enormous rocket engine, was too large to be placed in concrete silos and could only be deployed by rail. Sometime in mid-1958 Soviet leader Nikita Khrushchev had apparently decided to halt the production of the SS-6 on grounds that it was too large, too immobile, and too vulnerable to a first strike. Khrushchev, aware of the American progress on the second-generation Polaris and Minuteman missiles, decided to scrap the SS-6 and develop the solid-fuel SS-7 in its place. As a result, as late as 1961 the Soviets had only deployed thirty-five ICBMs.[36]

Although Symington had been far off the mark in predicting three thousand Soviet long-range missiles by 1962, he had succeeded in spotlighting the weakness of the CIA analysis of the Soviet missile program. Dulles's agency counted the number of ICBM tests correctly but failed to follow this evidence to its logical conclusion. Instead of determining that the Soviets had reached a dead end with the first-generation SS-6 in 1958, the CIA tried to compromise with the public and congressional pressures generated by the *Sputnik* scare by offering only a modest scaling down of its inflated estimate of Soviet ICBM capabilities. The prediction of five hundred Russian SS-6 missiles by 1962, while better than the original estimate of one thousand, still went far beyond the available evidence to suggest a serious missile gap opening—500 Soviet ICBMs to only 130 for the United States.

President Eisenhower had been right in reacting prudently to the cries for a massive buildup of first-generation American missiles. His concern for a balanced budget and his instinctive caution in judging probable Soviet behavior, rather than theoretical capabilities, led him to place a sensible limit on the first generation of American missiles and put a greater emphasis on the development of the solid-fuel Polaris and Minuteman as the basis for American deterrence in the future. However, he failed in his fundamental responsibility of reassuring a badly shaken nation. He refused to compromise the U-2 program by disclosing the lack of Russian progress in the ICBM race, and he was almost arrogant in insisting that the Congress and the people accept his strategic judgments without question. In the wake of *Sputnik*, Americans wanted more than broad verbal reassurances from the hero of World War II. Unable to persuade the American people that the dawn of the space age had not eroded the nation's security, Eisenhower found himself continuing to retreat from his goal of a balanced budget. Thus despite his own better judgment, he was forced to preside over a massive arms buildup that far transcended any possible Soviet threat.

CHAPTER TWELVE

"The excitement has now died down to a large extent, and much of the chagrin has vanished, too," commented the *Washington Post* on the first anniversary of *Sputnik*. The five-part series, entitled "Sputnik plus One," portrayed the American people as having recovered from the uproar that followed the first Soviet satellite a year before. Hanson Baldwin, writing in the *New York Times*, agreed, as he noted that public opinion was much less frantic a year later. In part, the Eisenhower administration had reassured the nation by the actions it had taken; in part, new issues such as the forced resignation of White House Chief of Staff Sherman Adams and a serious crisis in the Formosa Straits over Quemoy and Matsu had replaced the post-*Sputnik* concerns.

The belated American successes in space had helped reduce public anxiety. With ARPA and NASA, the Eisenhower administration had created vigorous new agencies to plan and conduct space activities. A year after *Sputnik*, the United States had caught up with and passed the Soviets in space, launching a total of four satellites (three *Explorers* and one *Vanguard*) compared to the three *Sputniks*. On October 4, 1958, three American satellites were still circling the earth, while only the last *Sputnik* remained in orbit. Yet the Soviets had used more powerful rockets, capable of delivering objects weighing as much as a typical American automobile into space; *Sputnik III* was eighty times heavier than *Explorer III*.[1]

In the all-important missile race, the American people still believed the Russians had a slight lead. A Gallup poll released on October 3, 1958, revealed that 40 percent of those questioned thought that the Soviet Union was "ahead in the field of long-range missiles," compared with 37 percent who thought the United States led. Hanson Baldwin felt that the Russian lead had been exaggerated after *Sputnik* and that a year later "across the board the United States is probably abreast or ahead of the Soviet Union." But he and others noted a sense of complacency within the administration and a tendency to give too much weight to budgetary concerns. Critics, notably Democrats, sensed that President Eisenhower had been hurt politically by the post-*Sputnik* concern over national defense; "his halo had slipped," one commented. As a result Democrats were hoping to make significant gains in the upcoming congressional elections.

Education proved more difficult to evaluate. The *Washington Post* commented on the way that the "beep-beep-beep of Sputnik" had become "a rallying-cry for critics of American education." But many felt that the National Defense Education Act was disappointing and that American schools a year later remained "more or less what they were." At the same time, there seemed to be greater attention paid to "intellectual values" and encouraging signs of greater emphasis on the teaching of math, science, and foreign language at the expense of "frill" electives. Although some critics were hoping that the Russians would be the first to land a rocket on the moon in order to stimulate greater public efforts for education, a majority of Americans did not share this concern. A Gallup poll indicated that a surprising 68 percent felt that the United States had "a better educational program" than the Soviet Union, and only 19 percent disagreed.

Overall the American people seem to have regained their composure a year after the initial panic over *Sputnik*. "Some are indifferent," commented the *Washington Post,* "perhaps a majority are complacent, but a vigorous minority are disturbed and apprehensive." It was this lingering feeling that the United States had not done enough to meet the Soviet challenge that cast doubt on the nature of Eisenhower's leadership. In all the post mortems on *Sputnik,* the question of whether the administration had done enough kept recurring. Hanson Baldwin referred to both "the limited imagination and the limited budget of our space program," while Chalmers Roberts concluded "Sputnik plus One" with a wistful observation: "The great question today is: Will America get the leadership it needs?"[2]

I

Eisenhower's determination to play down the feeling of a race with the Soviets became clear in his conduct of space policy in the fall of 1958. With NASA due to begin functioning on October 1, 1958, Killian began making preparations for the first meeting of the new Space Council in late September. Although it was to be modeled after the National Security Council, the president recommended that the new body meet only once a month, not weekly like the NSC. He told Killian that he did not want the members of the council to play too active a role; he viewed them as a board of directors whose job was simply to review and approve the policies set forth by NASA administrator Keith Glennan.

At the first meeting of the Space Council, on September 24, 1958, the president read a statement prepared by Killian that spelled out his views. "I shall look to this Council," Eisenhower began, "for advice on the broad policy aspects of our national aeronautics and space program." The group quickly agreed to meet once a month, primarily to listen to and comment on items presented by NASA Director Glennan. The council's main purpose would be to clear up ambiguities in the space program, particularly by settling jurisdictional disputes regarding what would be considered peaceful space activities assigned to NASA as opposed to military projects to be retained by the Pentagon's Advanced Research Projects Agency (ARPA).[3]

Most of the discussion centered on plans for a large rocket booster, in excess of one million pounds thrust, that would be needed for deep space flight such as sending men to the moon. ARPA had already asked Wernher Von Braun's team at the Army Ballistic Missile Agency (ABMA) at Huntsville to begin designing such a huge booster. Von Braun began to develop plans to cluster eight Jupiter rockets together to achieve an engine capable of delivering more than a million pounds of thrust. Eisenhower expressed a preference for placing this key project under NASA's control, but he agreed with the Space Council's decision to let the two agencies try to work out their own arrangement, with the council to make the final decision if they reached a stalemate.[4]

On October 1 the White House released an executive order establishing NASA by giving it authority over three former NACA research laboratories as well as over most of the nation's existing space programs, including ARPA's *Explorer* satellites and planned moon probes as well as the Navy's Vanguard effort. NASA was put in charge of the million-pound booster, but the question of shifting both the Jet Propulsion Laboratory (JPL) at Cal Tech and Von Braun's ABMA from the army to NASA was left open for negotiation. The order also confirmed the transfer of $117 million from the Pentagon to NASA in the 1958 budget to pay for these space programs.[5]

The new space agency now was in charge of two of the nation's three major space activities. The first, earth satellites, was already beginning to lose public interest now that the United States had overcome the initial Soviet advantage. Vanguard had achieved just one successful launch, a tiny three-and-a-quarter-pound sphere that was predicted to orbit the earth for two hundred years. After a seventh Vanguard attempt failed in late September, NASA suspended the program while it studied the reasons for the lack of success of the original American satellite effort. Despite a failure in August, NASA continued the Explorer program, which used Von Braun's reliable Jupiter-C booster to send up satellites designed to gain more information about the risks and hazards astronauts would encounter in the first manned space flights.[6]

There was far more interest in NASA's second area of responsibility, lunar probes to be conducted by the air force and the army. After the failure of the first moon shot in August, the president worried about how to "avoid undue suspense and expectations" when Glennan briefed the cabinet on October 9 on plans for a second lunar probe designed to place a television camera in orbit around the moon. Recalling wistfully the secrecy surrounding the wartime Manhattan Project, Eisenhower suggested referring vaguely to "space probes" and disguising the actual purpose of the flight "unless and until it should be a success."

Pioneer I, launched by the air force from Cape Canaveral on October 11, proved to be a near miss that captured the public's imagination. A four-stage rocket powered by a modified Thor with an eighty-five-pound instrumented pay load, the lunar probe performed well, reaching a top speed of 23,450 miles per hour and traveling nearly eighty thousand miles into space, thirty times farther than any of the Russian or American satellites. It went one-third of the way to the moon, missing its goal only because of a trajectory that was slightly too shallow to enable it to escape from the earth's gravitational pull.

American space enthusiasts hailed *Pioneer I* as an "unprecedented shot." "The all-important fact," claimed *Time,* "was that the bird had plumbed the black beyond and had climbed to unheard-of-heights." Missile-builder Simon Ramo put it more succinctly: "What we gained this weekend was a few seconds on infinity." *Life* presented five pages of color pictures on *Pioneer I,* which it called "a priceless package of Liliputian instruments," the product of the "best brains of the Air Force." The editors talked of the important data gathered on the limits of the Van Allen radiation belts, which indicated that manned space flight would be possible. Despite the fact that *Pioneer I* did not reach the moon, *Life* called the launch "historic," proclaiming that "its record-setting flight must be counted not a failure but a major triumph of man."[7]

The near euphoria over *Pioneer I* quickly faded as subsequent American lunar probes failed to reach their goal. In early November *Pioneer II,* the final air force effort, climbed to an altitude of only one thousand miles before its third stage failed to ignite. Traveling at sixteen thousand miles per hour, the instrument package fell back into the earth's atmosphere over Central Africa and quickly disintegrated. The army's first effort at a lunar probe came in early December. *Pioneer III,* a sixty-ton, four-stage rocket powered by a Jupiter IRBM and carrying a thirteen-pound payload, fared better, traveling some sixty-six thousand miles into space but failing to go fast enough to escape the earth's gravity. Like the first *Pioneer,* the army's moon probe did bring back valuable information about the radiation belts surrounding the earth.

The public interest in these lunar probes reflected the desire to have the United States beat the Russians to the moon and thus wipe out some of the lingering aftereffects of *Sputnik*. American confidence suffered another setback in early January when *Luna I*, the first Soviet lunar probe, flew within thirty-two hundred miles of the moon before going into solar orbit. Despite the Russian failure actually to reach the moon, *Luna I* maintained the Soviet lead in space by becoming the first man-made object to escape the earth's gravitational pull.[8]

ARPA, rather than NASA, retained control over the third U.S. space effort, the reconnaissance satellite, which Eisenhower felt was far more important than either scientific satellites or lunar probes. Worried that continued U-2 overflights of the Soviet Union might create an international incident, ever since the first *Sputnik* the president had looked forward to the day when American satellites would replace the vulnerable spy plane. He and his advisers had defended the high cost of the WS-117L program, allocating $186 million in the 1959 budget, nearly as much as the total for all NASA activities. Defense Secretary Neil McElroy had put the case for the reconnaissance satellite most forcefully, terming it "vital to the security of the United States." "The prior warning which the reconnaissance satellite might well provide," McElroy believed, "could save the country from heavy destruction in the event of a Soviet nuclear attack."

Given the importance of a spy satellite to American security, the president decided in February 1958 to put the CIA in charge of the effort, now code-named Corona. The air force, operating under orders from ARPA, would develop a special Thor booster to place a CIA-designed capsule, complete with camera, into a polar orbit that would offer the best possible view of Soviet territory from space. As the time for the first launch neared, ARPA decided to give out a cover story to the press. On December 3, 1958, the Pentagon announced Project Discoverer, described as a "long-range satellite program aimed at placing mice, monkeys, then man in space." Launched from Vandenberg Air Force Base in California rather than Florida's Cape Canaveral, these satellites would weigh about a thousand pounds, lighter than *Sputnik III* but much heavier than the American *Explorers*. Despite the scientific cover, experts speculated that the California site would permit the launch of reconnaissance satellites that required a polar orbit.[9]

Members of the President's Science Advisory Committee worried about what one termed the "political vulnerability" of the American spy satellite. O. G. Villard of the Space Science Board of the National Academy of Sciences objected to trying to pass off Discoverer as a purely scientific experiment. People were bound to learn its real purpose, he claimed, favoring instead a forthright policy of disclosing its reconnaissance mission. Another scientist suggested offering all the data gathered to the United Nations as part of a claim to a policy of freedom of space.[10]

The president was more concerned with the slow pace of Discoverer. The first flight, scheduled for January 1958, ran into technical difficulties and did not take place until late February. Meanwhile Eisenhower grew increasingly worried about the U-2 flights. Noting that the Russians were tracking these overflights with radar, he told his Board of Consultants on Foreign Intelligence Activities on December 22, 1958, that he wondered "whether the intelligence which we receive from this source is worth the exacerbation of international tension which results." Two months later, he informed advisers pressing for more U-2 flights that he felt they represented "undue provocation." "Nothing," he added, "would make him request authority to declare war more quickly than violation of our air space by Soviet aircraft." Referring obliquely to Discoverer, he said this project was coming along "nicely," and he would prefer to avoid U-2 overflights until the "new equipment" was ready. Unfortunately, as Donald Quarles pointed out, the reconnaissance satellites would not be ready for another eighteen months to two years.[11]

Quarles was very accurate in his prediction. The early Discoverer flights met with difficulty after difficulty; first the satellites did not go into the proper orbit, then the air force had trouble capturing the film packages that floated back to earth by parachute. Finally, in August 1960, Discoverer flights 13 and 14 succeeded in taking very revealing pictures of Soviet territory. By that time, however, the international incident that Ike had feared had already occurred when the Soviets shot down Francis Gary Powers's U-2 on May 1, 1960, leading the president to suspend the overflights. The success of Project Discoverer meant there was only a three-month gap in aerial surveillance of the Soviet Union; the spy satellite that Eisenhower had so strongly backed since *Sputnik* proved invaluable in protecting American security in the early 1960s, the period when the missile gap was supposed to be at its height.[12]

While NASA began to take control over all space activity except the spy satellite, two issues developed that required action by the Space Council. The first was the question of whether or not to transfer the army's two space activities—the Jet Propulsion Laboratory and the Army Ballistic Missile Agency—to NASA. Glennan thought he had worked out an agreement with Deputy Secretary of Defense Quarles for NASA to acquire both, but Secretary of the Army Wilber Brucker fought hard to hang onto the Huntsville operation. Leaks to the press, including a threat by Von Braun to quit if NASA took over his team, placed great pressure on the administration. The president expressed disgust at bureaucratic maneuvering and "the lack of any spirit of give and take" over this issue. Although he thought NASA should take charge of both activities, he accepted a compromise worked out between Glennan and Brucker that transferred the JPL to NASA but kept ABMA under army control for a year, with work on the million-pound booster at Huntsville to be done under contract to the space agency. On December 3, 1958, the Space Council formally accepted this solution.[13]

The second item on the agenda was a NASA request that Project Mercury, the plan for manned space flight, be given "highest priority." In arguing for this step, as well as for a budget commitment of over $100 million in 1959 and 1960, NASA claimed that putting man in space was "the cornerstone on which true space exploration will be built" and was "of utmost importance to the national prestige in the eyes of the world." In a meeting with Eisenhower prior to the formal Space Council session, Quarles and Killian both dissented on the designation of "highest priority" for manned space flight, claiming it would distort the entire priority system. The president also expressed reservations, preferring to save highest priority for "things of great importance or time-urgency." The Space Council, nevertheless, voted on December 3, 1958, to grant Project Mercury "highest priority" in order to achieve manned orbital flights by mid-1960.

Despite this action, President Eisenhower was clearly reluctant to commit the United States to an all-out space race with the Soviet Union. Although he approved a substantial increase in NASA's budget for 1960, from $240 to $370 million, he resisted a request by Glennan for an additional $125 million in early 1959 to develop a booster for manned flight to the moon in the 1960s. While admitting that we were in a contest with Russia for world prestige, he still felt "we must lay more stress on not going into debt by spending beyond our receipts."[14]

The president's personal reservations about manned space flight came out most clearly when he asked NASA to modify public statements on its goals. He urged "less emphasis" on ultimate applications and greater stress on "more limited objectives." When Glennan asked him for permission to recruit members of the military for space flight, the president agreed but then asked the NASA chief not to publicize the astronauts, in order "to avoid generating a great deal of premature press build-up." These words fell on deaf ears; soon NASA would embark on an extensive publicity campaign centering on the selection and training of the first Americans to venture into space. The president, however, remained skeptical of the space race between the United States and the Soviet Union that had begun with *Sputnik*. He gave ground grudgingly to the public and congressional pressure for space spectaculars, all the while ensuring that the American response included the spy satellite that he deemed essential to national security.[15]

II

Steady progress in the American missile program in the fall of 1958 appeared to justify the president's deliberate response to the *Sputnik* crisis. The main focus was on the Atlas ICBM, scheduled for deployment before the end of 1959. The air force completed the first set of tests in September, with three successful flights of the first stage at a distance of six hundred miles. The first test of the two-stage Atlas at intercontinental range, however, ended in an explosion only eighty seconds after it left the launch pad. In October McElroy informed Eisenhower that on the second try an Atlas had "accomplished a significant milestone in that the full ICBM 5500 nautical mile range was achieved." He added, however, that accuracy was still a problem; the dummy warhead landed twenty-four miles from the target area.[16]

The first fully successful Atlas test at its full range of sixty-three hundred miles in late November led to new assertions that the United States had met the Soviet missile challenge. *Time* praised both the Air Force and Convair, builder of the Atlas, for sticking to a "schedule that was programed for maximum effort long before Sputnik." Claiming that the Atlas was close to becoming "a real operational weapon," the magazine concluded that "Russia has no monopoly" on the ICBM and that the American missile program was "coming and coming fast." *U.S. News & World Report* agreed, asserting that even before the most recent Atlas tests the United States possessed "a formidable arsenal" of missiles. "The U.S. is clearly superior to Soviet Russia in military strength today," the editors boasted. "That superiority rests both in nuclear weapons and the means of delivering those weapons to a target."[17]

The air force, however, did not want to rely exclusively on the first-generation Atlas ICBM. Within the Pentagon it fought hard for both the more sophisticated Titan, which could be placed in a hardened silo with its storable liquid fuel, and the Minuteman, the true second-generation solid-fuel ICBM. General Bernard Schriever, head of the Ballistic Missile Division, resisted attempts to slash the Minuteman budget in half or to terminate the Titan and use its funds to pay the high cost of Minuteman development. Schriever was able to defend his ICBMs from budgetary attacks by both the army and navy. He countered with a request to expand the Titan deployment from four to eleven squadrons and thus raise the planned ICBM force from 130 missiles to 200 by 1962. The Joint Chiefs forwarded this proposal to the White House, where it would be considered in the final deliberations over the fiscal 1960 budget later in the fall of 1958.[18]

Final testing and deployment of IRBMs also proceeded on schedule in the second half of 1959. Although both the Thor and Jupiter experienced failures in early tests, by December both missiles had been fired successfully. The army sent a Jupiter some fifteen hundred miles downrange, while the air force Thor went nearly as far. Neither missile, however, had yet achieved a high degree of accuracy. Nevertheless, the United States went ahead with plans to place four Thor squadrons in Great Britain and continued negotiations for Jupiter bases in other European countries, primarily Italy and Turkey.[19]

In September components of the first Thors began to arrive in England. By the end of the year, the air force had announced the arrival of all four squadrons, some sixty missiles, at the British bases, where they were within range of Moscow. Training of English crews who would fire the Thors under American command and control took another six months. Yet even when the first squadron became operational in June 1959, the Thors were rated at only 50 percent reliability. And they remained vulnerable to a Soviet first strike, since it took at least fifteen minutes to fill them with liquid fuel prior to launch.[20]

It was this inherent weakness of the IRBMs, together with the prospect of early ICBM deployment, that led Secretary of Defense McElroy to announce a surprising revision in American strategic policy in November 1958. Answering a question at a press conference on when the Pentagon would make a choice between Thor and Jupiter, he replied that both would be produced, but only in limited numbers. In view of the vulnerability of IRBMs to a Soviet first strike, he felt it would be unwise to deploy additional Thors and Jupiters since "we are coming closer to the time of the operational capability of the Atlas." Two days later, however, the State Department, in an apparent effort to reassure the NATO allies, issued a statement saying that there was "no lessening" of the American intention of basing Thors and Jupiters in Europe. "The IRBM program," the State Department affirmed, "is best suited to strengthening that part of the free world's defenses which lie in Europe."

McElroy was furious at what he considered unwarranted State Department interference in strategic policy. He called John Foster Dulles on November 17 to protest, saying he found it "strange for one Dept. to put out an interpretation of another Dept.'s press statement." The secretary of state claimed it was done without his knowledge when he was out of town; he said he was "disturbed" and agreed that "it never should have happened."[21]

The press quickly noted the rift between the Defense and State Departments. The initial American response to the apparent Soviet lead in the ICBM race signaled by *Sputnik* had been to rely on IRBMs in Europe to protect the NATO countries from Soviet missile blackmail, as well as to add to the American bomber deterrent before the Atlas and Titan ICBMs could be deployed. The editors of the *Nation* and the *Reporter* observed that it was the United States who had taken the initiative on placing IRBMs in Europe and that the NATO allies had been quite reluctant about accepting them, fearing that the American Thors and Jupiters would be a likely target for a Soviet nuclear strike. Both journals backed McElroy, stating that it made more sense for the United States to rely on ICBMs on its own territory to deter the Soviet Union. In contrast to the State Department, they believed that removal of the American IRBMs would reassure rather than alarm Europeans.

In the ensuing controversy, some observers began to question the wisdom of relying so heavily on missiles for deterrence. William J. Newman, a Boston University government professor, argued that it was dangerous to use missiles, which reached their targets within thirty minutes, to deliver nuclear weapons. B-52 bombers were much safer, since they could be kept on aerial alert and called back hours after an initial attack order. The early missiles, moreover, were notoriously unreliable and quite inaccurate. Carl Dreher, writing in the *Nation,* agreed with this assessment of the lack of precision and reliability of first-generation missiles. He also favored depending on bombers for the next few years until a more sophisticated second generation of missiles came on line, the Polaris and Minuteman. He stressed the very high costs of missiles compared to aircraft and bemoaned the "gargantuan" waste involved in building duplicate ICBMs, such as the Atlas and Titan. Yet it was the huge expense that doomed all efforts at making rational choices in the missile age. "So much money is invested in a single big missile," Dreher pointed out, "that its discontinuance is inconceivable until at least a few units have been fired in a final demonstration of its obsolescence."[22]

This criticism had little effect on the administration's decision to make ICBMs the heart of the American nuclear deterrent. On October 4, 1958, the air force opened a second major American launch complex in California both as a missile test and training ground and as a site for the deployment of the first Atlas squadron. Located on the Pacific coast 170 miles northwest of Los Angeles, Camp Cooke, an inactive army post, became Vandenberg Air Force Base. Launch pads completed in the fall of 1958 were used to test Thor and Titan missiles while work continued on facilities to house both Atlas and Titan missiles when they became operational. The new base, boasted *U.S. News & World Report* in December, was "the world's biggest and most elaborately equipped missile center."[23]

One great advantage of Vandenberg over Cape Canaveral in Florida lay in the way it could launch satellites in a north-south polar orbit. Vandenberg became the home base for Project Discoverer, the spy satellite operation announced in December 1958. The president originally had hoped that Vandenberg would provide greater secrecy than Canaveral, where the press regularly observed all launches from beaches only a few miles away. In November the Pentagon press office informed the White House that reporters could follow all the Pacific launches from nearby public property. Reluctantly Eisenhower agreed to the same policy followed in Florida: "giving to the press the information that they could get in any event, but giving it to them in an orderly, embargoed way, and specifying that firings which would reveal classified information will not be open to press coverage."[24]

The administration went ahead with plans to deploy the first Atlas squadron at Vandenberg, but it decided to place the other twelve ICBM squadrons at air force bases in the interior of the nation, primarily in the Great Plains region. Warren Air Force Base outside Cheyenne, Wyoming, received the second group of Atlas ICBMs, while future squadrons were programmed for bases in Idaho, Washington, Nebraska, Kansas, Colorado, and South Dakota. The first Atlas squadrons were completely exposed to enemy attack; subsequent ones were placed in concrete bunkers that offered some protection. The Atlas, which took more than ten minutes to be filled with thirty thousand gallons of highly explosive RP-1 fuel and liquid oxygen, could not be fired from hardened silos. The air force relied on dispersal for minimal protection against a first strike, placing the nine missiles in a squadron in three widely scattered groups. Titan missiles, using a storable liquid fuel, were programmed for silos hardened to withstand a blast of 100 psi, with each silo located several miles away from the next.

The need to protect American missiles from a Soviet first strike slowed down the projected deployment of the first generation of ICBMs. The widely spaced concrete silos created a huge engineering complex that required nearly three years to complete from the time construction began. The first Atlas squadron at Vandenberg was deployed on open launch pads in stages in 1959, beginning with three missiles in July and only six by the end of the year. Gradually the other sites were finished, with the second Atlas squadron becoming operational in Wyoming in September 1960 and the remaining squadrons in 1961 and 1962. By December 1962 the United States had deployed nineteen ICBM squadrons—thirteen Atlas and six Titan. Minuteman became operational in late 1962, and one thousand of these second generation missiles replaced all but fifty-four of the Titans by the end of 1965.[25]

It is now clear that there was no missile gap in the early 1960s. The Soviet Union deployed fewer than a dozen of its first generation SS-6 missiles by 1960, fewer even than the first American Atlas missiles at Vandenberg and Warren. The year 1962, cited by Joseph Alsop as the time of maximum danger when it was believed the Russians would have 1,000 ICBMs to only 130 for the United States, was the year of the Cuban missile crisis. By that time, there was a missile gap in reverse: The United States had about two hundred ICBMs compared to fewer than one hundred for the Soviet Union. Add the nine American submarines carrying 144 Polaris missiles, and the American retaliatory advantage became overwhelming in the early 1960s.[26]

Eisenhower had been right all along. The missile program that he had begun in 1955 provided more than an ample margin of security for the United States as it made the transition from B-52 bombers to long-range missiles in the late 1950s and early 1960s. The president had resisted the pressures of the Gaither committee and the Democratic opposition in Congress for massive increases in defense spending to ward off a mythic Soviet threat. Yet he had proved unable to convince either Congress or the American people that there was no danger. His stubborn insistence on trying to hold down defense spending spared the nation untold billions, but he did agree to increases that he felt were not truly necessary. Eisenhower deserves high marks for protecting the national security without overreacting; as a political leader, however, he failed to persuade the American people that they were safe from foreign danger.

III

The congressional election of 1958 confirmed Eisenhower's inability to reassure a worried American electorate. His personal popularity, which had fallen to an all-time low of 49 percent in the Gallup poll in April, rose to 58 percent over the summer and then fell back to 56 percent by October. Despite the fact that more than half the people gave his presidential performance a positive rating, reporters pressed him hard on his administration's achievements as the fall election approached. Asked at an October 1, 1958, press conference to comment on America's military position on the anniversary of *Sputnik,* the president cited the four satellites the United States had put in orbit in the last seven months. On missiles, he claimed the Russians had a head start as a result of lethargy in the Truman years but that his administration had greatly narrowed their lead. "I believe we have the biggest, strongest, finest body of scientists," he concluded, "amply armed with money to do the job, and that's that."

Some commentators thought that Eisenhower's rather abrupt press conference remarks had ignored political realities. "What Ike misses was that it is his own leadership, his ability to dramatize the record, that is a key issue—perhaps the only real issue—in Election Year 1958," observed *Time.* Samuel Lubell noted that the Republican candidates for Congress badly needed all the help the president could offer them in the midst of a recession that gave Democrats a great advantage. Although the outcome would probably turn on local issues, Lubell felt the GOP needed to draw upon Eisenhower's personal appeal to many voters. The people still liked Ike, he commented, although he did detect "a deep concern that Eisenhower may no longer be the master of the White House."[27]

One source of political weakness was the president's insistence on stressing fiscal restraint at a time when the Democrats were calling for more spending, both to overcome the recession at home and match the Soviet challenge abroad. Asked about the 1960 budget in mid-October, Eisenhower said he was doing everything he could "to get it down to the last cent that I think is needed" for national security and safety, adding "I believe we are spending too much money." Referring to Democratic campaign calls for greater expenditures, the president voiced his objection to the theory "that just money alone is going to make the United States greater, stronger both at home and abroad." The same day, he complained to a Republican group that as a result of *Sputnik* Congress had voted for "additional sums" that were unnecessary and had led to a big deficit, which he vowed to eliminate in the future.[28]

Aware that he had to answer the charge that his administration had allowed the Soviets to open up a missile gap, Eisenhower began to prepare a campaign speech on national defense. He told his speechwriters to develop the theme that the Democrats had "completely neglected" missiles and that since 1955 the administration had worked hard to narrow the Russian lead. Usually reluctant to engage in political infighting, the president said he felt a tragic error had been made and that the Republicans had to be "almost barbed" in telling this story.[29]

In his basic campaign speech, given first in Los Angeles on October 20 and then repeated with only minor variations to audiences in Chicago, Pittsburgh, and Baltimore later in the month, Eisenhower strongly defended his record on space and missiles. Claiming that he had inherited a "missile gap" from Truman, who spent only $1 million a year on rockets, the president pointed out that he followed the recommendations of his scientific advisers in 1955 and gave both the IRBM and the ICBM "the nation's highest priority." "No effort, no talent, no expense has since been spared," Eisenhower boasted, "to speed these projects." "Today America—and all the world—knows that in less than four years we are rapidly closing the missile gap that we inherited," the president concluded. "The Sputniks have been matched by Explorers, Vanguards, and Pioneers."

At the same time, Eisenhower insisted on continuing his crusade against "wasteful government spending." He denounced the pleas of Democratic critics for even greater expenditures for missiles and other weapons. Pointing out that these "self-styled liberals" call for both more spending and tax cuts, he asked, "Now, just how gullible do these spenders think Americans really are?" Above all, he stressed America's nuclear superiority, stating that SAC's striking power was "beyond imagination." In running for office, he recalled, he had "promised a strong national defense." "No matter what the political merchants of fear and defeat would have you believe," he told the voters, "we have kept the promise."[30]

Despite the president's fervid appeals, the electorate gave the administration a stern rebuff. The Democrats won a sweeping victory, gaining thirteen seats in the Senate and forty-seven in the House and adding five governorships to control thirty-four statehouses. As a result, those whom the president denounced as irresponsible spenders would command a 62 to 34 vote margin in the Senate and 282 to 153 in the House. Speaking to his aides, Eisenhower admitted that the Democrats had scored a "sweep" of "devastating proportions." He realized that the figures were so bad "that there are scarcely enough Republican votes to sustain a veto." The only bright spot, he noted, was that the defeat might unify the Republicans and end the party feuding he had found so distasteful.[31]

Political commentators cited many factors that contributed to the Democratic victory. Local issues, as always, played a big role in the outcome: a rejection of Secretary of Agriculture Ezra Taft Benson's policies in the farm states, right-to-work measures in several industrial states that brought out a heavy labor vote, and the recession, which took its toll on the party in power. Liberal analyst Carey McWilliams noted the lack of any commanding national issues and called it a "landslide in a vacuum." *Life* claimed that personalities played a larger role than issues and took some solace in the success of moderate Republicans like Governor Nelson Rockefeller in New York and the defeat of Old Guard Senators William Knowland in California and John W. Bricker in Ohio.

Nearly everyone, however, viewed the outcome as a reflection of the loss of national confidence in Eisenhower's leadership. The *Wall Street Journal* declared it was Ike "who had the sense of direction and lost it." The *Denver Post* spoke of "weak, distracted and irrationalized leadership"; the *Atlanta Constitution* accused the president of being "indecisive, uncertain and hesitant"; the *Providence Journal* claimed that "dissatisfaction" with Eisenhower "was at the root of the results." A GOP national committeeman from Utah expressed his disgust with the president's "aloofness from politics," claiming that "his attitude of being above it all has made us all just a bit ashamed to be politicians." What seemed most important of all was Eisenhower's inability to stem a growing feeling of national uneasiness, a feeling of what the *Wall Street Journal* termed "impending disaster." Samuel Lubell attributed the loss of confidence in Eisenhower to "a sense that as a nation we are beset by problems which are slipping beyond our control."[32]

The president understood that he had suffered a personal defeat. At his press conference the day after the election, he appeared tired and dispirited. "It was plain that the Democratic landslide had jolted Dwight Eisenhower badly—that he found it painful to talk about," noted *Time*. The president tried to put the best face on the outcome, saying that he hoped that many of the Democrats shared his concern for fiscal integrity and would join him in doing what was "best for the country." He pointed out that the deficit was approaching a record $12 billion for the current fiscal year and warned against the possibility of inflation. Regretting that the 1958 vote marked a "complete reversal" after his reelection just two years before, he still planned to oppose excessive spending and work for the fiscal soundness of the country.[33]

The president may not have known how difficult a time he would have in holding down spending in the 1960 budget. Even members of his own cabinet felt that Eisenhower was obsessed with economy measures. HEW Secretary Arthur Flemming, upset by the president's insistence on a balanced budget at a cabinet meeting three days after the election, told a sympathetic John Foster Dulles that both the Congress and the people wanted more spending. Worried about the influence of conservatives like Secretary of the Treasury Robert Anderson, Flemming suggested that Dulles and Vice-President Richard Nixon try to help Ike see the need for more creative policies.[34]

Knowing that the Democrats in Congress were crucial to his goal of "holding the line on our expenditures" in the 1960 budget, the president allowed Secretary of the Treasury Anderson to arrange a private meeting with a fellow Texan, Senate Majority Leader Lyndon Johnson, on November 18. Eisenhower tried to solicit LBJ's help in curbing some of the Democrats in Congress who favored "rapid expansion in a number of military programs." Johnson replied that many Democrats would prefer cuts in foreign aid to hold down the deficit. When Eisenhower said that during his final two years in office "his single and only concern was the welfare of the country as a whole" and asked for Johnson's "close cooperation" in holding down spending, LBJ was noncommittal. Johnson did suggest that the president consult with Richard Russell on defense issues, and he agreed to meet with Eisenhower from time to time in an effort to achieve bipartisan consensus.[35]

The outcome of the 1958 elections left Eisenhower in a difficult political position. There is no evidence that *Sputnik* or talk of a missile gap was directly responsible for the Republican defeat.[36] Yet the Soviet satellite had begun an erosion of public confidence in Eisenhower's ability to lead the nation amid the uncertainties of the new space age. The success in launching satellites and testing ICBMs helped restore some measure of pride in American technology, but few Americans seemed to share the president's overriding concern with fiscal restraint. Fearful that the Russians might soon regain the lead with either a moon shot or a missile breakthrough, the voters had turned to the Democrats as a better bet to deal with the unknown dangers that lay ahead.

IV

The 1958 congressional elections undermined Eisenhower's determination to limit defense spending. Before the Democratic victory, he tried to persuade the Pentagon to hold the 1960 defense budget to a ceiling of $40 billion, just above the current level of military expenditures. Outraged by the high cost of new weapons—airplanes and missiles that cost as much as $23 million apiece—the president warned Joint Chiefs Chairman Nathan Twining on September 29 that the military must help him achieve a balanced budget. Russian moves in the Cold War, he suggested, included "efforts to make us spend ourselves into weakness."

Eisenhower targeted the duplication of weapons, especially missiles with similar missions, as the best place to economize. He asked his aides to prepare a "graphic chart to illustrate those duplications." The president kept pointing out the overlap between Thor and Jupiter IRBMs and Atlas and Titan ICBMs. As new weapons were developed, he explained in his postelection press conference on November 5, it was necessary to cut out the older ones "that they are displacing." We could not, he added, "just pile one weapon and one system of weapons on another, and so in the long run break ourselves." Later the same day he reiterated this point to a group of scientists, calling the budget situation "intolerable unless we are able to bring expenditures in line with receipts." We had to find "a mechanism which will disclose and assist in the elimination of duplicating weapons systems," he insisted.[37]

The Pentagon failed to heed the president's warnings. Although Secretary Neil McElroy was able to pare down the original service requests to a total of $43 billion, this figure was still $3 billion over the president's goal for 1960. Instead of cutting back the Titan as Eisenhower and others urged, the air force recommended increasing the number of ICBMs to be deployed by 1962 from 130 to 200 by adding seven additional Titan squadrons. The navy wanted a second nuclear-powered aircraft carrier without sacrificing the Polaris program that Congress favored. Even McElroy refused to make a choice between the Thor and the Jupiter, finally deciding to produce both but in smaller numbers than the original projection.[38]

Faced with this apparent impasse, in late November the president summoned both his economic and military advisers to Augusta, where he was spending the Thanksgiving holiday. Secretary of the Treasury Robert Anderson and Budget Director Maurice Stans informed the president that they could balance the 1960 budget at about $77 billion if defense spending did not increase. Stans submitted a memorandum in which he stated, "It is my strong recommendation that the Department of Defense be held to a level of $40 billion [in] expenditures," adding that in his judgment this figure "will not significantly impair the security of the country."

Events beyond the president's control made it impossible for him to accept this advice. Nikita Khrushchev had just begun the second Berlin crisis by threatening to turn the Soviet zone of the city over to East

Germany, an action the United States objected to adamantly. With the Democrats already calling for higher defense spending, the Pentagon could now argue that the intensified Cold War required increases rather than cuts in the military budget.[39]

Neil McElroy opened the Augusta meeting in a conciliatory way by pointing out that he had reduced the original Pentagon request to less than $43 billion in new obligational authority and to just under $42 billion in actual expenditures for 1960. This represented an increase of only $2 billion at a time of grave national crisis. He went on to make the case for adding seven additional Titan squadrons, for a total of two hundred ICBMs, and for expanding the navy's Polaris program from five to nine submarines. His main concession to economy was cutting back the IRBM allotment from the authorized twelve squadrons to just eight, despite the objections of the State Department.

Anderson and Stans repeated their pleas for a $40 billion ceiling for the Defense Department. They pointed out that domestic agencies had cut their original requests from $42 to $36.5 billion; if the Pentagon would only match half these reductions, the administration could balance the budget. Eisenhower asked more pointed questions, wondering why the defense budget still included so many duplicate weapons. "How many times do we have to destroy Russia?" he asked. He particularly objected to the Titan, which he considered a costly and unnecessary duplication of the Atlas ICBM. McElroy introduced a political angle when he replied that the elimination of the Titan program would cost twenty-five thousand jobs and add greatly to the unemployment rolls.

Realizing that further discussion was futile, Eisenhower adjourned the Augusta conference with a request that the two opposing sides try to work out a compromise and present it at the next scheduled National Security Council meeting in Washington on December 4. Leaving the meeting, Nathan Twining said the president was angry at the military ("full of red meat," he told Ann Whitman, Ike's secretary) as he insisted they go at least part way to prevent a deficit. The next day, Eisenhower vented his anger at the air force for asking for what he termed "fantastic" sums for weapons "that were still in someone's mind." He objected above all to the idea of funding three different ICBMs—the Atlas, Titan, and Minuteman—simultaneously. He told McElroy that "the Air Force felt, unsoundly to him, that they had to develop, produce and procure weapons all at the same time."[40]

John Foster Dulles, whose failing health would prevent him from attending the upcoming NSC meeting, still tried to back the president. He told Robert Anderson that he had urged Eisenhower to resist the "terrific amount of overlapping" in new weapons and to use the savings to prevent cuts in conventional forces. Dulles, known to the public as the architect of massive retaliation, had learned from experience, notably in the Formosa Straits crisis and the Lebanon intervention, the importance of "conventional forces which we use every day in our business." Fearful that the Pentagon would reduce ground troops to save the new weapons, he warned that "if we have nothing but nuclear warfare, we will be in a bad spot."[41]

When Eisenhower returned to Washington on December 3, 1958, Maurice Stans informed him that he could achieve a balanced budget for 1960 if foreign aid could be held to $3.5 billion and defense spending to $40.8 billion. The president, stressing his "strong desire for a balanced budget," agreed to the cut in foreign aid and asked his aides to meet with McElroy to work out a deal "along these lines." In effect Eisenhower wanted the Bureau of the Budget and the Pentagon to split the difference on defense spending.

The NSC meeting, which finally took place on Saturday, December 6, after a two-day delay, proved to be what Ann Whitman termed a "bloody" showdown that ended in a draw. "Apparently the Navy refused to give one inch," she commented, "and if the Navy would not give in, neither would any other service." McElroy presented the Defense Department recommendations for seven additional Titan squadrons, four more Polaris submarines for 1960 with three more planned for 1961 (a total of twelve), and for a reduction from twelve to eight IRBM squadrons in Europe—five Thor and three Jupiter. The president withheld comment but indicated he would approve if offsetting savings could be found in other Defense Department programs. He instructed Anderson and McElroy to meet over the weekend and reach agreement on a figure, telling Ann Whitman that if they did he would consider it a "miracle."[42]

Eisenhower gave in on Monday, December 8, accepting a final sum of just under $41 billion for defense expenditures in 1960. While the increase in defense spending was only about $1 billion, the new budget figures that the president approved represented a significant increase in the size of American nuclear striking forces. The number of ICBMs planned for 1962 would go from 130 to 200, while the doubling of Polaris submarines would add 112 IRBMs, more than offsetting the reduction of 60 Thor and Jupiter missiles in Europe.

From Eisenhower's standpoint, the most regrettable result was to build huge increases into future defense budgets. When the cost of Minuteman—which went up from just $26 million in FY 1958 to $276 million in 1960—was added in, the American ICBM budget would reach a peak of over $1.5 billion in 1961, with the accelerated Polaris program adding $2 billion more. Altogether the strategic weapons authorized by the Eisenhower administration would eventually cost the American taxpayer more than $15 billion (see Table 7).[43]

In giving his final approval, the president made clear his feeling of helplessness. He told Gordon Gray, who had succeeded Robert Cutler as national security adviser in the summer of 1958, that "if he were in

TABLE 7: Table of Projected ICBM and Polaris Missile Costs
(in millions of dollars)

	1958	1959	1960	1961	1962	1963
Atlas	653.7	665.4	558.8	493.1	142.0	72.0
Titan	365.4	560.5	636.7	821.0	421.0	133.0
Minuteman	26.0	233.0	276.0	308.0	240.0	185.0
Polaris	966.7	1,180.4	1,600.0	2,000.0	2,000.0	600.0
Total	2,002.8	2,639.3	3,071.5	3,622.1	2,803.0	990.0

charge [of the Pentagon] he felt that he could take $5 billion out of the Defense budget." But since the military asserted that the programs they presented at the NSC meeting on Saturday "were essential to the national security, he had little choice but to approve them."

The president was equally candid with McElroy, claiming that he had been "dragooned" into approving the Pentagon's proposals. He expressed special distaste for the increase in ICBM squadrons, saying he still did not understand why "it was necessary to program" both Titan and Atlas missiles. He then made it clear to the defense secretary that "his approval was reluctant but was given only because he felt he had no choice."[44]

One reason the president had not fought harder was his realization that, if he held the military in check during the budget process, the generals and admirals could simply have gone to Congress to ask for higher appropriations. On December 15, in a meeting with Republican congressional leaders, he went over the defense budget explaining the reasons for the increases and counseling moderation. But he admitted that, in this regard, "I'm still a reactionary." Usually, he observed, in peacetime Congress gave the president less for defense than he asked for, but this year he expected the Democrats to insist on more funding than he thought reasonable. Urging the GOP leaders to help him hold the line, he concluded, "If anyone were to take the sum of all the estimates of requirements based on the aggregates of their fears, the result would be out of this world."[45]

Thus the president knew that the nearly $41 billion figure that Anderson and McElroy finally compromised on for defense spending in 1960 was at best a minimum. In his final two years in office, Eisenhower would do all he could to hold back the tide of military expenditures, at times even refusing to spend the additional funds appropriated by Congress. Forced to ask for more than he felt was necessary for national defense, he still fought hard to achieve what he termed "security with prudence." The vast sums spent for new weapons after *Sputnik* came in spite of rather than in response to Eisenhower's strategic vision.[46]

V

On December 18, 1958, President Eisenhower made a dramatic announcement during a diplomatic dinner at the White House. The United States had just carried out Project Score, placing an entire Atlas missile into orbit around the earth; at four and a half tons, the fuel tank and engine of the rocket made it by far the largest object ever sent into space. More important, Score had put a 150-pound communications satellite into orbit, complete with a Christmas message to the world that would be beamed back to earth in the next day or two. The president took obvious pride in what he claimed "constitutes a distinct step forward in space operations." His dinner guests shared in the mood of celebration. "Of course," commented Ann Whitman, "everyone was elated."

The next day the Score satellite broadcast the president's recorded message to the entire world. "Through the marvels of scientific advance," Eisenhower began, "my voice is coming to you from a satellite circling in outer space." He went on to "convey to you and all mankind America's wish for peace on earth and good will toward men everywhere."[47]

The American press hailed Score as the final American answer to *Sputnik*. *U.S. News & World Report* headlined its story "4½-TON SATELLITE SHOWS WHAT U.S. CAN DO." The editors pointed out that the latest edition of *Jane's All the World's Aircraft* ranked the United States ahead of the Soviet Union in air power and then concluded that the United States had clearly established "a lengthening lead in the space race." Although *Time* admitted that sending a spent rocket into space was a stunt that served no useful scientific purpose, it nevertheless stressed the fact that Score proved that the United States had solved the critical guidance problem in launching the Atlas into orbit. The editors of *Newsweek* drew a contrast with the preceding year, when the Russians could boast of two *Sputniks* compared to the American failure to launch *Vanguard*. "Now the whole picture had changed," they commented; "the 'missile gap' has been closed."[48]

Critics were quick to point out the hollowness of these claims. The actual communications satellite that Score put into orbit weighed just over 150 pounds, far less than the 3,000-pound instrumented payload of *Sputnik III*. Orbiting the empty fuel tank and engine of the Atlas missile was a meaningless feat that failed to demonstrate any new technical capability. Calling Score "an extravagant propaganda stunt," the *New Republic* argued that it wasted money desperately needed for genuine scientific research.[49]

In a sense, the critics were right. When Eisenhower first approved Project Score in August 1958, he insisted that it be kept absolutely secret, with no advance word to the press. Aware of the highly publicized failures of the first American satellite launches and moon shots, the president wanted to be able to control the public reaction. At the same time, he ordered the originating agency, ARPA, to play down the military's role by turning the project over to NASA as soon as possible. And Eisenhower made sure that Killian was assigned general oversight of the project. The science adviser, in turn, informed the president at the outset that orbiting a spent rocket "does not represent a true technological advance vis-à-vis the Russians." Therefore, Killian told Eisenhower, the administration "at all levels should refrain from playing up the '9,000 pounds in orbit' aspect of this test."[50]

In the year following *Sputnik,* however, Dwight Eisenhower had learned how much more important appearances were than reality when it came to space feats. In his public statements, he stressed the value of the 150-pound communication satellite in helping the people of the world exchange ideas and information rapidly. At the same time, he did nothing to discourage the euphoria of the press over the huge size of the orbiting Atlas. The American people, he had come to realize, were more impressed by spectacular deeds in space than by scientifically correct experiments.

The lesson of *Sputnik* was clear. The Soviets had won a sweeping propaganda victory by upstaging the United States and placing the first artificial satellite into orbit around the globe. Eisenhower had seen from the beginning that the real significance of this feat lay in demonstrating the feasibility of, and even offering a legal precedent for, a future reconnaissance satellite that could replace the vulnerable U-2. While the public worried about losing the space race and allowing the Soviets to open up a dangerous missile gap, the president concentrated on a prudent and limited expansion of American missile programs, a speedup in the reconnaissance satellite effort, a modest extension of federal aid to education in the name of national defense, and the creation of a civilian agency devoted to the peaceful exploration of outer space. Yet in achieving these goals, he had failed to quiet the fears of the American people that *Sputnik* represented a fundamental shift in military power and scientific achievement from the United States to the Soviet Union. Project Score was the president's belated recognition that appearances were of primary importance in the new space age; during his last two years in the White House, Eisenhower would give as much weight to intangible factors such as world opinion and prestige as to missiles and spacecraft.

NOTES

List of Manuscript Collections Cited in Notes

Dwight D. Eisenhower Presidential Library, Abilene, Kansas
    John Foster Dulles Papers (Dulles Telephone Calls)
    Dwight D. Eisenhower Papers of the President of the United States (Ann
        Whitman File)
        Administrative Series
        Dwight D. Eisenhower Diary Series (DDE Diary)
        NSC Series
    T. Keith Glennan Diary
    Bryce Harlow Papers
    Office of the Special Assistant for National Security Affairs (OSANSA):
        NSC Series, Briefing Notes Subseries (NSC Briefing Notes)
            Policy Papers Subseries
        OCB Series, Subject Subseries (OSANSA OCB)
        Special Assistant Series, Chronological Subseries
            Presidential Subseries
            Subject Subseries
    Office of the Special Assistant for Science and Technology (OSAST)
    President's Science Advisory Committee (PSAC)
    Staff Secretary, Cabinet Series, Minnich notes (SS Cabinet Series)
            Legislative Meeting Series, Minnich notes (SS LM)
            Subject Series, Alphabetical Subseries (SS Alpha)
            Department of Defense Subseries (SS DOD)
            White House Subseries (SS WH)
    White House Central Files, Confidential File (WHCF CF)
    Ann Whitman Diary (ACW Diary)
Lyndon B. Johnson Presidential Library, Austin, Texas
    Lyndon B. Johnson Papers
        Senate Papers
        Statements File

Richard B. Russell Memorial Library, University of Georgia, Athens, Georgia
    Richard B. Russell Papers
University of Missouri Western Historical Manuscript Collection, Columbia,
    Missouri Stuart Symington Papers

List of Published Sources Cited in Notes

Albrook, Robert A. "How Good Are Our Missiles?" *Reporter* 18 (Feb. 6, 1958).
Ambrose, Stephen E. *Eisenhower the President*. New York, 1984.
Armacost, Michael H. *The Politics of Weapons Innovation: The Thor-Jupiter Controversy*. New York, 1969.
Ascoli, Max. "Our Cut Rate Education." *Reporter* 18 (Feb. 20, 1958).
Augenstein, Bruno W. "Evolution of U.S. Military Space Program, 1945–1960." *International Security Dimensions of Space*. Ed. Uri Ra'anan and Robert L. Pfaltzgraff, Jr. Hampden, Conn., 1984.
Baar, James, and William E. Howard. *Polaris!* New York, 1960.
Baldwin, Hanson. *The Great Arms Race: A Comparison of U.S. and Soviet Power Today*. New York, 1958.
Ball, Desmond. *Politics and Force Levels: The Strategic Missile Program of the Kennedy Administration*. Berkeley, 1980.
Barr, Stringfellow. "Idiot's Orbit: Cold War in a Lunar Age." *Nation* 186 (Jan. 25, 1958).
Bean, Louis. "Happy, Hopeful Democrats." *New Republic* 138 (March 24, 1958).
Beard, Edmund. *Developing the ICBM: A Study in Bureaucratic Politics*. New York, 1976.
Bendiner, Robert. "Who Owns Outer Space?" *Reporter* 18 (June 12, 1958).
Beschloss, Michael R. *Mayday: Eisenhower, Khrushchev and the U-2 Affair*. New York, 1986.
Bottome, Edgar M. *The Missile Gap: A Study of the Formulation of Military and Political Policy*. Rutherford, N.J., 1971.
Burns, Arthur J. "Some Lessons of the Recession." *Reporter* 19 (Dec. 11, 1958).
Burrows, William E. *Deep Black: Space Espionage and National Security*. New York, 1986.
Caidin, Mark. *Red Star in Space*. New York, 1963.
Cline, Ray S. *Secrets, Spies and Scholars: Blueprint of the Essential CIA*. Washington, 1976.
Clowse, Barbara Barksdale. *Brainpower for the Cold War: The Sputnik Crisis and the National Defense Education Act of 1958*. Westport, Conn., 1981.
Cutler, Robert. *No Time for Rest*. Boston, 1965.
Dale, Edwin L. "Are We Americans Going Soft?" *New York Times Magazine*. Dec. 1, 1957.
Dick, James C. "The Strategic Arms Race, 1957–1961: Who Opened the Missile Gap?" *Journal of Politics* 34 (1972).
Divine, Robert A. "Johnson and the Politics of Space." *The Johnson Years*, vol. 2: *Vietnam, the Environment, and Science*. Ed. Robert A. Divine. Lawrence, Kan., 1987.
Dreher, Carl. "Missile Madness." *Nation* 187 (Dec. 13, 1958).
Dulles, Allen. *The Craft of Intelligence*. New York, 1963.

Eisenhower, Dwight D. *Mandate for Change.* Garden City, N.Y., 1963.
———. *Waging Peace, 1956–1961.* Garden City, N.Y., 1965.
Eurich, Alvin C. "Russia's New Schooling." *Atlantic Monthly* 201 (April 1958).
Evans, Rowland, and Robert Novak. *Lyndon B. Johnson: The Exercise of Power.* New York, 1966.
Fischer, John. "Who's in Charge Here?" *Harper's* 216 (Feb. 1958).
Gavin, James W. *War and Peace in the Space Age.* New York, 1958.
Geelhoed, E. Bruce. *Charles E. Wilson and Controversy at the Pentagon, 1953–1957.* Detroit, 1979.
Goldwater, Barry M. *With No Apologies.* New York, 1970.
Griffith, Allison. *The National Aeronautics and Space Act: A Study of the Development of Public Policy.* Washington, 1962.
Hagan, John P. "The Viking and the Vanguard," *The History of Rocket Technology.* Ed. Eugene M. Emme. Detroit, 1964.
Halperin, Morton H. "The Gaither Committee and the Policy Process." *World Politics* 13 (April 1961).
Hayes, E. Nelson. "Tracking Sputnik I." *The Coming of the Space Age.* Ed. Arthur C. Clarke. New York, 1967.
Hessler, William H. "The Navy's Submersible Missile-Launching Base." *Reporter* 18 (June 12, 1958).
Hymoff, Edward. "Some of Our Launching Pads Are Missing." *Reporter* 20 (June 25, 1959).
Joint Committee on Defense Production. *Deterrence and Survival in the Nuclear Age.* 94th Congress, 2d Session. Washington, 1976.
Kaplan, Fred. *The Wizards of Armageddon.* New York, 1983.
Katzenbach, Edward L. "The Pentagon's Reorganization Muddle." *Reporter* 18 (May 15, 1958).
Killian, James R., Jr. *Sputnik, Scientists, and Eisenhower.* Cambridge, Mass., 1977.
Kinnard, Douglas. *President Eisenhower and Strategy Management: A Study in Defense Politics.* Lexington, Ky., 1977.
Kolodziej, Edward A. *An Uncommon Defense and Congress, 1945–1963.* Columbus, Ohio, 1966.
Koppes, Clayton R. *JPL and the American Space Program.* New Haven, 1982.
Korb, Lawrence J. *The Joint Chiefs of Staff: The First Twenty-five Years.* Bloomington, 1976.
Lapp, Ralph E. *The New Priesthood: The Scientific Elite and the Uses of Power.* New York, 1965.
Licklider, Roy E. "The Missile Gap Controversy." *Political Science Quarterly* 85 (Dec. 1970).
Loeb, Larry M. "Jupiter Missiles in Europe: A Measure of Presidential Power." *World Affairs* 139 (1976).
Lubell, Samuel. "Sputnik and American Public Opinion." *Columbia University Forum* 1 (1957).
Macmillan, Harold. *Riding the Storm, 1956–1959.* New York, 1971.
McDougall, Walter A. . . . *the Heavens and the Earth: A Political History of the Space Age.* New York, 1985.
McWilliams, Carey. "Landslide in a Vacuum." *Nation* 187 (Nov. 15, 1958).
Manno, Jack. *Arming the Heavens.* New York, 1984.
Medaris, John B. *Countdown for Decision.* New York, 1960.

Miles, Wyndam D. "The Polaris." *A History of Rocket Technology.* Ed. Eugene M. Emme. Detroit, 1964.

Millis, Walter. "The Road to Nowhere." *Nation* 185 (Dec. 14, 1957).

Mills, C. Wright. "Program for Peace." *Nation* 185 (Dec. 7, 1957).

Morgenthau, Hans J. "The Decline of America." *New Republic* 137 (Dec. 9, 1957).

Murphy, Charles J. V. "The White House Since Sputnik." *Fortune* 57 (Jan. 1958).

———. "The Embattled Mr. McElroy." *Fortune* 59 (April 1959).

———. "Khrushchev's Paper Bear." *Fortune* 70 (Dec. 1964).

Neufeld, Jacob. *Ballistic Missiles in the United States Air Force, 1945–1960.* Washington, 1990.

Nitze, Paul H. *From Hiroshima to Glasnost: At the Center of Decision.* New York, 1989.

Oakley, J. Ronald. *God's Country: America in the Fifties.* New York, 1986.

O'Donovan, Patrick. "Rude Awakening." *Nation* 185 (Oct. 26, 1957).

Perry, Robert L. "The Atlas, Thor, Titan and Minuteman." *The History of Rocket Technology.* Ed. Eugene M. Emme. Detroit, 1964.

Power, Thomas S. *Design for Survival.* New York, 1965.

Prados, John. *The Soviet Estimate: U.S. Intelligence Analysis & Russian Military Strength.* New York, 1982.

Prochnau, William N., and Richard W. Larsen. *A Certain Democrat: Senator Henry M. Jackson, a Political Biography.* Englewood Cliffs, N.J., 1972.

Ramo, Simon. *The Business of Science: Winning and Losing in the High-Tech Age.* New York, 1988.

Ravitch, Diane. *The Troubled Crusade: American Education, 1945–1980.* New York, 1983.

Raymond, Jack. "How Much Must We Spend for Defense?" *New Republic* 139 (Dec. 22, 1958).

Rockefeller Brothers Fund. *Prospects for America: The Rockefeller Panel Reports.* Garden City, N.Y., 1961.

Rosholt, Robert L. *An Administrative History of NASA, 1958–1963.* Washington, 1966.

Sapolsky, Harvey M. *The Polaris System Development: Bureaucratic and Programmatic Success in Government.* Cambridge, Mass., 1972.

Schoettle, Enid Curtis Bok. "The Establishment of NASA." *Knowledge and Power: Essays on Science and Government.* Ed. Sanford A. Lakoff. New York, 1966.

Schuman, Frederick L. "How Real Is the Soviet Military Threat?" *New Republic* 137 (Dec. 23, 1957).

Schwiebert, Ernest G. *A History of the U.S. Air Force Ballistic Missiles.* New York, 1965.

Senate Armed Services Committee. "Inquiry into Satellite and Missile Programs." *Hearings Before the Preparedness Investigating Subcommittee of the Senate Committee on Armed Services,* 85th Congress, 1st and 2d Sessions. Washington, 1958. (Cited in notes as Senate Inquiry.)

Senate Foreign Relations Committee. *Executive Sessions,* 85th Congress, 2d Session, vol. 10. Washington, 1980.

———. *Executive Sessions,* 86th Congress, 1st Session, vol. 11. Washington, 1982.

Shapiro, Karl. "Why Out-Russia Russia?" *New Republic* 138 (June 9, 1958).

Shapley, Harlow. "Satellite Hysteria." *Nation* 185 (Oct. 25, 1957).

Shepley, James R. "Life-and-Death Debate over Missile Program." *Life* 46 (March 9, 1959).

Silberman, Charles E., and Sanford S. Parker. "The Economic Impact of Defense." *Fortune* 57 (June 1958).

Stares, Paul B. *The Militarization of Space: U.S. Policy, 1945–1984.* Ithaca, N.Y., 1985.

Stebbins, Richard P. *The United States in World Affairs, 1957.* New York, 1958.

Swenson, Loyd S., Jr., James M. Grimwood, and Charles C. Alexander. *This New Ocean: A History of Project Mercury.* Washington, 1966.

Tokaty, G. A. "Soviet Rocket Technology." *The History of Rocket Technology.* Ed. Eugene M. Emme. Detroit, 1964.

U.S. Department of State. *Foreign Relations of the United States, 1954–1957,* vol. 4. Washington, 1986.

Von Braun, Wernher. "The Redstone, Jupiter, and Juno." *The History of Rocket Technology.* Ed. Eugene M. Emme. Detroit, 1964.

Wilson, Sloan. "It's Time to Close Our Carnival." *Life* 44 (March 24, 1958).

York, Herbert. *Race to Oblivion.* New York, 1970.

———. *Making Weapons, Talking Peace: A Physicist's Odyssey from Hiroshima to Geneva.* New York, 1987.

List of Abbreviations

ABMA	Army Ballistic Missile Agency
ACW	Ann C. Whitman
Alpha	Alphabetical File
ARPA	Advanced Research Projects Agency
BAS	*Bulletin of the Atomic Scientists*
BOB	Bureau of the Budget
CF	Confidential File
DDE	Dwight David Eisenhower
DOD	Department of Defense
JPL	Jet Propulsion Laboratory
LBJ	Lyndon B. Johnson
NACA	National Advisory Committee for Aeronautics
NASA	National Aeronautics and Space Administration
NDEA	National Defense Education Act
NIE	National Intelligence Estimate
NSC	National Security Council
NYT	*New York Times*
OCB	Operations Coordinating Board
OSANSA	Office of the Special Assistant for National Security Affairs
OSAST	Office of the Special Assistant for Science and Technology
PPP	*Public Papers of the Presidents of the United States*
PPS	Policy Papers Subseries

PSAC   President's Science Advisory Committee
SNIE   Special National Intelligence Estimate
SS   Staff Secretary
USN   *U.S. News & World Report*
WH   White House
WHCF   White House Central File
WSEG   Weapon System Evaluation Group

Introduction

1. E. Nelson Hayes, "Tracking Sputnik I," in Arthur C. Clarke, ed., *The Coming of the Space Age* (New York, 1967), 5–11; Mark Caidin, *Red Star in Space* (New York, 1963), 132–33.

2. *Time* 70 (Oct. 14, 1957), 29; ibid. 70 (Oct. 21, 1957), 50; Senate Armed Services Committee, "Inquiry into Satellite and Missile Programs," *Hearings Before the Preparedness Investigating Subcommittee of the Senate Committee on Armed Services*, 85th Congress, 1st and 2d Sessions (Washington, 1958; hereafter cited as Senate Inquiry), 147; Caidin, *Red Star,* 132.

3. *Time* 70 (Oct. 14, 1957), 29; *Science* 126 (Oct. 18, 1957), 739; ibid. 70 (Nov. 15, 1957), 1007.

4. October 1957 schedules, DDE Diary, Box 27; telephone calls, Oct. 5, 1957, DDE Diary, Box 27; Hagerty to Dulles, Oct. 5, 1957, Dulles Telephone Calls, Microfilm Reel 10; *NYT,* Oct. 6, 1957, p. 1.

5. *Newsweek* 50 (Oct. 14, 1957), 37; *Time* 70 (Oct. 14, 1957), 27; *New Republic* 137 (Oct. 14, 1957), 3–4; *Life* 43 (Oct. 14, 1957), 34–35.

6. *Time* 70 (Oct. 21, 1957), 21; Symington to Eisenhower, Oct. 8, 1957, Symington Papers, Com. Box 28; *Washington Post,* Oct. 6, 1957, clipping in Symington Papers, Com. Box 48; *NYT,* Oct. 20, 1957, p. 1.

7. *USN* 43 (Oct. 18, 1957), 86; *NYT,* Oct. 20, 1957, sec. 4, p. 1; list of quotations, Oct. 1957, Symington Papers, Welsh Box 172.

8. James R. Killian, Jr., *Sputnik, Scientists, and Eisenhower* (Cambridge, Mass., 1977), 7–8; *USN* 43 (Oct. 18, 1957), 31; *Reporter* 17 (Nov. 28, 1957), 2.

9. *Time* 70 (Oct. 14, 1957), 29; Edwin L. Dale, Jr., "Are We Americans Going Soft?," *NYT Magazine,* Dec. 1, 1957, p. 21; *Saturday Review* 40 (Nov. 16, 1957), 26.

10. *Life* 43 (Oct. 21, 1957), 35; *Reporter* 17 (Oct. 31, 1957), 10, 12.

11. Harlow Shapley, "Satellite Hysteria," *Nation* 185 (Oct. 25, 1957), 55, 60.

12. Ibid., 104; G. A. Tokaty, "Soviet Rocket Technology," in Eugene M. Emme, ed., *The History of Rocket Technology* (Detroit, 1964), 279; Caidin, *Red Star,* 87–97; *Look* 22 (Feb. 4, 1958).

13. *Saturday Review* 40 (Oct. 19, 1957), 26; C. Wright Mills, "Program for Peace," *Nation* 185 (Dec. 7, 1957), 420–21.

14. *USN* 43 (Oct. 18, 1957), 160; ibid. (Dec. 6, 1957), 136; *Nation* 185 (Oct. 19, 1957), 253.

15. Walter Millis, "The Road to Nowhere," *Nation* 185 (Dec. 14, 1957), 449; *New Republic* 137 (Dec. 23, 1957), 13; Frederick L. Schumann, "How Real Is the Soviet Military Threat?," ibid., 10.

16. *Atlantic Monthly* 200 (Dec. 1957), 4; *Time* 70 (Oct. 28, 1957), 18–19; *NYT,* Oct. 20, 1957, sec. 4, pp. 3, 10.

17. Patrick O'Donovan, "Rude Awakening," *Nation* 185 (Oct. 26, 1957), 278; *Time* 70 (Oct. 21, 1957), 23.

Chapter One

1. Charles J. V. Murphy, "The White House Since Sputnik," *Fortune* 57 (Jan. 1958), 100; Howard Pyle to Adams, Oct. 8, 1957, SS Alpha, Box 23; ACW Diary, Oct. 8, 1957, Box 9.

2. Staff notes, Oct. 7, 1957, DDE Diary, Box 27; Foster to Allen Dulles, Oct. 7, 1957, Hagerty to Foster Dulles, Oct. 7 and 8, 1957, Dulles Telephone Calls, Box 7.

3. Andrew Goodpaster memcon, Oct. 9, 1957 (of White House conference, Oct. 8, 1957), SS DOD, Box 6; Robert Cutler memcon, Oct. 8, 1957 (of White House conference, Oct. 8, 1957), NSC Briefing Notes, Box 13; and memo from Sec. of Defense McElroy to Eisenhower, Oct. 7, 1957, ibid., Box 7.

4. McElroy to Eisenhower, Oct. 7, 1957, NSC Briefing Notes, Box 7; "Satellite Programs in the Department of Defense," Oct. 25, 1957, Harlow Papers, Box 1; John P. Hagan, "The Viking and the Vanguard," in Emme, *History of Rocket Technology,* 125–26.

5. Hagan, "Viking and Vanguard," 127–35; "Satellite Programs," Oct. 25, 1957, Harlow Papers, Box 1; Rabi to Arthur S. Fleming, Oct. 10, 1956, NSC Briefing Notes, Box 7; Dwight D. Eisenhower, *Waging Peace, 1956–1961* (Garden City, N.Y., 1965), 209.

6. McElroy to Eisenhower, Oct. 7, 1957, NSC Briefing Notes, Box 7.

7. Goodpaster memcon, Oct. 9, 1957 (of White House conference, Oct. 8, 1957), SS DOD, Box 6; Cutler memcon, Oct. 8, 1957 (of White House conference, Oct. 8, 1957), NSC Briefing Notes, Box 13.

8. Killian, *Sputnik,* 12; Goodpaster memcons, Oct. 9, 1957 (of White House conference, Oct. 8, 1957), and Oct. 9, 1957 (of White House Conference, Oct. 9, 1957), SS DOD, Box 6.

9. *PPP,* Eisenhower, 1957, pp. 733–35.

10. Ibid., 719–32.

11. *Nation* 185 (Oct. 26, 1957), 278; *New Republic* 137 (Oct. 28, 1957), 2; *NYT,* Oct. 20, 1957, sec. 4, p. 3.

12. Minnich notes, Oct. 18, 1957, SS Cabinet Series, Box 4; Gates to McElroy, Oct. 22, 1957, and McElroy to Gates, Oct. 29, 1957, OSAST, Box 15.

13. Wernher Von Braun, "The Redstone, Jupiter, and Juno," in Emme, *History of Rocket Technology,* 108–11; John B. Medaris, *Countdown for Decision* (New York, 1960), 119–22, 144, 154–56; Herbert York, *Race to Oblivion* (New York, 1970), 105.

14. Goodpaster memcon, Oct. 9, 1957 (of White House meeting, Oct. 8, 1957), SS DOD, Box 6; Goodpaster memcon, Oct. 31, 1957 (of White House meeting, Oct. 30, 1957), SS DOD, Box 2.

15. Staff notes, Oct. 25, 1957, DDE Diary, Box 27; satellite chronology, Dec. 12, 1957, Harlow Papers, Box 1.

16. *PPP,* Eisenhower, 1957, p. 724; Goodpaster memcon, Oct. 9, 1957 (of White House meeting, Oct. 8, 1957), SS DOD, Box 6.

17. Paul B. Stares, *The Militarization of Space: U.S. Policy, 1945–1984*

(Ithaca, N.Y., 1985), 30–31; Bruno W. Augenstein, "Evolution of U.S. Military Space Program, 1945–1960," in Uri Ra'anan and Robert L. Pfaltzgraff, Jr., eds., *International Security Dimensions of Space* (Hampden, Conn., 1984), 274–75; Jack Manno, *Arming the Heavens* (New York, 1984), 27, 32.

18. Ibid., 43–44; memo by John Irwin, Nov. 29, 1957, OSAST, Box 15; "Satellite Programs," Oct. 25, 1957, Harlow Papers, Box 1.

19. Robert Bendiner, "Who Owns Outer Space?," *Reporter* 18 (June 12, 1958), 17–20; Manno, *Arming the Heavens,* 36.

20. Cabinet minutes, Oct. 18, 1957, DDE Diary, Box 27.

21. Eisenhower, *Waging Peace,* 211; David Beckler to Gordon Gray, May 22, 1959, OSAST, Box 17; Michael R. Beschloss, *Mayday: Eisenhower, Khrushchev and the U-2 Affair* (New York, 1986), 75–76, 81.

22. Murphy, "White House Since Sputnik," 100–101; Goodpaster memcon, Oct. 16, 1957 (of White House meeting, Oct. 15, 1957), DDE Diary, Box 27; Cutler handwritten notes of White House meeting, Oct. 15, 1957, OS-ANSA, Special Assistant Series, Subject Subseries, Box 7.

23. Cutler handwritten notes of Pentagon meeting, Oct. 15, 1957, ibid.

24. Cutler to Rabi, Oct. 15, 1957, OSAST, Box 1.

25. Eisenhower, *Waging Peace,* 211–12.

26. *Time* 70 (Nov. 18, 1957), 21, 23–24; *USN* 43 (Oct. 25, 1957), 45–50.

27. *Time* 70 (Nov. 18, 1957), 24; *USN* 43 (Nov. 15, 1957), 65; *Life* 43 (Nov. 18, 1957), 126, 128.

28. *Time* 70 (Dec. 2, 1957), 76; *BAS* 13 (Dec. 1957), 347, 349, 358.

29. *Nation* 185 (Dec. 7, 1957), 427; *Saturday Review* 40 (Dec. 14, 1957), 20; *BAS* 13 (Dec. 1957), 348.

30. Quarles to Sherman Adams, Oct. 31, 1957, Alan Waterman to Killian, Nov. 29, 1957, and Neil Carothers to Henry Loomis, Jan. 22, 1958, OSAST, Box 15; Cutler to Eisenhower, Nov. 4, 1957, SS WH, Box 2; Eisenhower to Preston Hotchkis, Nov. 15, 1957, DDE, Box 28.

31. *PPP,* Eisenhower, 1957, pp. 737, 755, 760; Eisenhower, *Waging Peace,* 215–16.

32. Killian, *Sputnik,* 10; Eisenhower to Hamilton D. Schwarz, Nov. 4, 1957, DDE Diary, Box 28.

33. Dean Alfange to Eisenhower, Oct. 15, 1957, and Eisenhower to Alfange, Oct. 25, 1957, DDE Diary, Box 27.

Chapter Two

1. ACW Diary, Oct. 9, 1957, Box 9; *PPP,* Eisenhower, 1957, pp. 735–36.

2. E. Bruce Geelhoed, *Charles E. Wilson and Controversy at the Pentagon, 1953–1957* (Detroit, 1979), 60, 100–104, 140–44, 173–75.

3. Charles J. V. Murphy, "The Embattled Mr. McElroy," *Fortune* 59 (April 1959), 147–50.

4. Murphy, "White House Since Sputnik," 232.

5. Cabinet minutes, Oct. 11, 1957, DDE Diary, Box 27; Minnich notes, Oct. 11, 1957, SS Cabinet Series, Box 4.

6. Symington press release, Oct. 15, 1957, Symington Papers, Welsh Box 156; *Time* 70 (Oct. 21, 1957), 21; *USN* 43 (Oct. 25, 1957), 38–41.

7. Cabinet minutes, Oct. 11, 1957, DDE Diary, Box 27; Dulles to Nixon, Oct. 15, 1957, Dulles Telephone Calls, Box 7.

8. Goodpaster memcon, Oct. 15, 1957 (of White House meeting, Oct. 14, 1957), SS DOD, Box 1; ACW Diary, Oct. 14, 1957, Box 9; *PPP,* Eisenhower, 1957, pp. 784–85.

9. Cabinet minutes, Oct. 18, 1957, DDE Diary, Box 27.

10. Minnich notes, Nov. 1, 1957, SS Cabinet Series, Box 4.

11. Edmund Beard, *Developing the ICBM: A Study in Bureaucratic Politics* (New York, 1976), 5–6, 8, 140–41.

12. Ibid., 145–56; Simon Ramo, *The Business of Science: Winning and Losing in the High-Tech Age* (New York, 1988), 85–87; Eisenhower, *Waging Peace,* 208; York, *Race to Oblivion,* 83–84; Quarles memo, undated, NSC Briefing Notes, Box 13.

13. Beard, *ICBM,* 160–62; Ramo, *Business of Science,* 92–93; York, *Race,* 86; "Intercontinental Ballistic Missile," undated history, Harlow Papers, Box 1.

14. Beard, *ICBM,* 185–88; William N. Prochnau and Richard W. Larsen, *A Certain Democrat: Senator Henry M. Jackson, a Political Biography* (Englewood Cliffs, N.J., 1972), 163–67; Anderson and Jackson to Eisenhower, June 30, 1955, NSC Briefing Notes, Box 13.

15. Beard, *ICBM,* 189; "Intercontinental Ballistic Missile," undated history, Harlow Papers, Box 1.

16. Killian, *Sputnik,* 68–76; "Intermediate Range Ballistic Missile," undated history, Harlow Papers, Box 1.

17. "Intercontinental Ballistic Missile," undated history, Harlow Papers, Box 1; Eisenhower to Wilson, Dec. 15, 1955, NSC Briefing Notes, Box 13.

18. Ibid.

19. Beard, *ICBM,* 172, 174; Robert L. Perry, "The Atlas, Thor, Titan and Minuteman," in Emme, *History of Rocket Technology,* 145, 149–50.

20. Ibid., 148–49; Ramo, *Business of Science,* 93–94; Ernest G. Schwiebert, *A History of the U.S. Air Force Ballistic Missiles* (New York, 1965), 189–91.

21. Perry, "Atlas," 145–46, 149; York, *Race,* 95.

22. Ibid., 97; Perry, "Atlas," 155–57.

23. Beard, *ICBM,* 208; Perry, "Atlas," 151, 157.

24. Dwight D. Eisenhower, *Mandate for Change* (Garden City, N.Y., 1963), 457.

25. York, *Race,* 94; Schwiebert, *History of Ballistic Missiles,* 114–15; Perry, "Atlas," 150–51.

26. Michael H. Armacost, *The Politics of Weapons Innovation: The Thor-Jupiter Controversy* (New York, 1969), 71–72; Medaris, *Countdown,* 67–74, 125–26; Von Braun, "Redstone," 117.

27. Medaris, *Countdown,* 133, 137, 148–49.

28. Armacost, *Politics,* 104–10; James Baar and William E. Howard, *Polaris!* (New York, 1960), 73; Wyndham D. Miles, "The Polaris," in Emme, *History of Rocket Technology,* 161–66; Harvey M. Sapolsky, *The Polaris System Development: Bureaucratic and Programmatic Success in Government* (Cambridge, Mass., 1972), 29–34, 182.

29. Ibid., 170–72; Wilson to Eisenhower, May 7, 1957, NSC Briefing Notes, Box 13.

30. "U.S. Missile Programs," undated, SS, Alpha, Box 18.

31. Beard, *ICBM,* 202; Armacost, *Politics,* 112–13, 166; Geelhoed, *Wilson,* 131–33; Senate Inquiry, 344–45.

32. Eisenhower to Wilson, July 8, 1957, and Wilson to Eisenhower, Aug. 9, 1957, NSC Briefing Notes, Box 13; Murray Snyder to General Hauck, Sept. 5, 1957, Harlow Papers, Box 1; Welsh to Symington, Feb. 20,1958, Symington Papers, Welsh Box 172; Beard, *ICBM*, 207–8.

33. Eisenhower to McElroy, Oct. 17, 1957, DDE Diary, Box 28; Welsh to Symington, Oct. 29, 1957, Symington Papers, Welsh Box 150.

34. A. G. Waggoner to Bryce Harlow, Feb. 23, 1960, Harlow Papers, Box 2; Schwiebert, *History of Ballistic Missiles*, 222; Wilson to Eisenhower, May 7, 1957, NSC Briefing Notes, Box 13; Jacob Neufeld, *Ballistic Missiles in the United States Air Force, 1945–1960* (Washington, 1990), 162, 167.

35. John Prados, *The Soviet Estimate: U.S. Intelligence Analysis & Russian Military Strength* (New York, 1982), 58–61; Charles J. V. Murphy, "Khrushchev's Paper Bear," *Fortune* 70 (Dec. 1964), 224, 227; Allen Dulles, *The Craft of Intelligence* (New York, 1963), 67–68.

36. Prados, *Soviet Estimate*, 41–47, 62; Murphy, "Khrushchev's Paper Bear," 227; classified testimony of Allen Dulles and Herbert Scoville to Senate Preparedness Subcommittee, in Dulles to Goodpaster, Nov. 29, 1957, Harlow Papers, Box 1.

37. Prados, *Soviet Estimate*, 62; Ray S. Cline, *Secrets, Spies and Scholars: Blueprint of the Essential CIA* (Washington, 1976), 154–55.

38. Prados, *Soviet Estimate*, 53–56; York, *Race*, 109.

39. Murphy, "Khrushchev's Paper Bear," 227; *Newsweek* 50 (Sept. 9, 1957), 43–44; *NYT*, Aug. 27, 1957; *PPP*, Eisenhower, 1957, 639–40.

40. Dulles and Scoville testimony, in Dulles to Goodpaster, Nov. 29, 1957, Harlow Papers, Box 1.

41. CIA consultants to Dulles, Oct. 23, 1957, in Dulles to Goodpaster, Oct. 28, 1957, OSAST, Box 1.

42. Prados, *Soviet Estimate*, 65; Fred Kaplan, *The Wizards of Armageddon* (New York, 1983), 155–60; Murphy, "Khrushchev's Paper Bear, 227–28; Dulles and Scoville testimony, in Dulles to Goodpaster, Nov. 29, 1957, Harlow Papers, Box 1.

43. Murphy, "White House Since Sputnik," 99; Robert Cutler to Eisenhower, Oct. 25, 1957, OSANSA, Special Assistant Series, Chronological Subseries, Box 5.

44. Harold Macmillan, *Riding the Storm, 1956–1959* (New York, 1971), 245, 260–61; Richard P. Stebbins, *The United States in World Affairs, 1957* (New York, 1958), 97.

45. Macmillan, *Riding*, 315–16; telephone conversation between Eisenhower and Dulles, Oct. 16, 1957, DDE Diary, Box 27; *PPP*, Eisenhower, 1957, pp. 768–73; *USN* 43 (Nov. 1, 1957), 32.

46. Macmillan, *Riding*, 325; Goodpaster memcon, Oct. 31, 1957 (of White House meeting, Oct. 22, 1957), DDE Diary, Box 27; *State Department Bulletin* 37 (Dec. 9, 1957), 916.

47. Macmillan, *Riding*, 320–21; *Life* 43 (Nov. 4, 1957), 24; *Time* 70 (Nov. 18, 1957), 29; Hagerty to Dulles, Oct. 25, 1957, Dulles Telephone Calls, Reel 10.

48. Eisenhower, *Waging Peace*, 219–20; Prados, *Soviet Estimate*, 68, 73; Morton H. Halperin, "The Gaither Committee and the Policy Process," *World Politics* 13 (April 1961), 361–63; Killian, *Sputnik*, 96–97; roster of Security Resources Panel, Nov. 4, 1957, OSAST, Box 14.

49. Kaplan, *Wizards*, 118–19, 128–32; Prados, *Soviet Estimate*, 70.

50. Halperin, "Gaither Committee," 364; Kaplan, *Wizards*, 136–41; Paul H. Nitze, *From Hiroshima to Glasnost: At the Center of Decision* (New York, 1989), 167.

51. Halperin, "Gaither Committee," 364, 368; Prados, *Soviet Estimate*, 72; Murphy, "White House Since Sputnik," 230–32.

52. Joint Committee on Defense Production, *Deterrence and Survival in the Nuclear Age*, 94th Congress, 2d Session (Washington, 1976), 12, 15–16, 19–22.

53. Ibid., 17–18.

54. Ibid., 19–23.

55. Halperin, "Gaither Committee," 368; Kaplan, *Wizards*, 147; Goodpaster memcon, Nov. 6, 1957 (of White House meeting, Nov. 4, 1957), DDE Diary, Box 28; ACW Diary, Nov. 9, 1957, Box 9; Eisenhower, *Waging Peace*, 222.

56. Halperin, "Gaither Committee," 368–69, 373; Killian, *Sputnik*, 96–97; record of actions of NSC Meeting, Nov. 7, 1957, SS, Alpha, Box 19.

57. Kaplan, *Wizards*, 132–34, 148–52; Goodpaster memcon, Nov. 7, 1957 (of White House meeting, Nov. 7, 1957), DDE Diary, Box 28; Sprague to Eisenhower, Nov. 14, 1957, OSAST, Box 14.

58. Cutler to Eisenhower, Oct. 25, 1957, OSANSA, Special Assistant Series, Chronological Subseries, Box 5; Thomas S. Power, *Design for Survival* (New York, 1965), 155; Halperin, "Gaither Committee," 382; Eisenhower, *Waging Peace*, 221–23.

59. Beschloss, *Mayday*, 121–22, 139, 147, 150; Barry M. Goldwater, *With No Apologies* (New York, 1970), 73; Edgar M. Bottome, *The Missile Gap: A Study of the Formulation of Military and Political Policy* (Rutherford, N.J., 1971), 180–81; James C. Dick, "The Strategic Arms Race, 1957–1961: Who Opened the Missile Gap?," *Journal of Politics* 34 (1972), 1073–74, 1078.

60. Prados, *Soviet Estimate*, 69; Kaplan, *Wizards*, 142; Beschloss, *Mayday*, 148–49; Goodpaster memcon, Oct. 25, 1957 (of conversation between Goodpaster and Richard Bissell, Oct. 23, 1957), SS Alpha, Box 14.

61. Goldwater, *With No Apologies*, 76; Beschloss, *Mayday*, 156.

Chapter Three

1. *Life* 43 (Nov. 18, 1957), 43; *Washington Star*, Nov. 5, 1957, clipping in Harlow Papers, Box 2; *Time* 70 (Nov. 11, 1957), 49; ibid. (Nov. 18, 1957), 76; *Science* 126 (Nov. 8, 1957), 965.

2. *Newsweek* 50 (Nov. 11, 1957), 35; *Life* 43 (Nov. 18, 1957), 35.

3. *NYT*, Nov. 4, 1957, p. 1; Dulles to Eisenhower, Nov. 3, 1957, and F. Dulles to A. Dulles, Nov. 5, 1957, Dulles Telephone Calls, Reel 7; *State Department Bulletin* 37 (Nov. 25, 1957), 825.

4. *Life* 43 (Nov. 18, 1957); *Time* 70 (Nov. 11, 1957), 23; ibid. (Nov. 18, 1957), 75.

5. *New Republic* 137 (Nov. 11, 1957), 3; *Newsweek* 50 (Nov. 11, 1957), 36; *NYT*, Nov. 7, 1957, p. 31.

6. *USN* 43 (Nov. 8, 1957), 38; Dwight to Arthur Eisenhower, Nov. 8, 1957, DDE Diary, Box 28.

7. Sherman Adams to Dulles, Nov. 4, 1957, Dulles Telephone Calls, Reel

10; Eisenhower to Arthur Burns, Nov. 4, 1957, DDE Diary, Box 28; *NYT,* Nov. 6, 1957, p. 1.

8. Eisenhower to Larson, Nov. 5, 1957, DDE Diary, Box 28; ACW Diary, Nov. 7, 1957, Box 9.

9. *PPP,* Eisenhower, 1957, pp. 789–99.

10. *Life* 43 (Nov. 18, 1957), 41; *New Republic* 137 (Nov. 11, 1957), 2; ibid. (Nov. 18, 1957), 3–4; ibid. (Nov. 25, 1957), 2; *Nation* 185 (Nov. 16, 1957), 333; *Time* 70 (Nov. 18, 1957), 19.

11. Samuel Lubell, "Sputnik and American Public Opinion," *Columbia University Forum* 1 (1957), 18, quoted in Halperin, "Gaither Committee," 375n.

12. Eisenhower, *Waging Peace,* 226; Eisenhower to Swede Hazlett, Nov. 18, 1957, DDE Diary, Box 28.

13. Killian, *Sputnik,* 20–24; Robert Cutler, *No Time for Rest* (Boston, 1965), 352; unsigned handwritten notes and typed outline proposal, Oct. 23, 1957, SS WH, Box 4; ACW Diary, Oct. 24, 1957, Box 9.

14. Sherman Adams memo, Oct. 30, 1957, SS WH, Box 4; Adams to Dulles, Oct. 30, 1957, and Dulles to Adams, Nov. 4, 1957, Dulles Telephone Calls, Reel 10; ACW Diary, Nov. 4, 1957, Box 9; handwritten notes of meeting between Killian and Eisenhower, Nov. 4, 1957, SS WH, Box 4.

15. *Time* 70 (Nov. 18, 1957), 20; *Newsweek* 50 (Nov. 18, 1957), 52; *Saturday Review* 40 (Oct. 14, 1957), 54–55; *NYT,* Nov. 8, 1957, p. 10.

16. Killian, *Sputnik,* 3–7, 29; *Time* 70 (Nov. 18, 1957), 20.

17. *Life* 43 (Nov. 18, 1957), 48; *Newsweek* 50 (Nov. 18, 1957), 42; *Saturday Review* 40 (Dec. 14, 1957), 55; John Cassidy to Goodpaster, Nov. 15, 1957, SS WH, Box 4.

18. *Washington Post,* Nov. 10, 1957, clipping in Harlow Papers, Box 2; *NYT,* Nov. 24, 1957, p. 1; *USN* 43 (Nov. 22, 1957), 98–99; Killian, *Sputnik,* 31–32.

19. Cutler to Goodpaster and Cassidy to Goodpaster, Nov. 15, 1957, SS WH, Box 4; *NYT,* Nov. 16, 1957, pp. 1, 3; Killian, *Sputnik,* 275.

20. *Time* 70 (Dec. 23, 1957), 19; Killian, *Sputnik,* 29.

21. Ralph E. Lapp, *The New Priesthood: The Scientific Elite and the Uses of Power* (New York, 1965), 194–95; *Time* 70 (Dec. 9, 1957), 26; Killian, *Sputnik,* 107–9.

22. York, *Race,* 114; Killian, *Sputnik,* 212.

23. Ibid., 110, 241.

24. *Time* 70 (Nov. 25, 1957), 99.

25. Diane Ravitch, *The Troubled Crusade: American Education, 1945–1980* (New York, 1983), 228–29; Barbara Barksdale Clowse, *Brainpower for the Cold War: The Sputnik Crisis and the National Defense Education Act of 1958* (Westport, Conn., 1981), 32–34; J. Ronald Oakley, *God's Country: America in the Fifties* (New York, 1986), 348–49.

26. *Time* 70 (Nov. 25, 1957), 99; ibid. (Dec. 2, 1957), 53; *Life* 43 (Nov. 4, 1957), 26; Glen Wilson to Gerry Siegel, Dec. 9, 1957, Preparedness Subcommittee, Senate Papers, Box 355, LBJ Library.

27. Clowse, *Brainpower,* 15–16; *USN* 43 (Nov. 15, 1957), 137.

28. *Time* 70 (Dec. 2, 1957), 53–54; *USN* 43 (Dec. 6, 1957), 86–91.

29. *USN* 43 (Dec. 13, 1957), 86–87; *Science* 126 (Nov. 15, 1957), 997; *Time* 70 (Nov. 25, 1957), 99.

30. *NYT Magazine,* Nov. 10, 1957, p. 95.

31. David Beckler to Goodpaster, Nov. 6, 1957, PSAC, Box 5.

32. *PPP,* Eisenhower, 1957, pp. 808–16.

33. *Time* 70 (Nov. 25, 1957), 26; *New Republic* 137 (Nov. 25, 1957), 4–5.

34. Clowse, *Brainpower,* 40–48.

35. Wilton Persons memo of White House conference, Nov. 6, 1957, DDE Diary, Box 28.

36. Cabinet minutes, Nov. 15 and Dec. 2, 1957, DDE Diary, Boxes 28 and 29; Minnich notes, Nov. 15 and Dec. 2, 1957, SS Cabinet Series, Box 4.

37. Minutes of leadership conference, Dec. 4, 1957, DDE Diary, Box 29; Minnich notes, Dec. 4, 1957, SS LM, Box 4.

38. Eisenhower, *Waging Peace,* 216–17; Minnich notes, Dec. 4, 1957, SS LM, Box 4.

39. Stephen E. Ambrose, *Eisenhower the President* (New York, 1984), 436–37; *NYT,* Dec. 1, 1957, sec. 4, p. 1; Murphy, "White House Since Sputnik," 232; Foster to Allen Dulles, Nov. 26, 1957, Dulles Telephone Calls, Reel 7.

40. Adams to Dulles, Nov. 25, 1957, Dulles to Hagerty, Nov. 27, 1957, and Adams to Dulles, Nov. 27, 1957, Dulles Telephone Calls, Reel 10; *USN* 43 (Dec. 6, 1957), 43.

41. Murphy, "White House Since Sputnik," 232; Ambrose, *Eisenhower,* 437–38; Adams and Nixon to Dulles, Nov. 29, 1957; Goodpaster to Dulles, Nov. 29, 1957; Adams to Dulles, Nov. 30, 1957, and Eisenhower to Dulles, Dec. 4, 1957, Dulles Telephone Calls, Reel 10; ACW Diary, Dec. 2, 1957, Box 9.

42. Ambrose, *Eisenhower,* 437, 440–41.

43. *USN* 43 (Dec. 6, 1957), 6; *Life* 43 (Dec. 9, 1957), 42; *Time* 70 (Dec. 9, 1957), 21; Murphy, "White House Since Sputnik," 228.

Chapter Four

1. *NYT,* Nov. 26, 1957, p. 1; *New Republic* 137 (Dec. 9, 1957), 2; telephone conversation between Eisenhower and Strauss, Nov. 25, 1957, DDE Diary, Box 27.

2. *NYT,* Oct. 13, 1957, sec. 4, p. 3; *USN* 43 (Nov. 22, 1957), 31.

3. Robert A. Divine, "Johnson and the Politics of Space," in Robert A. Divine, ed., *The Johnson Years,* vol. 2: *Vietnam, the Environment, and Science* (Lawrence, Kan., 1987), 218–20; telephone conversation between Johnson and Styles Bridges, Nov. 5, 1957, Preparedness Subcommittee, Senate Papers, Box 355, LBJ Library.

4. Divine, "Johnson and the Politics of Space," 219–20; Johnson press release, Nov. 4, 1957, Statements File, Box 23, LBJ Library.

5. Dulles to Johnson, Oct. 23, 1957, and Oct. 31, 1957, Dulles Telephone Calls, Reel 10; Walter Jenkins to Lyndon Johnson, Oct. 29, 1957, Preparedness Subcommittee, Senate Papers, Box 355, LBJ Library; Edwin L. Weisl to Killian, Nov. 14, 1957, OSAST, Box 6.

6. Robert Cutler to Frederick Dearborn, Oct. 19, 1957, OSANSA OCB, Box 4; Harkey Reiter to Harlow, undated, Harlow Papers, Box 1; staff notes, Nov. 4, 1957, DDE Diary, Box 28; Symington to Thomas Lanphier, Dec. 14, 1957, Symington Papers, Alpha Correspondence File, 1958.

7. "History of Long-range Ballistic Missiles," undated, Harlow Papers, Box 1.

8. Diary entry, Nov. 6, 1957, DDE Diary, Box 28; ACW Diary, Nov. 6, 1957, Box 9.

9. Divine, "Johnson and the Politics of Space," 222; Johnson to Symington, Nov. 7, 1957, Symington Papers, Com. Box 48; Symington to Johnson, Nov. 21 and 26, 1957, and Johnson to Symington, Dec. 2, 1957, Symington Papers, Com. Box 46; minutes of Preparedness Subcommittee meeting, Nov. 22, 1957, Preparedness Subcommittee, Senate Papers, Box 405, LBJ Library.

10. Divine, "Johnson and the Politics of Space," 219–20; Rowland Evans and Robert Novak, *Lyndon B. Johnson: The Exercise of Power* (New York, 1966), 209.

11. Senate Inquiry, 6–8, 60, 87, 112.

12. Ibid., 21, 28, 60, 63–65, 113.

13. Ibid., 198–99, 243, 265.

14. Ibid., 227–28, 230–31, 258, 282; Phillip Areeda to Bryce Harlow, Dec. 2, 1957, Harlow Papers, Box 1.

15. Classified testimony of Allen Dulles and Herbert Scoville to Senate Preparedness Subcommittee, in Dulles to Goodpaster, November 29, 1957, Harlow Papers, Box 1.

16. *USN* 43 (Dec. 6, 1957), 67; *Time* 70 (Dec. 9, 1957), 27.

17. Senate Inquiry, 351, 356, 491–93, 509, 917; *Time* 70 (Dec. 23, 1957), 12.

18. *Time* 70 (Dec. 30, 1957), 14; press release, Dec. 5, 1957, Symington Papers, Com. Box 46; text of speech, Dec. 5, 1957, Symington Papers, Com. Box 48.

19. *Reporter* 17 (Dec. 26, 1957), 4; *Nation* 185 (Dec. 7, 1957), 417.

20. Goodpaster memo, Oct. 31, 1957 (of Oct. 30, 1957 meeting), SS DOD, Box 2; cabinet minutes, Jan. 3, 1958, Minnich notes, SS Cabinet Series, Box 4.

21. Goodpaster memcon, Nov. 15, 1957 (of White House meeting, Nov. 11, 1957), and Goodpaster memcon, Dec. 5, 1957 (of White House meeting, Dec. 5, 1957), SS DOD, Box 2.

22. Goodpaster memcon, Nov. 15, 1957 (of White House meeting, Nov. 11, 1957), and Nov. 23, 1957 (of White House meeting, Nov. 22, 1957), SS DOD, Box 2; Eisenhower to McElroy, telephone call, Nov. 21, 1957, DDE Diary, Box 29; undated memo, S. M. Keeny to James Killian, OSAST, Box 6.

23. George Kistiakowsky memo, Dec. 19, 1957, OSAST, Box 12; Senate Inquiry, 194; Goodpaster memcon, Dec. 2, 1957 (of White House meeting, Nov. 26, 1957), SS DOD, Box 6.

24. Humphrey to Eisenhower, Nov. 21, 1957, and Eisenhower to Humphrey, Nov. 22, 1957, DDE Diary, Box 28; minutes of bipartisan congressional meeting, Dec. 3, 1957, DDE Diary, Box 27; minutes of legislative leadership meeting, Dec. 4, 1957, DDE Diary, Box 29; Goodpaster memcon, Dec. 5, 1957 (of White House meeting, Dec. 5, 1957), SS DOD, Box 2.

25. Hagan, "Viking and Vanguard," 136–37; Robert Cutler to Neil McElroy, Oct. 17, 1957, OSAST, Box 15.

26. *USN* 43 (Dec. 13, 1957), 33; *Time* 70 (Dec. 16, 1957), 9; Donald Quarles to Eisenhower, Dec. 6 and 9, 1957, SS Alpha, Box 23.

27. *Life* 43 (Dec. 16, 1957), 25; *Nation* 185 (Dec. 21, 1957), 466; *Time* 70 (Dec. 16, 1957), 9, 12.

28. *USN* 43 (Dec. 13, 1957), 33; Dulles to Nixon, Dulles to Hagerty, and Quarles to Dulles, Dec. 6, 1957, Dulles Telephone Calls, Reels 7, 9.

29. Killian to John Stennis, Dec. 20, 1957, OSAST, Box 6; Killian to Eisenhower, Dec. 6, 1957, SS WH, Box 2; Killian to Eisenhower, Dec. 9, 1957, SS Alpha, Box 23.

30. PSAC minutes, Dec. 11, 1957, PSAC, Box 1; York, *Race*, 135.

31. Dulles to Quarles, Nov. 4, 1957, Dulles Telephone Calls, Reel 7; Goodpaster memcon, Nov. 23, 1957 (of White House meeting, Nov. 22, 1957), DDE Diary, Box 28; U.S. Department of State, *Foreign Relations of the United States, 1954–1957* (Washington, 1986), vol. 4, p. 215; Macmillan, *Riding*, 335–36.

32. *PPP*, Eisenhower, 1957, p. 835; *NYT*, Dec. 19, 1957, p. 1; *Time* 70 (Dec. 23, 1957), 17.

33. Macmillan, *Riding*, 337; Larry M. Loeb, "Jupiter Missiles in Europe: A Measure of Presidential Power," *World Affairs* 139 (1976), 28–29; *Time* 70 (Dec. 23, 1957), 17–18.

34. *USN* 43 (Dec. 27, 1957), 28; *Time* 70 (Dec. 23, 1957), 9, 11; ibid. 71 (Jan. 6, 1958), 11; *PPP*, Eisenhower, 1957, 847–49; *New Republic* 138 (Jan. 6, 1958), 2.

35. Dulles to LBJ, Dec. 23, 1957, Dulles Telephone Calls, Reel 7; Loeb, "Jupiter Missiles," 36.

36. *Time* 71 (Jan. 6, 1958), 16; *New Republic* 137 (Dec. 30, 1957), 2; *USN* 43 (Dec. 20, 1957), 42–43.

37. Hans J. Morgenthau, "The Decline of America," *New Republic* 137 (Dec. 9, 1957), 9–14; ibid. 137 (Dec. 16, 1957), 7–11.

38. *Time* 70 (Dec. 30, 1957), 12; *USN* 43 (Dec. 27, 1957), 31; Killian to Eisenhower, December 28, 1957, Administrative Series, Box 23.

Chapter Five

1. *Time* 70 (Dec. 2, 1957), 13; ibid. (Dec. 30, 1957), 55–56; Arthur F. Burns, "Some Lessons of the Recession," *Reporter* 19 (Dec. 11, 1958), 16–17.

2. *Washington Post* clipping, Dec. 20, 1957, Symington Papers, Com. Box 48.

3. Halperin, "Gaither Committee," 373–77; Killian, *Sputnik*, 98–100; memorandum of discussions with executive branch on Gaither report, Jan. 6, 1958, Senate Papers, Box 433, LBJ Library.

4. Rockefeller Brothers Fund, *Prospects for America: The Rockefeller Panel Reports* (Garden City, N.Y., 1961), 108; *Life* 44 (Jan. 13, 1958), 13–15.

5. *Reporter* 18 (Jan. 23, 1958), 2–3; *Time* 71 (Jan. 6, 1958), 9; Johnson speech to Democratic Caucus, Jan. 7, 1958, Statements File, Box 23, LBJ Library.

6. *Nation* 186 (Jan. 18, 1958), 41–42; *USN* 44 (Jan. 17, 1958), 100–101; *Life* 44 (Jan. 20, 1958), 19.

7. Johnson to Eisenhower, Jan. 28, 1958, Harlow Papers, Box 1; undated memorandum by Gerald Siegal, Senate Papers, Box 405, LBJ Library.

8. Minutes of cabinet meeting, Jan. 3, 1958, and legislative leadership meeting notes, Jan. 7, 1958, DDE Diary, Box 30; Minnich notes, Jan. 7, 1958, SS LM, Box 4.

9. ACW Diary, Jan. 6, 7, and 9, 1958, Box 9.

10. *PPP*, Eisenhower, 1958, pp. 2–15.

11. *USN* 44 (Jan. 17, 1958), 53; *Time* 71 (Jan. 20, 1958), 15; *Life* 44 (Jan. 20, 1958), 24, 26.

12. ACW Diary, Jan. 9 and 10, 1958, Box 9; Nixon to Dulles, Jan. 9, 1958, Dulles Telephone Calls, Reel 7.

13. Eisenhower to John Hay Whitney, Jan. 13, 1958, and legislative leadership meeting notes, Jan. 7, 1958, DDE Diary, Box 30.

14. *PPP*, Eisenhower, 1958, pp. 17–19; cabinet meeting minutes, Jan. 3, 1958, DDE Diary, Box 30; White House press release, Jan. 7, 1958, Harlow Papers, Box 2; Ed Welsh to Stuart Symington, Jan. 13, 1958, Symington Papers, Com. Box 27; *USN* 44 (Jan. 24, 1958), 33; *Time* 71 (Jan. 20, 1958), 15.

15. *PPP*, Eisenhower, 1958, pp. 72–73; *New Republic* 138 (Jan. 27, 1958), 3; *Nation* 186 (Jan. 25, 1958), 61; *Time* 71 (Jan. 20, 1958), 15; *USN* 44 (Jan. 24, 1958), 33.

16. McElroy to Eisenhower, Jan. 21, 1958, and Goodpaster memcon, Jan. 22, 1958 (of White House meeting on Jan. 21, 1958), SS DOD, Box 6; Cutler to McElroy, Jan. 22, 1958, SS DOD, Box 9.

17. W. M. Minshull to James Killian, Dec. 26, 1957, OSAST, Box 14; Cutler briefing notes for President, Jan. 15, 1958, OSANSA, Special Assistant Series, Chronological Subseries, Box 5; ACW Diary, Jan. 16, 1958, Box 9.

18. James Perkins to James Killian, Jan. 7, 1958; William Foster to Killian, Jan. 13, 1958, Rowan Gaither to Killian, Jan. 14, 1958, E. P. Oliver to David Beckler, Jan. 15, 1958, Gaither to Killian, Jan. 17, 1958, and Killian to Gaither, Jan. 22, 1958, OSAST, Box 14; *PPP*, Eisenhower, 1958, pp. 117–18; Minnich notes, Jan. 28, 1958, SS LM, Box 4.

19. Bottome, *Missile Gap*, 36–37, 57.

20. Brian Duchin, "Dwight D. Eisenhower and the Reorganization of the Department of Defense," pp. 5–9, unpublished paper in the author's possession.

21. *USN* 44 (Jan. 10, 1958), 80–81; *Time* 70 (Oct. 28, 1957), 18.

22. ACW Diary, Jan. 6, 1958, Box 9.

23. Goodpaster memcon, Nov. 4, 1957 (of White House meeting, Nov. 4, 1957), DDE Diary, Box 28.

24. Goodpaster memcon, Nov. 6, 1957 (of White House meeting with JCS and service secretaries, Nov. 6, 1957), DDE Diary, Box 28.

25. Brundage and Rockefeller to Eisenhower, Nov. 12, 1957, OSAST, Box 6.

26. David Beckler to Andrew Goodpaster, Nov. 6, 1957, PSAC, Box 5; Killian to McElroy, Dec. 30, 1957, and Jan. 14, 1957, OSAST, Box 6; Killian, *Sputnik*, 235.

27. Eisenhower, *Waging Peace*, 244–45; Ann Whitman to Eisenhower, Dec. 31, 1957, and ACW Diary, Jan. 1, 1957, Box 9; Goodpaster memcon, Jan. 10, 1958 (of White House meeting, Jan. 9, 1958), DDE Diary, Box 30.

28. Killian, *Sputnik*, 235; *PPP*, Eisenhower, 1958, pp. 9, 92; *Time* 71 (Jan. 27, 1958), 13.

29. ACW Diary, Jan. 11 and 15, 1958, Box 9; legislative leadership meeting notes, Jan. 14, 1958, DDE Diary, Box 30; Minnich notes, Jan. 14, 1958, SS LM, Box 4.

30. ACW Diary, Jan. 20, 21, 25, and 28, 1958; Eisenhower telephone call to

Nelson Rockefeller, Jan. 20, 1958, and Harlow memcon, Jan. 30, 1958 (of Pentagon meeting, Jan. 25, 1958), DDE Diary, Box 30.

31. Legislative leadership meeting notes, Jan. 28, 1958, DDE Diary, Box 30; Eisenhower, *Waging Peace*, 245.

32. Killian, *Sputnik*, 194–95; Waterman to Eisenhower, Nov. 20, 1957, PSAC, Box 4; *Time* 71 (March 17, 1958), 41; John Stambaugh to Killian, Nov. 26, 1957, Lee DuBridge to Killian, Dec. 17, 1957, and Maurice Stans to Sherman Adams, Dec. 11, 1957, OSAST, Box 8.

33. *USN* 44 (Jan. 10, 1958), 85–87; *Time* 71 (Jan. 13, 1958), 63.

34. Ann Whitman notes of Eisenhower meeting with Folsom, Dec. 30, 1957, ACW Diary, Box 9.

35. Ann Whitman to Sherman Adams, Dec. 31, 1957, ACW Diary, Box 9; Milton Eisenhower memorandum, Jan. 3, 1958, DDE Diary, Box 30.

36. *PPP*, Eisenhower, 1958, pp. 46–50, 127–32; Eisenhower, *Waging Peace*, 241–42.

37. "HEW Press Survey," staff notes, Jan. 3, 1958, DDE Diary, Box 29; ACW Diary, Jan. 28, 1959, Box 9; Clowse, *Brainpower*, 81; *Time* 71 (Jan. 13, 1958), 63; *Life* 44 (Jan. 13, 1958), 16; *Nation* 186 (Jan. 11, 1958), 21; *New Republic* 138 (Feb. 3, 1958), 5–6.

38. Stringfellow Barr, "Idiot's Orbit: Cold War in a Lunar Age," *Nation* 186 (Jan. 25, 1958), 63–65; *USN* 44 (Jan. 24, 1958), 68–77; Max Ascoli, "Our Cut Rate Education," *Reporter* 18 (Feb. 20, 1958), 8–9.

39. *USN* 44 (Feb. 21, 1958), 66–67; *New Republic* 138 (Jan. 27, 1958), 5; *Time* 71 (Jan. 13, 1958), 63.

40. *Science* 127 (Jan. 31, 1958), 228; *Time* 71 (Feb. 17, 1958), 72; *USN* 44 (Feb. 21, 1958), 66, 75.

41. Donald Quarles to Eisenhower, Jan. 7, 1958, SS Alpha, Box 23; ACW Diary, Jan. 22, 1958, Box 9; *New Republic* 138 (Feb. 3, 1958), 2.

42. *Time* 71 (Feb. 10, 1958), 15; Medaris, *Countdown*, 190, 201.

43. Ibid., 206–12; Goodpaster memcon, Feb. 1, 1958 (of White House meeting on Jan. 31, 1958), DDE Diary, Box 30; *USN* 44 (Jan. 24, 1958), 8; Ann Whitman memorandum of telephone calls on Jan. 31 and Feb. 1, 1958, ACW Diary, Box 9.

44. *Life* 44 (Feb. 10, 1958), 13, 18; *Time* 71 (Feb. 10, 1958), 15; *USN* 44 (Feb. 14, 1958), 33–35.

45. *Time* 71 (Feb. 10, 1958), 23; special staff note, Feb. 3, 1958, DDE Diary, Box 30.

46. Eisenhower, *Waging Peace*, 257; Killian, *Sputnik*, 119.

47. *Life* 44 (Feb. 17, 1958), 37–38; Killian draft of Eisenhower statement, Feb. 5, 1958, OSAST, Box 4; *Science* 127 (Feb. 14, 1958), 330–31; *Time* 71 (Feb. 10, 1958), 49, 52.

48. *USN* 44 (Feb. 7, 1958), 34.

Chapter Six

1. Robert Truax to I. I. Rabi, Nov. 6, 1957, OSAST, Box 15.

2. Senate Inquiry, 615–16; *Life* 43 (Nov. 18, 1957), 133, 136.

3. *USN* 44 (Jan. 17, 1958), 68.

4. *Time* 71 (March 10, 1958), 56; *USN* 44 (Feb. 7, 1958), 54.

5. *Time* 71 (March 31, 1958), 50, 52.

6. *Science* 127 (Jan. 3, 1958), 9, 15, 17.

7. *New Republic* 138 (Feb. 3, 1958), 5, 10–13; *Life* 44 (March 17, 1958), 36.

8. *Time* 71 (Feb. 17, 1958), 19–20; *Science* 127 (Feb. 14, 1958), 331; ibid. (Feb. 21, 1958), 392; ibid. (Feb. 28, 1958), 449; York, *Race*, 117; Walter A. McDougall, . . . *the Heavens and the Earth: A Political History of the Space Age* (New York, 1985), 166–67, 169.

9. Goodpaster memcon, Feb. 6, 1958 (of White House meeting, Feb. 3, 1958), SS DOD, Box 6.

10. Legislative leadership meeting notes, Feb. 4, 1958, DDE Diary, Box 30; Minnich notes, Feb. 4, 1958, SS LM, Box 4.

11. Killian, *Sputnik*, 122; pre–press conference notes, Feb. 5, 1958, DDE Diary, Box 30; *PPP*, Eisenhower, 1958, p. 143.

12. Legislative leadership meeting notes, Feb. 4, 1958, DDE Diary, Box 30; Goodpaster memcon, Feb. 6, 1958 (of White House meeting, Feb. 4, 1958), SS DOD, Box 6; Goodpaster memcon, Feb. 10, 1958 (of White House meeting, Feb. 7, 1958), DDE Diary, Box 30.

13. Killian, *Sputnik*, 122–23; PSAC minutes, Dec. 10, 1957, PSAC, Box 1.

14. Killian memorandum, Dec. 30, 1957, PSAC, Box 4.

15. Loyd S. Swenson, Jr., James M. Grimwood, and Charles C. Alexander, *This New Ocean: A History of Project Mercury* (Washington, 1966), 7–9, 55–56; McDougall, *Heavens and Earth*, 164–65.

16. PSAC minutes, Dec. 10, 1957, PSAC, Box 1; Killian memorandum, Dec. 30, 1957, PSAC, Box 4.

17. Killian, *Sputnik*, 129–32; Enid Curtis Bok Schoettle, "The Establishment of NASA," in Sanford A. Lakoff, ed., *Knowledge and Power: Essays on Science and Government* (New York, 1966), 199–212; Herbert York, *Making Weapons, Talking Peace: A Physicist's Odyssey from Hiroshima to Geneva* (New York, 1987), 114–15; memorandum by H. W. Bode, Feb. 24, 1958, PSAC, Box 4; PSAC minutes, Feb. 7, 1958, PSAC, Box 1.

18. Killian, *Sputnik*, 133, 280–87; Goodpaster memcon, March 5, 1958 (of White House meeting, March 5, 1958), SS Alpha, Box 18.

19. PSAC minutes, Feb. 7 and March 12, 1958, PSAC, Box 1.

20. Killian, *Sputnik*, 124; draft of presentation to NSC by Killian, Purcell, and York, March 7, 1958, OSAST, Box 15; record of action at NSC meeting, March 6, 1958, SS Alpha, Box 20.

21. Cutler to Goodpaster, March 6, 1958, SS Alpha, Box 18; Minnich notes, March 14, 1958, SS Cabinet Series, Box 5; cabinet minutes, March 14, 1958, DDE Diary, Box 31. York's time estimate of ten to fifteen years to send a man to the moon proved remarkably accurate, but the program would cost ten times his original projection; see York, *Making Weapons*, 113.

22. Minnich notes, April 1, 1958, SS LM, Box 5.

23. *PPP*, Eisenhower, 1958, p. 233; Killian, *Sputnik*, 289–98.

24. Col. James Sutherland to Secretary of the General Staff, March 12, 1958, SS DOD, Box 6; *USN* 44 (March 14, 1958), 48; *Time* 71 (April 7, 1958), 18.

25. Telephone call, Waterman to Eisenhower, March 17, 1958, DDE Diary, Box 31; ACW Diary, March 17, 1959, Box 9; *Science* 127 (March 28, 1958), 688; *Time* 71 (March 31, 1958), 11; ibid. (April 28, 1958), 46.

26. *PPP*, Eisenhower, 1958, p. 215; *Life* 44 (March 31, 1958), 38; *USN* 44 (March 28, 1958), 37–39.

27. Legislative leadership meeting notes, March 18, 1958, DDE Diary, Box 31; Minnich notes, March 18, 1958, SS LM, Box 5.

28. Johnson to McElroy and McElroy to Eisenhower, March 19, 1958, York to Killian, Feb. 18, 1958, and Killian to Eisenhower, March 20, 1958, OSAST, Box 15.

29. Eisenhower to McElroy, March 24, 1958, OSAST, Box 15; Murray Snyder to Goodpaster, March 26, 1958, WHCF CF, Subject Series, Box 65.

30. Augenstein, "Evolution of U.S. Military Space Program," 278–79; Terry to Loomis, Jan. 13, 1958, OSANSA OCB, Box 4.

31. PSAC minutes, Dec. 11, 1957, PSAC, Box 1; ACW Diary, March 17, 1958, Box 9; Waterman to Eisenhower, telephone call, March 17, 1958, DDE Diary, Box 31.

32. Paul Johnston to Killian, March 25, 1958, PSAC, Box 4; Killian, *Sputnik,* 133–35.

33. *PPP,* Eisenhower, 1958, pp. 269–72.

34. Eisenhower to Secretary of Defense and Chairman of NACA, April 2, 1958, Symington Papers, Com. Folder 5; undated draft memorandum, Secretary of Defense and Chairman of NACA to Eisenhower, and Robert Piland to Killian, April 10, 1958, OSAST, Box 15.

35. *Nation* 186 (April 12, 1958), 306; *Time* 71 (April 14, 1958), 15; *New Republic* 138 (April 14, 1958), 5; *Life* 44 (April 7, 1958), 20.

Chapter Seven

1. Goodpaster memcon, Feb. 6, 1958 (of White House meeting, Feb. 4, 1958), SS DOD, Box 6.

2. Ibid.; Prados, *Soviet Estimate,* 76.

3. Killian, *Sputnik,* 222.

4. Killian to McElroy, undated, SS Alpha, Box 18.

5. Neufeld, *Ballistic Missiles,* 222–23; *New Republic* 186 (March 22, 1958), 247.

6. Ibid. 186 (March 8, 1958), 197; Robert A. Albrook, "How Good Are Our Missiles?," *Reporter* 18 (Feb. 6, 1958), 21–22.

7. *Time* 71 (March 3, 1958), 15; *USN* 44 (March 21, 1958), 68.

8. Miles, "Polaris," 168; Baar and Howard, *Polaris,* 149–50, 154–56; Senate Inquiry, 2319, 2353.

9. Perry, "Atlas," 157–58; Schwiebert, *History of Ballistic Missiles,* 124–26; Neufeld, *Ballistic Missiles,* 187, 227; *Time* 71 (March 10, 1958), 16; Sapolsky, *Polaris System Development,* 40.

10. Senate Inquiry, 2318–19, 2336, 2338.

11. McElroy presentation to NSC, Feb. 27, 1958, SS DOD, Box 6; Kistiakowsky to Killian, Feb. 28, 1958, OSAST, Box 1; Neufeld, *Ballistic Missiles,* 151, 176.

12. ACW Diary, Feb. 5, 6, and 7, 1958, Box 9; Killian, *Sputnik,* 234.

13. John Fischer, "Who's In Charge Here?," *Harper's* 216 (Feb. 1958), 10, 18; *Reporter* 18 (March 6, 1958), 4; *Time* 71 (March 3, 1958), 11–12.

14. Ann Whitman memo, Feb. 25, 1958, DDE Diary, Box 30; ACW Diary, March 1, 1958, Box 9; *PPP,* Eisenhower, 1958, p. 185.

15. *Life* 44 (March 3, 1958), 91, 94; *USN* 44 (March 29, 1958), 10; *Time* 71 (March 31, 1958), 13.

16. Ibid. (March 17, 1958), 13–15; telephone call, Dwight to Milton Eisenhower, March 14, 1958, DDE Diary, Box 31; *New Republic* 138 (March 17, 1958), 2; Louis Bean, "Happy, Hopeful Democrats," ibid. (March 24, 1958), 8–9.

17. Senate Inquiry, 2384; *USN* 44 (June 6, 1958), 10.

18. Telephone call, Dwight to Milton Eisenhower, March 14, 1958, DDE Diary, Box 31; Goodpaster handwritten notes, undated, SS Alpha, Box 18.

19. Dulles to Anderson, March 3, 1958, Dulles Telephone Calls, Reel 7.

20. Charles E. Silberman and Sanford S. Parker, "The Economic Impact of Defense," *Fortune* 57 (June 1958), 102–5, 215–18.

21. Missile panel memo to Killian, March 4, 1958, SS DOD, Box 6. In addition to Kistiakowsky, the other members of the panel were R. F. Bacher, L. E. Hyland, J. W. McRae, and Herbert York.

22. Killian to Eisenhower, March 8, 1958, SS DOD, Box 6.

23. Goodpaster memcon, March 11, 1958 (of White House meeting, March 10, 1958), DDE Diary, Box 31.

24. Goodpaster memcon, March 21, 1958 (of White House meeting, March 20, 1958), DDE Diary, Box 31.

25. Goodpaster memcon, March 21, 1958 (of White House meeting with McElroy, March 20, 1958), DDE Diary, Box 9; Goodpaster memcon, March 21, 1958 (of White House meeting with Killian, March 20, 1958), SS DOD, Box 6; Minnich notes, March 25, 1958, SS LM, Box 5.

26. ACW Diary, April 1, 1958, Box 10; telephone call, McElroy to Eisenhower, April 1, 1958, DDE Diary, Box 31.

27. Edward A. Kolodziej, *An Uncommon Defense and Congress, 1945–1963* (Columbus, Ohio, 1966), 278; Senate Inquiry, 2359–61, 2381, 2411, 2414.

28. Summary of discussion by S. Everett Gleason, April 25, 1958 (of NSC Meeting, April 24, 1958), NSC Series, Box 10; record of NSC action, April 24, 1958, SS Alpha, Box 20; Herbert York report on history of missile program to NSC, May 5, 1965, *Declassified Documents,* 1989, #1589.

29. Roy E. Licklider, "The Missile Gap Controversy," *Political Science Quarterly* 85 (Dec. 1970), 601; Dick, "Strategic Arms Race," 1064, 1080–81; Bottome, *Missile Gap,* 206–7; telephone call, McElroy to Eisenhower, April 1, 1958, DDE Diary, Box 31.

Chapter Eight

1. Goodpaster memcon, Feb. 28, 1958 (of White House meeting, Feb. 27, 1958), SS DOD, Box 1.

2. Goodpaster memcon, March 12, 1958 (of White House meeting, March 28, 1958), SS DOD, Box 1; Bryce Harlow to Eisenhower, March 27, 1958, DDE Diary, Box 31; ACW Diary, March 31, 1958, Box 9.

3. Eisenhower, *Waging Peace,* 246; ACW Diary, March 28, 1958, Box 9.

4. Legislative leadership meeting notes, April 1, 1958, DDE Diary, Box 32; Minnich notes, April 1, 1958, SS LM, Box 5.

5. Eisenhower to Lodge, April 1, 1958, and Hagerty to Eisenhower, April 2, 1958, DDE Diary, Box 32; ACW Diary, April 2, 1958, Box 10; *PPP,* Eisenhower, 1958, pp. 259–60.

6. Eisenhower, *Waging Peace,* 247–48; *PPP,* Eisenhower, 1958, pp. 274–85.

7. Ibid., 285; *Time* 71 (April 14, 1958), 15–16; ibid. (April 21, 1958), 12; *New Republic* 138 (April 14, 1958), 2; *Atlantic Monthly* 201 (June 1958), 12; Edward L. Katzenbach, Jr., "The Pentagon's Reorganization Muddle," *Reporter* 18 (May 15, 1958), 15–17; Eisenhower, *Waging Peace*, 250.

8. Ibid.; Goodpaster memorandum for the record, April 9, 1958, DDE Diary, Box 32.

9. *PPP*, Eisenhower, 1958, pp. 297–98, 332.

10. Legislative leadership meeting notes, April 15, 1958, DDE Diary, Box 32; *PPP*, Eisenhower, 1958, pp. 311–14, 320.

11. ACW Diary, April 9, 1958, Box 10; *PPP*, Eisenhower, 1958, pp. 327–34.

12. *Time* 71 (April 28, 1958), 18; *USN* 44 (April 28, 1958), 80, 123.

13. Douglas Kinnard, *President Eisenhower and Strategy Management: A Study in Defense Politics* (Lexington, Ky., 1977), 92; Goodpaster memcon, April 24, 1958 (of White House meeting, April 21, 1958), SS DOD, Box 1; telephone call, Brucker to Eisenhower, May 7, 1958, DDE Diary, Box 33; *Time* 71 (May 12, 1958), 24.

14. *PPP*, Eisenhower, 1958, p. 343; *New Republic* 138 (May 5, 1958), 2; *Life* 44 (May 5, 1958), 40.

15. *Time* 71 (May 5, 1958), 12; telephone call, Lodge to Eisenhower, April 28, 1958, DDE Diary, Box 31; typed notes of congressional testimony by Twining and McElroy, April 23–28, 1958, and Bryce Harlow memcon, May 27, 1958 (of White House meeting, April 28, 1958), DDE Diary, Box 32.

16. *USN* 44 (May 9, 1958), 50; *PPP*, Eisenhower, 1958, pp. 357–58.

17. Ibid., 365, 373–75, 378–86, 392.

18. ACW Diary, April 21, 1958, Box 10; Eisenhower, *Waging Peace*, 251; Karl Bendetsen to Killian, June 4, 1958, OSAST, Box 6; B. E. Hutchinson to Symington, May 29, 1958, J. K. Evans to Symington, May 29, 1958, Ward M. Canaday to Symington, June 2, 1958, and Gardner Wright to Symington, June 5, 1958, Symington Papers, Box 169.

19. *Time* 71 (May 19, 1958), 14; Eisenhower to John McCloy, May 10, 1958, DDE Diary, Box 33.

20. Eisenhower, *Waging Peace*, 252–53.

21. Harlow memcon, May 26, 1958 (of White House meeting, May 12, 1958), DDE Diary, Box 32; ACW Diary, May 14 and 16, 1958, Box 10; Eisenhower to Vinson, May 16, 1958, DDE Diary, Box 33.

22. *USN* 44 (May 23, 1958), 6; Minnich notes, May 19, 1958, SS LM, Box 5.

23. Telephone call, Eisenhower to General Persons, May 30, 1958, DDE Diary, Box 33; Minnich notes, June 5, 1958, SS LM, Box 5.

24. *PPP*, Eisenhower, 1958, pp. 439–43.

25. Eisenhower to Krock, May 30, 1958, DDE Diary, Box 33.

26. Minnich notes, May 27, 1958, SS LM, Box 5; *PPP*, Eisenhower, 1958, p. 444; telephone call, Eisenhower to General Persons, May 30, 1958, DDE Diary, Box 33; Harlow memcon, May 28, 1958 (of White House meeting, May 27, 1958), DDE Diary, Box 32.

27. Minnich to Maurice Stans, June 10, 1958, DDE Diary, Box 33; Minnich notes, June 10, 1958, SS LM, Box 5; *Time* 71 (June 23, 1958), 16–17.

28. Roswell Gilpatrick to Symington, March 26, 1958, Neil McElroy to Symington, March 31, 1958, and Symington to Herbert Moloney, April 17, 1958, Symington Papers, Box 169.

29. Douglas and Mansfield to Symington, June 19, 1958, and Symington to Douglas and Mansfield, June 25, 1958, Symington Papers, Box 58; Symington to all senators, June 26, 1958, ibid., Box 169; Symington to Russell, June 30 and July 23, 1958, ibid., Box 30.

30. ACW Diary, June 24, 1958, Box 10; Minnich notes, June 24, 1958, SS LM, Box 5; Eisenhower, *Waging Peace*, 252; telephone call, Eisenhower to McElroy, June 30, 1958, DDE Diary, Box 34.

31. ACW Diary, June 26 and July 16 and 18, 1958, Box 10; telephone call, Eisenhower to Russell, July 16, 1958, DDE Diary, Box 34.

32. Telephone call, Eisenhower to Taylor, July 3, 1958, DDE Diary, Box 34; *USN* 45 (July 4, 1958), 13; *Time* 72 (July 7, 1958), 10.

33. *USN* 45 (July 14, 1958), 14; Goodpaster memcon, June 23, 1958 (of White House meeting, June 23, 1958), DDE Diary, Box 33.

34. *Time* 72 (July 28, 1958), 13; ibid. (August 4, 1958), 14; *USN* 45 (Aug. 1, 1958), 68; Eisenhower, *Waging Peace*, 252; *PPP*, Eisenhower, 1958, p. 564.

35. Ibid., p. 597; Eisenhower, *Waging Peace*, 253; Lawrence J. Korb, *The Joint Chiefs of Staff: The First Twenty-Five Years* (Bloomington, 1976), 18–20.

36. *Science* 128 (Aug. 15, 1958), 349.

37. Goodpaster memcon, Sept. 15, 1958 (of White House meeting, Sept. 11, 1958), DDE Diary, Box 36; Beckler to Killian, Oct. 10, 1958, OSAST, Box 6; York, *Making Weapons*, 166–67.

38. Eisenhower to Barry Leithead and William Robinson, Aug. 2, 1958, DDE Diary, Box 35.

Chapter Nine

1. *Science* 127 (June 6, 1958), 1328; McDougall, *Heavens and Earth*, 175; *Time* 71 (May 26, 1958), 16; *USN* 44 (May 23, 1958), 54; minutes of cabinet meeting, May 16, 1958, DDE Diary, Box 32.

2. *New Republic* 138 (June 2, 1958), 2; ibid. (June 16, 1958), 2.

3. Killian, *Sputnik*, 136–37; Schoettle, "Establishment of NASA," pp. 251–52; *USN* 44 (May 16, 1958), 8.

4. Goodpaster memcon, May 12, 1958 (of White House meeting, May 12, 1958), and Harlow memcon, May 26, 1958 (of White House meeting, May 12, 1958), DDE Diary, Box 32.

5. Alison Griffith, *The National Aeronautics and Space Act: A Study of the Development of Public Policy* (Washington, 1962), 85–86; *PPP*, Eisenhower, 1958, p. 407.

6. Griffith, *National Aeronautics and Space Act*, 75–89; Schoettle, "Establishment of NASA," 256–59.

7. Killian, *Sputnik*, 136–37; Killian memo, June 6, 1958, PSAC, Box 4; Minnich notes, June 17, 1958, SS LM, Box 5; Whitman to Eisenhower, July 7, 1958, DDE Diary, Box 35.

8. Harlow memcon, May 28, 1958 (of White House meeting, May 27, 1958), DDE Diary, Box 32; Welsh to Symington, June 19, 1958, Symington Papers, Com. Folder 6.

9. Eisenhower, *Waging Peace*, 257; Killian, *Sputnik*, 137; Wilton Person memo, July 7, 1958, DDE Diary, Box 35.

10. Schoettle, "Establishment of NASA," 260–61; Griffith, *National Aeronautics and Space Act,* 90–96.

11. Goodpaster memcon, July 18, 1958 (of White House meeting, July 17, 1958), DDE Diary, Box 35; Goodpaster to Gordon Gray, July 22, 1958, SS WH, Box 3; Killian, *Sputnik,* 138.

12. Victor Emanuel to Killian, July 15, 1958, PSAC, Box 4; *Time* 72 (July 28, 1958), 13; *USN* 45 (July 25, 1958), 8; *PPP,* Eisenhower, 1958, p. 273; Schoettle, "Establishment of NASA," 261.

13. Unsigned BOB memo, undated; Piland to Killian, June 30, 1958; Piland notes, July 8, 1958 (on space panel meeting, July 2, 1958), OSAST, Box 15.

14. Piland notes, July 8 and 11, 1958 (on space panel meetings, July 2 and 10, 1958), and Charles Zimmermann memo, July 15, 1958, OSAST, Box 15; John Clark to Killian, July 23, 1958, and Hugh Dryden to Killian, July 18, 1958, OSAST, Box 16.

15. Piland to Killian, July 7, 1958; Piland notes, July 11, 1958 (of space panel meeting, July 10, 1958); Piland to Killian, July 11, 23, and 24, 1958, OSAST, Box 15.

16. Piland notes, July 8 and 11, 1958 (on space panel meetings, July 2 and 10, 1958), and W. H. Pickering to Killian, July 9, 1958, OSAST, Box 15.

17. Piland notes, July 8 and 11, 1958 (on space panel meetings, July 2 and 10, 1958), and Piland memo, July 14, 1958 (of meeting between Killian and Stans, July 12, 1958), OSAST, Box 15.

18. Piland to Killian, July 16, 1958, OSAST, Box 16; Piland to Killian, July 25 and 28, 1958, OSAST, Box 15.

19. Stans to Eisenhower, July 29, 1958, DDE Diary, Box 35; Eisenhower, *Waging Peace,* 260.

20. Killian, *Sputnik,* 141–43; *Time* 72 (July 14, 1958), 20.

21. Killian, *Sputnik,* 138–39; Goodpaster memcon, July 18, 1958 (of White House meeting, July 17, 1958), DDE Diary, Box 35; Goodpaster memcon, July 25, 1958 (of White House meeting, July 25, 1958), SS Alpha, Box 18; T. Keith Glennan Diary, p. 3; Robert Rosholt, *An Administrative History of NASA, 1958–1963* (Washington, 1966), 40–41; McDougall, *Heavens and Earth,* 195–96.

22. Swenson, Grimwood, and Alexander, *This New Ocean,* 101–6.

23. Record of action at NSC meeting, July 3, 1958, SS Alpha, Box 20; "Preliminary U.S. Policy on Outer Space," NSC-5814/1, Aug. 18, 1958, NSC Series, Policy Papers Subseries, Box 25; McDougall, *Heavens and Earth,* 180–94.

24. *USN* 45 (July 4, 1958), 10; *Science* 128 (Aug. 15, 1958), 349; *Time* 72 (Aug. 4, 1958), 16, 55; Killian to Eisenhower, Aug. 23, 1958, OSAST, Box 15.

25. *Time* 71 (June 23, 1958), 44; *Nation* 186 (June 21, 1958), 555.

26. Goodpaster memo, July 3, 1958, SS DOD, Box 6; *USN* 45 (July 25, 1958), 27; ibid. (Aug. 8, 1958), 31–32.

27. Minnich handwritten notes, Aug. 15, 1958, SS Cabinet Series, Box 5; *Time* 72 (Aug. 18, 1958), 58; Johnson to Killian, Aug. 15, 1958, OSAST, Box 6; *USN* 45 (Aug. 15, 1958), 70.

28. Ibid. (Aug. 29, 1958), 8; *Time* 71 (May 12, 1958), 10.

Chapter Ten

1. *PPP*, Eisenhower, 1958, 150.

2. Clowse, *Brainpower*, 66–77; *Science* 127 (Feb. 21, 1958), 389–90.

3. Eisenhower, *Waging Peace*, 243; cabinet minutes, March 28, 1958, DDE Diary, Box 31; Minnich notes, March 28, 1958, SS Cabinet Series, Box 5.

4. Ed McCabe memcon, June 6, 1958 (of Whte House meeting, June 6, 1958), and Eisenhower to Conant, June 13, 1958, DDE Diary, Box 33; ACW Diary, June 12, 1958, Box 10.

5. *New Republic* 138 (May 19, 1958), 4; Clowse, *Brainpower*, 106–7.

6. "Crisis in Education," *Life* 44 (March 24, 1958), 25, 27; ibid. (April 14, 1958), 117–24; ibid. (April 21, 1958), 34; Sloan Wilson, "It's Time to Close Our Carnival," ibid. (March 24, 1958), 36–37.

7. Eisenhower to Jackson, March 26, 1958, DDE Diary, Box 31; ACW Diary, March 26, 1958, Box 9.

8. Clowse, *Brainpower*, 111; *Time* 71 (April 7, 1958), 77; ibid. (April 14, 1958), 77, 78.

9. Alvin C. Eurich, "Russia's New Schooling," *Atlantic Monthly* 201 (April 1958), 57–58; Clowse, *Brainpower*, 113; Karl Shapiro, "Why Out-Russia Russia?" *New Republic* 138 (June 9, 1958), 10, 12.

10. *Time* 72 (July 7, 1958), 55–56; Rockefeller Brothers Fund, *Prospects for America*, pp. 356, 375, 390.

11. PSAC education panel minutes, March 7, 1958, OSAST, Box 14; Killian to Allen Ellender, March 26, 1958, OSAST, Box 16; *USN* 44 (May 16, 1958), 98.

12. Killian to DuBridge, May 23, 1958, and Robert Briber to members of PSAC, July 15, 1958, OSAST, Box 8; PSAC education panel minutes, May 24, 1958, OSAST, Box 13.

13. Killian to DuBridge, May 23, 1958, Robert Briger to J. R. Zacharias, June 25, 1958, and Briber to Dean Burchard, Nov. 19, 1958, OSAST, Box 14. Killian presented the PSAC panel's white paper, "Education for the Age of Science," to the cabinet on May 15, 1959, and it was made public ten days later. Briber to members of PSAC education panel, May 15, 1959, OSAST, Box 14.

14. Clowse, *Brainpower*, 116–17; *PPP*, Eisenhower, 1958, pp. 518–19.

15. ACW Diary, July 2, 1958, Box 10; McCabe memcon, July 2, 1958 (of White House meeting, July 2, 1958), and Wainwright to Eisenhower, July 2, 1958, DDE Diary, Box 35; *PPP*, Eisenhower, 1958, pp. 527–28.

16. Minnich notes, July 22, 1958, SS LM, Box 5; legislative leadership meeting notes, July 22, 1958, and Minnich to Stans, July 22, 1958, DDE Diary, Box 35.

17. *Time* 72 (Aug. 11, 1958), 58; *Science* 128 (Aug. 8, 1958), 289–90; *PPP*, Eisenhower, 1958, p. 585; Clowse, *Brainpower*, 126–38.

18. *Time* 72 (Sept. 1, 1958), 16, 52; *Science* 128 (Sept. 5, 1958), 521–22.

19. *PPP*, Eisenhower, 1958, p. 671; Eisenhower, *Waging Peace*, 243.

20. *Life* 45 (Sept. 1, 1958), 26; *Nation* 187 (Sept. 6, 1958), 102–3; *Science* 128 (Sept. 5, 1958), 521–22.

21. BOB memo to Eisenhower, Dec. 8, 1958, OSAST, Box 8.

22. *USN* 45 (Dec. 19, 1958), 12; ibid. (Oct. 3, 1958), 48–50; Robert Briber memo, Feb. 20, 1959, and Briber to Killian, May 11, 1959, OSAST, Box 8; Clowse, *Brainpower*, 152–61.

Chapter Eleven

1. Goodpaster memcon, June 18, 1958 (of White House meeting, June 18, 1958), DDE Diary, Box 33; ballistic missile panel to Killian, July 18, 1958, *Declassified Documents,* 1988, #1141.

2. Goodpaster memcon, Aug. 4, 1958 (of White House meeting, Aug. 4, 1958), DDE Diary, Box 35; *Time* 72 (Aug. 11, 1958), 10; *USN* 45 (Aug. 15, 1958), 10; ballistic missile panel to Killian, July 18, 1958, *Declassified Documents,* 1988, #1141.

3. Senate Inquiry, 2433; *Life* 45 (July 21, 1958), 85; *Time* 72 (July 28, 1958), 14; ibid. (Aug. 18, 1958), 58.

4. Ballistic missile panel to Killian, July 18, 1958, *Declassified Documents,* 1988, #1141.

5. *Life* 45 (Aug. 18, 1958), 36; ibid. (Sept. 1, 1958), 42; William H. Hessler, "The Navy's Submersible Missile-Launching Base," *Reporter* 18 (June 12, 1958), 16.

6. Kolodziej, *Uncommon Defense,* 277–78.

7. *PPP,* Eisenhower, 1958, pp. 435, 513.

8. Senate Inquiry, 2474–75; Symington to Johnson, July 26, 1958, Symington Papers, Subj. Box 172.

9. Baar and Howard, *Polaris,* 158; *NYT,* July 25, 1958, p. 1; ibid., July 31, 1958, pp. 1, 9; *USN* 45 (Aug. 8, 1958), 8.

10. Goodpaster memcon, June 23, 1958 (of White House meeting, June 23, 1958), and legislative leadership meeting notes, June 24, 1958, DDE Diary, Box 33; Minnich to Stans, July 22, 1958, and legislative leadership meeting, July 22, 1958, DDE Diary, Box 35; Minnich notes, June 24 and July 29, 1958, SS LM, Box 5.

11. *Washington Post,* July 25, 1958, p. 2; *NYT,* Aug. 7, 1958, p. 3; ibid., Aug. 8, 1958, p. 1; *PPP,* Eisenhower, 1958, p. 635.

12. Prados, *Soviet Estimate,* 9, 65, 78; memo for the record, June 9, 1958, DDE Diary, Box 33; Senate Foreign Relations Committee, *Executive Sessions,* 85th Congress, 2d Session (Washington, 1980), vol. 10, p. 64.

13. Prados, *Soviet Estimate,* 79; Dick, "Strategic Arms Race," 1070–71; Dulles to Eisenhower, Oct. 10, 1958, Harlow Papers, Box 2.

14. Kistiakowsky to Killian, undated, OSAST, Box 7; Goodpaster memcon, April 17, 1958 (of White House meeting, April 17, 1958), DDE Diary, Box 32.

15. Dulles to Killian, May 2, 1958, OSAST, Box 1; Kistiakowsky to Killian, June 19, 1958, OSAST, Box 7.

16. Minutes of NSC meeting, May 8, 1958, *Declassified Documents,* 1990, #298; James S. Lay to Robert Cutler, May 9, 1958, NSC Briefing Notes, Box 14.

17. Prados, *Soviet Estimate,* 79; memo for the record, June 9, 1958, DDE Diary, Box 33.

18. Prados, *Soviet Estimate,* 80; Goodpaster memcon, June 18, 1958 (of White House meeting, June 17, 1958), DDE Diary, Box 33.

19. NSC directive, June 25, 1958, Patrick Coyne to Gordon Gray, June 30, 1959, and Cutler memo for the record, May 21, 1958, NSC Briefing Notes, Box 14; *USN* 44 (June 20, 1958), 41; WSEG report, Aug. 8, 1958, *Declassified Documents,* 1988, #1505.

20. Goodpaster memo for the record, March 7, 1958, SS Alpha, Box 14; Prados, *Soviet Estimate*, 85; Beschloss, *Mayday*, 150–52.

21. Minutes of PSAC meeting, December 15 and 16, 1958, PSAC, Box 5.

22. Hanson Baldwin, *The Great Arms Race: A Comparison of U.S. and Soviet Power Today* (New York, 1958), 12, 15–16, 54, 56–57, 65–66, 100, 102–3.

23. James W. Gavin, *War and Peace in the Space Age* (New York, 1958), 4, 11; *Life* 45 (Aug. 4, 1958), 75, 82.

24. *Washington Post*, July 30, 1958, p. 17; ibid., Aug. 1, 1958, p. 19; ibid., Aug. 3, 1958, sec. E, p. 5.

25. Russell to J. Howard Tumlin, Aug. 12, 1958, Russell Papers, Series 15, Box 394.

26. *PPP*, Eisenhower, 1958, pp. 649–50.

27. Prados, *Soviet Estimate*, 81–83; Dulles to Eisenhower, Oct. 10, 1958, Harlow Papers, Box 2.

28. Howard Stoertz memcon, Aug. 18, 1958 (of meeting between Dulles and Symington, Aug. 6, 1958), SS Alpha, Box 24; Licklider, "Missile Gap Controversy," 605; Goodpaster memcon, Aug. 29, 1958 (of White House meeting, Aug. 25, 1958), DDE Diary, Box 35.

29. Symington to Eisenhower, Aug. 29, 1958, SS Alpha, Box 24; Goodpaster memcon, Aug. 30, 1958 (of White House meeting, Aug. 29, 1958), DDE Diary, Box 35.

30. Telephone call, Eisenhower to Quarles, Aug. 29, 1958, DDE Diary, Box 35; Harlow to Symington, Sept. 4, 1958, Harlow Papers, Box 2.

31. Dulles to Eisenhower, Oct. 10, 1958, Harlow Papers, Box 2.

32. Dulles memo, Oct. 9, 1958, enclosed in Goodpaster to Harlow, Oct. 18, 1958, Harlow Papers, Box 2; Robert Briber to Killian, Oct. 9, 1958, OSAST, Box 1.

33. Prados, *Soviet Estimate*, 83; James R. Shepley, "Life-and-Death Debate over Missile Program," *Life* 46 (March 9, 1959), 120.

34. Dulles memcon of meeting with Symington, Dec. 16, 1958, SS Alpha, Box 24.

35. Prados, *Soviet Estimate*, 83–84; Bottome, *Missile Gap*, 96–97.

36. Prados, *Soviet Estimate*, 84, 118; Murphy, "Khrushchev's Paper Bear," 228.

Chapter Twelve

1. *Washington Post*, Sept. 30, 1958, pp. 1, 4; *NYT*, Oct. 5, 1958, sec. 4, p. 6.

2. Ibid.; *Washington Post*, Oct. 1, 1958, pp. 1, 4; ibid., Oct. 3, 1958, pp. 1, 7, 14; ibid., Oct. 4, 1958, p. 1.

3. Killian to Eisenhower, Aug. 23, 1958, Robert Piland to Killian, Sept. 11, 1958, and Piland to Finan, Sept. 22, 1958, PSAC, Box 4; Goodpaster memcon, Sept. 25, 1958 (of White House meeting, Sept. 23, 1958), SS Alpha, Box 18.

4. Roger Jones to Goodpaster, Sept. 15, 1958, SS Alpha, Box 18; *New Republic* 139 (Oct. 20, 1958), 10; minutes of Space Council meeting, Sept. 24, 1958, SS Alpha, Box 23.

5. *Science* 128 (Oct. 10, 1958), 826; Hagerty press release, Oct. 1, 1958, OSANSA OCB, Box 6; Keith Glennan to Lyndon Johnson, Oct. 21, 1958, Symington Papers, Com. Folder 8.

6. Pre–press conference notes, Oct. 1, 1958, DDE Diary, Box 36; *USN* 45 (Oct. 3, 1958), 6; *Time* 72 (Sept. 1, 1958), 15; Swenson, Grimwood, and Alexander, *This New Ocean,* 49.

7. Cabinet minutes, Oct. 9, 1958, DDE Diary, Box 36; *USN* 45 (Oct. 24, 1958), 79; *Time* 72 (Oct. 20, 1958), 17–18; *Life* 45 (Oct. 27, 1958), 120, 125, 132.

8. *NYT,* Nov. 8, 1958, pp. 1, 10; ibid., Nov. 9, 1958, p. 1; ibid., Dec. 7, 1958, sec. 4, p. 1; Von Braun, "Redstone," 118; *Time* 72 (Dec. 15, 1958), 41; Clayton R. Koppes, *JPL and the American Space Program* (New Haven, 1982), 92–93; Caidin, *Red Star,* 166–71.

9. Summary of NSC meeting, July 3, 1958, *Declassified Documents,* 1990, #336; William E. Burrows, *Deep Black: Space Espionage and National Security* (New York, 1986), 104, 107; Prados, *Soviet Estimate,* 105–6; *NYT,* Dec. 4, 1958, p. 1; *Time* 72 (Dec. 15, 1958), 42.

10. Villard to Lloyd Berkner, Jan. 22, 1959, and memo by R.S.L., April 24, 1959, OSAST, Box 15.

11. John Eisenhower memcons, Dec. 22, 1958 (of White House meeting, Dec. 16, 1958), and Feb. 12, 1959 (of White House meeting, Feb. 12, 1959), SS Alpha, Box 15.

12. Burrows, *Deep Black,* 109–11; Prados, *Soviet Estimate,* 107–9.

13. Glennan Diary, pp. 14, 17; Goodpaster to Glennan, Oct. 15, 1958, Brucker to McElroy, Oct. 28, 1958, and Goodpaster memcon, Oct. 31, 1958 (of White House meeting, Oct. 30, 1958), SS Alpha, Box 18; Edward Welsh to Symington, Oct. 16, 1958, Symington Papers, Welsh Box 172; *USN* 45 (Oct. 24, 1958), 12; Koppes, *JPL,* 98–99; Space Council minutes, Dec. 3, 1958, OSANSA OCB, Box 6.

14. Robert Piland memo to Space Council, Nov. 25, 1958, SS Alpha, Box 23; Goodpaster memcons, Dec. 3, 1958 (of White House meeting, Dec. 3, 1958), and Feb. 24, 1959 (of White House meeting, Feb. 17, 1959), SS Alpha, Box 18.

15. Space Council minutes, Dec. 3, 1958, OSANSA OCB, Box 6; Goodpaster memcon, Dec. 22, 1958 (of White House meeting, Dec. 18, 1958), DDE Diary, Box 38.

16. Neufeld, *Ballistic Missiles,* 205; *Time* 72 (Sept. 29, 1958), 12; McElroy to Eisenhower, Dec. 3, 1958, SS DOD, Box 6.

17. *Time* 72 (Dec. 8, 1958), 15; *USN* 45 (Oct. 10, 1958), 35–36; ibid. (Nov. 14, 1958), 75.

18. Neufeld, *Ballistic Missiles,* 228–29; Kistiakowsky to Killian, Sept. 25, 1958, *Declassified Documents,* 1987, #2319.

19. *USN* 45 (Oct. 17, 1958), 14; *Time* 72 (Dec. 22, 1958), 17; ibid. (Dec. 27, 1958), 8; Neufeld, *Ballistic Missiles,* 186, 223; NSC memo for the record, Jan. 16, 1959, *Declassified Documents,* 1987, #144.

20. *Time* 72 (Sept. 22, 1958), 21; *USN* 45 (Dec. 5, 1958), 6.

21. *USN* 45 (Nov. 21, 1958), 8; Charles H. Donnelly, "The United States Guided Missile Program," Jan. 13, 1959, Symington Papers, Welsh Box 156; McElroy to Dulles, Dulles Telephone Calls, Reel 8.

22. *Nation* 187 (Nov. 29, 1958), 397; *Reporter* 19 (Nov. 27, 1958), 2; ibid. (Dec. 25, 1958), 4; Carl Dreher, "Missile Madness," *Nation* 187 (Dec. 13, 1958), 447–48.

23. Neufeld, *Ballistic Missiles*, 177–78; *Time* 72 (Dec. 15, 1958), 15; *USN* 45 (Dec. 12, 1958), 35.

24. Murray Snyder to Goodpaster, Nov. 19, 1958, and Goodpaster memo for the record, Nov. 24, 1958, SS Alpha, Box 18.

25. *USN* 45 (Dec. 12, 1958), 36; Neufeld, *Ballistic Missiles*, 178, 186–89, 201–4, 242; Charles Haskins to Gordon Gray, Dec. 5, 1958, *Declassified Documents*, 1987, #2902; Edward Hymoff, "Some of Our Launching Pads Are Missing," *Reporter* 20 (June 25, 1959), 27–28.

26. Bottome, *Missile Gap*, 211–12; Desmond Ball, *Politics and Force Levels: The Strategic Missile Program of the Kennedy Administration* (Berkeley, 1980), 47.

27. *PPP*, Eisenhower, 1958, pp. 720–21; *Time* 72 (Oct. 6, 1958), 15; ibid. (Oct. 13, 1958), 19.

28. *PPP*, Eisenhower, 1958, pp. 739, 746.

29. ACW Diary, Sept. 30, 1958, Box 10.

30. *PPP*, Eisenhower, 1958, pp. 761–62, 791, 804, 823.

31. *Time* 72 (Nov. 10, 1958), 25; *USN* 45 (Nov. 14, 1958), 33–38; pre–press conference briefing, Nov. 5, 1958, DDE Diary, Box 37.

32. *Time* 72 (Nov. 17, 1958), 17, 20; *Life* 45 (Nov. 17, 1958), 36G; *New Republic* 139 (Nov. 17, 1958), 3; Carey McWilliams, "Landslide in a Vacuum," *Nation* 187 (Nov. 15, 1958), 351–52.

33. *PPP*, Eisenhower, 1958, pp. 827–31; *Time* 72 (Nov. 17, 1958), 19.

34. Flemming to Dulles, Nov. 7, 1958, Dulles Telephone Calls, Reel 10.

35. Anderson memcon, Nov. 18, 1958 (of White House meeting, Nov. 18, 1958), DDE Diary, Box 37.

36. Bottome, *Missile Gap*, 83.

37. Goodpaster memcon, Sept. 30, 1958 (of White House meeting, Sept. 9, 1958), DDE Diary, Box 36; Goodpaster memcon, Nov. 3, 1958 (of White House meeting, Nov. 3, 1958), and Gordon Gray memcon, Nov. 6, 1958 (of White House meeting, Nov. 5, 1958), DDE Diary, Box 37; *PPP*, Eisenhower, 1958, p. 836.

38. *Time* 72 (Dec. 1, 1958), 13; ibid. (Dec. 8, 1958), 17; Neufeld, *Ballistic Missiles*, 190–91.

39. Stans to Eisenhower, Nov. 28, 1958, DDE Diary, Box 37; Dulles to Eisenhower, Nov. 24, 1958, Dulles Telephone Calls, Reel 9.

40. John Eisenhower memcon, Dec. 9, 1958 (of Augusta conference, Nov. 28, 1958), and telephone call, Eisenhower to McElroy, Nov. 29, 1958, DDE Diary, Box 37; ACW Diary, Nov. 28, 1958, Box 10.

41. Anderson to Dulles, Dec. 3, 1958, Dulles Telephone Calls, Reel 8.

42. Stans memcon, Dec. 10, 1958 (of White House meeting, Dec. 3, 1958), DDE Diary, Box 38; Gordon Gray memcon, Dec. 5, 1958 (of White House meeting, Dec. 3, 1958), Special Assistant Series, Presidential Subseries, Box 3; record of action at NSC meeting, Dec. 6, 1958, SS Alpha, Box 20; diary entry, Dec. 6, 1958, DDE Diary, Box 37.

43. Military budget for FY 1960, Dec. 8, 1958, *Declassified Documents*, 1986, #81; undated chart of missile funding, ibid., #1409.

44. Gray memcon, Dec. 9, 1958 (of White House meeting and telephone call, Dec. 8, 1958), Special Assistant Series, Presidential Subseries, Box 3.

45. Jack Raymond, "How Much Must We Spend for Defense?," *New Republic* 139 (Dec. 22, 1958), 9; ACW Diary, Dec. 15, 1958, Box 10; Minnich notes,

Dec. 15, 1958, SS LM, Box 5; legislative meeting notes, Dec. 15, 1958, DDE Diary, Box 38.

46. Neufeld, *Ballistic Missiles,* 190–91; speech notes, Dec. 8, 1958, DDE Diary, Box 38.

47. ACW Diary, Dec. 17, 18, and 19, 1958, Box 10; *PPP,* Eisenhower, 1958, p. 865.

48. *USN* 45 (Dec. 26, 1958), 6, 27–28; *Time* 72 (Dec. 29, 1958), 7; *Newsweek* 52 (Dec. 29, 1958), 13.

49. *New Republic* 139 (Dec. 29, 1958), 4.

50. Piland to Killian, July 31, 1958, Eisenhower to McElroy, Aug. 15, 1958, and Killian to Goodpaster, Aug. 8, 1958, OSAST, Box 15.

INDEX

237